Fortune's L

The Magical Record contained within this book details the work of two senior magicians within the Fraternity of the Inner Light during the years 1937-39. The adepts are Charles Seymour and Christine Campbell Thomson, better known as Christine Hartley.

Although the diaries of Seymour and Hartley form the nucleus of this book, it is the magical system of their nominal superior, Dion Fortune, that provides the focus for everything. Founder of the Fraternity of the Inner Light, Ms. Fortune brought a clarity, depth, excitement and sheer power to the magical revival which has never been equalled.

Hartley—a young priestess making her way between the worlds—and Seymour—an Irishman with rare gifts who wrote some of the best essays on Magic of all time—were in their own ways extraordinary figures. Seymour and Hartley will in time come to be analyzed and judged along with Fortune, patterned by the myths that have come to surround their teacher. Their own magic has played no small part in the re-discovery of the Pagan heritage.

Originally published as *Dancers to the Gods*, this new edition contains Seymour's long essay "The Old Religion," which many think is the finest piece of magical writing in this century. A true manual of self-initiation, this essay covers more ground in a few dozen pages than most writers on the topic can manage in a dozen books.

Be warned. In a strange way these same Magical Diaries can have a mystical effect upon the reader. For those who know how to listen, there is a song behind the prose which is at once yearning, thrilling, wistful—and utterly compelling. The simple act of reading these juxtaposed diaries of a true priest and priestess can cause a resonance within the soul which will, ultimately, transform those who so desire it.

About the Author

Alan Richardson was born in Northumberland, England, in 1951, and has been writing on the topic of magic for many years. He does not belong to any occult group or society, does not take pupils, and does not give lectures or any kind of initiation. He insists on holding down a full-time job in the real world like any other mortal. That, after all, is part and parcel of the real magical path. He is married with two children and lives very happily in a small village in the southwest of England.

To Write to the Author

We cannot guarantee that every letter written to the author can be answered, but all will be forwarded. Both the author and the publisher appreciate hearing from readers, learning of yur enjoyment and benefit from this book. Llewellyn also publishes a bi-monthly news magazine with news and reviews of practical esoteric studies and articles helpful to the student, and some readers' questions and comments to the author may be answered through this magazine's columns if permission to do so is included in the original letter. The author sometimes participates in seminars and workshops, and dates and places are announced in *The Llewellyn New Times*. To write to the author, or to ask a question, write to:

Alan Richardson
c/o THE LLEWELLYN NEW TIMES
P.O. Box 64383-673, St. Paul, MN 55164-0383, U.S.A.

Please enclose a self-addressed, stamped envelope for reply, or $1.00 to cover costs.

LLEWELLYN'S HIGH MAGICK SERIES

20th Century Magic
and The Old Religion
Dion Fortune,
Christine Hartley,
Charles Seymour

Alan Richardson

A New, Expanded and Revised Publication of
Dancers to the Gods

1991
Llewellyn Publications
St. Paul, Minnesota 55164-0383, U.S.A.

20th Century Magic: And The Old Religion / Dion Fortune, Christine Hartley, Charles Seymour. Copyright © 1991 by Alan Richardson. All rights reserved. Printed in the United States of America. No part of this book may be used or reproduced in any manner whatsoever without permission in writing from Llewellyn Publications except in the case of brief quotations embodied in critical articles and reviews.

FIRST LLEWELLYN EDITION
Originally published as *Dancers to the Gods*, Aquarian Press, 1985

Library of Congress-in-Publication Data:
Richardson, Alan, 1951-
    20th century magic: Dion Fortune, Christine Hartley, Charles Seymour/ Alan Richardson. — 1st Llewellyn ed., rev.
    p. cm. — (Llewellyn's western magick historical series)
    Rev. ed. of: Dancers to the gods. c1985.
    Includes edited diaries of Dion Fortune and Christine Hartley and The old religion by Charles Seymour.
    Includes bibliographical references.
    ISBN 0-87542-673-5
    1. Fortune, Dion. 2. Seymour, C. R. F. (Charles Richard Foster). 1880-1943. 3. Hartley, Christine. 4. Fraternity of the Inner Light. 5. Seymour, C. R. F. (Charles Richard Foster), 1880-1943—Diaries. 6. Hartley, Christine—Diaries. 7. Paganism. 8. Magic. 9. Occultist—England—Biography. I. Richardson, Alan, 1951- Dancers to the gods. II. Seymour, C. R. F. (Charles Richard Foster), 1880-1943. Old religion. 1991. III. Title. IV. Title: Twentieth century magic. V. Series.
BF1408.R53 1991   90-28621
133.4'3'0922—dc20   CIP
[B]

Llewellyn Publications
A Division of Llewellyn Worldwide, Ltd.
P.O. Box 64383, St. Paul, MN 55164-0383

About Llewellyn's High Magick Series

Practical Magick is performed with the aid of ordinary, everyday implements, is concerned with the things of the Earth and the harmony of Nature, and is considered to be the magick of the common people. *High Magick*, on the other hand, has long been considered the prerogative of the affluent and the learned. Some aspects of it certainly call for items expensive to procure and for knowledge of ancient languages and tongues, though that is not true of all High Magick. There was a time when, to practice High Magick, it was necessary to apprentice oneself to a Master Magician, or *Mage*, and to spend many years studying and, later, practicing. Throughout the Middle Ages there were many high dignitaries of the Church who engaged in the practice of High Magick. They were the ones with both the wealth and the learning.

High Magick is the transformation of the Self to the Higher Self. Some aspects of it also consist of rites designed to conjure spirits, or entities, capable of doing one's bidding. Motive is the driving force of these magicks and is critical for success.

In recent years there has been a change from the traditional thoughts regarding High Magick. The average intelligence today is vastly superior to that of four or five centuries ago. Minds attuned to computers are finding a fascination with the mechanics of High Magical conjurations (this is especially true of the mechanics of Enochian Magick).

The Llewellyn High Magick Series has taken the place of the Mage, the Master Magician who would teach the apprentice. "Magick" is simply making happen what one desires to happen—as Aleister Crowley put it: "The Science and Art of causing Change to occur in conformity with Will." The Llewellyn High Magick Series shows how to effect that change and details the steps necessary to cause it.

Magick is a tool. High Magick is a potent tool. Learn to use it. Learn to put it to work to improve your life. This series will help you do just that.

Other Books by Alan Richardson

An Introduction to the Mystical Qabalah
Gate of Moon: Mythical & Magical Doorways to the Otherworld
Priestess: The Life and Magic of Dion Fortune
Earth God Rising: The Return of the Male Mysteries

With Geoff Hughes:

Ancient Magicks for a New Age

Table of Contents

Acknowledgments ix
Introduction xi

The Priestess in the Orchard 1
The Dancers to the Gods 45
The Magical Record 91
The Old Religion, by Charles Seymour 183

Index 235

To Paddy,
Hugs & Kisses
(chaste ones!)
Alan4 Richardson

Acknowledgments

The following people have given me a great deal of help in the preparation of this book:

Duncan Mirylees of the Local Studies Centre in Guildford for his expert and patient help. Brian Longman for his second opinions; Caroline Marshall of the British Library for the final diagnoses. I take my leave with thanks, promising never to mention Dr. Moriarty again.

Israel Regardie for his bemused comments which helped me in many ways; Susan Tolley for her long bike rides which found treasures, freely given; Bill and Bobbie Gray for their insight, anecdotes, and kindness; Mr. and Mrs. Firth (no relation) of Weston-super-Mare for their long hours of work; and Basil Wilby for his encouragement in gray areas.

John Winter for his masterful researches in musty corners at the expense of (he claims) his usual Buddha-like serenity; Philip and Jan Carver for helping the great serpent swallow its own tail once more; T. W. Shepherd for details that provided the foundation of my work; David Annwn, the Welsh rhymester, for his bard's eye view on some fishy matters; and Mike and Dolores Ashcroft-Nowicki for the background music and orchestration.

The Churches of Christ, Scientist in Llandudno, Sheffield, Weston-super-Mare, as well as the District Manager in London, Mr. Richard Robinson.

T. C. Charman for his priceless details on Colonel Seymour's military career.

The staff of the India Office Library.

Mr. A. E. Marshall and Mr. M. J. Stevens of Firth Brown Tools, Sheffield.

Clive Harper, Gregory Tillett and T. G. H. James for the unstinting use of their wide knowledge.

Mr. R. A. Gilbert of Bristol, for some useful clues.

The staff of the libraries at Winchester, Bristol, Sheffield, Trowbridge, Bradford on Avon, Weston-super-Mare, Bath and Llandudno.

And as always to Michelle, for providing the still center of my turning world.

These people do not necessarily share my views. The responsibility for interpreting or misinterpreting the information which follows is entirely mine.

And finally to DNF, FPD, M, and FAF. Them above all others.

Introduction

The Magical Record contained within this book details the work of two senior magicians within the Fraternity of the Inner Light during the years 1937-39. The adepts in question were Charles Seymour and Christine Campbell Thomson—who is rather better known as Christine Hartley. For the first time we can study in depth the rites and visions of two high-grade occultists within a genuine lodge, who functioned as priest and priestess, and whose magic has played no small part in the re-discovery of the Pagan heritage.

Seymour, Hartley and Dion Fortune were each in their own way extraordinary figures, although for the years in question CCT, as she was invariably known, was still very much a young priestess making her way between the worlds,

Seymour on the other hand was the forgotten mage, an Irishman with rare gifts who wrote some of the best essays on Magic of all time, and whose peculiar magnetism and interests helped the Western psyche open some all but forgotten gates.

While Dion Fortune herself was never less than one of the most extraordinary women of our century, who brought a clarity, depth, excitement and sheer power to the Magical revival which has never been equaled. Next to her shade, so many of the present-day shamans, priestesses and channels can seem rather shabby. Next to her living reality, they would have just looked silly.

It is difficult, however, to be objective when writing about magicians. They are a group of people who believe themselves possessed of profound psychic faculties which can reach into the future or remote past. They excite the imagination in a way that bare facts about their lives cannot express. Seymour and Hartley have been protected from the sort of calumny or eulogy that has been flung around Fortune, largely because they maintained very low profiles, were very private people. Yet they will in time be analyzed and hence judged along with her, patterned by the same myths which have come to surround their teacher like the walls of a labyrinth.

Everyone has their own ideas about Dion Fortune, but they rarely agree. Many, indeed, have vested interests in the way that she is interpreted, but that is just another sign of her importance. In talking to a great many people who knew her, I came away with completely divergent viewpoints, each of them vehemently expressed.

They ran something like this:

Dion Fortune's problem was that her pagan approach crippled her, spiritually, in her latter years;

In her latter years Dion Fortune's excessive Christianity caused her to decline;

She declined because she was a closet lesbian who appealed to impressionable women;

It was not impressionable women but weak men she preyed upon, because she was a sexual vampire—especially in her last years.

In her last years she was overshadowed by an Atlantean priestess, a primitive being all out for power;

In her last years she had nothing left within her—nothing at all,

And so on, around and around,

Even the very act of putting these down caused some people to take offense, feeling it better that any slurs should be suppressed, hoping that they might be forgotten if we all kept very quiet. But this was never going to happen. I had been hearing these opinions and more for twenty years and they were growing like long shadows. It was my approach that if I didn't tell the basic story as clearly as possible someone else would, and someone who might seize upon one angle and one only, thus defining and damning the woman for an eternity. I took as my defense, my justification for printing some of the things above, that the woman who could write in 1930 about how she had once been accused of being a man in drag, preying on weak women, would not worry in the least about the exposure of such things. It took no small amount of courage to write that, in 1930. So I hoped that the light would shorten the shadows a bit, and also forestall the sort of myths that were building up even then around the other two, Seymour in particular.

Even so, one can never write a biography of such people as much as a "mythography," to coin a word. It is the consequence of working with power, the result of invoking the gods. They become myths themselves. Therefore, if we are to get at any appoximation of the truth at all, it is this:

Dion Fortune created a style and system of magic, and in return her magicians recreated her in their own images. God had much the same problem.

So although the Diaries of Seymour and Hartley form the nucleus of the present book, it was the magical system of their nominal superior which provided the focus for everything. If Dion Fortune is badly out of focus, then the rest must be too. Which is why I went through several approaches in writing the first chapter, "Priestess in the Orchard." My own inclination is unabashedly Pagan. Christianity (though not its Christ) makes me feel quite ill. My first impulse was to advance the hypothesis that in the dichotomy which surely existed between Dion's Christian and Pagan sides, it was the Christian which eventually won, and so her whole fraternity took the Wrong Turning. I wanted to show that the path of Thomas Penry Evans (her husband), Charles Seymour and Christine Hartley was the Right Way. Yet by the time I had worked through several versions I became less inclined to think in such terms.

There are no Wrong Paths, of course. The way to work through a maze is to choose one wall and one wall only, touch and follow every inch of it, into and out of the dead ends, until it leads you into the center and out again with slow certainty. How you deal with the half-beast which roars at the heart of it is an individual matter.

Likewise the present-day Society of the Inner Light has been subject to its own share of abuse for moving away from the form and approach once used by its founder. This is the criticism that all occult groups get if they dare to outlast their founders. To a great extent it is an accolade: without motion it would be accused of being moribund.

The only criterion is whether or not a system works. If it works then it is the Right Way. It will draw the individual psyche into the mandala, the pattern.

I personally have no links whatsoever with the Society—none at all. I wrote to them once as a teenager asking details about Dion's birthdate, background, favourite color, etc., etc., and got a rather formal reply saying that they did not think my inquiries relevant, or important. The Work itself was the main thing. It is only now, when I have answered many of my own questions, that I accept that the Society was largely right. The fire that the likes of Fortune and Seymour and Hartley started within the Western spirit is the important thing; the precise nature of those idiosyncracies which led up to such a promethean act is, ultimately, so much trivia.

Still, I think that such trivia should at least be fair, and accurate. After that the reader must make his own sense of it all, choose his wall and then enter the labyrinth at his leisure, turning and searching to his own delight. Those who are frustrated by the obvious gaps in the biographical narrative should refer to *The Magical Life of Dion Fortune* (Aquarian Press, England, 1991),which is as yet the only full, general biography of that enigmatic woman, whose writings are still crying out for serious critical analysis. Further information can also be found in *Ancient Magicks for a New Age* (Llewellyn, 1989) which details the work done by Seymour and Hartley after they parted company with Dion Fortune. These three books together should provide a unique insight into the world of real Magic, though they are necessarily colored (as all biographies are) by the tone and peculiarites of my own marred self. If any would-be biographer or critic chooses to analyze these same personalities and their work from a totally opposite viewpoint to mine, then I will cheerfully provide them with whatever information I have left, or have found since, and give them every encouragement to pull my own literary vision to pieces. They have only to write to me care of the publishers (enclosing adequate return postage) and convince me of the seriousness of their intent.

In many ways being given these diaries by Christine Hartley in 1983 did no more than complete a process which had begun many years before, As a boy, riding in an old and rattling bus westward across the lonely moors of Northumberland, just below the Roman ruins of the once-massive Hadrian's Wall, I had always been eerily drawn to a sign which simply said MITHRAEUM, pointing off to the left beyond the dry-stone walls, and black-faced sheep, and the low, damp, glistening hills beyond.

I could never have explained to anyone why I always wanted to stop there and explore. I had no knowledge of Mithras, no clear interest in Romano-British archaeology, but still I could not avoid the sense that the place was important to me, and linked with... *someone*. The distant hills beyond had, and have, a message for me also, which I learned to read at the age of 18 when I lived among them for one of the bleakest, loneliest, and yet intensely romantic years of my life, but it was the linking of that Temple of Mithras with a particular sense of *someone* that over-rode all other impressions.

This was Seymour of course. I always knew exactly what he looked like, even before I'd heard the name, or knew anything about him.

So when those diaries arrived on my doorstep and I began the arduous task of typing them up from the handwritten originals, it was as though my boy-self in some parallel life had indeed stepped off the bus and made his way across the marsh, past the sacred well, and into the mystic precincts of a long-dead worship.

Indeed the very act of typing up the diaries affected me on very deep levels. Perhaps by a combination of physical and mental absorption, and the power inherent in the Workings, I found myself falling into states akin to those felt by those who look into crystal balls. Sometimes I seemed to peek in upon FPD and CCT as they worked their Magic all those years before; sometimes, I knew that in some sense I was actually involved in rites which had once been worked (in linear time) thousands of years earlier. For days, weeks, the entities that Seymour and Hartley had invoked seemed to live with me, and the atmosphere of our already haunted house became filled with the spirits of these Secret Chiefs that the world had almost forgotten.

Be warned... In a strange way these same Magical Diaries can have a similar effect upon the reader. For those who know how to listen, there is a song behind the prose which is at once yearning, thrilling, wistful—and utterly compelling. The simple act of reading these juxtaposed diaries of a true priest and priestess can cause a resonance within the soul which will, ultimately, transform those who so desire it.

And if this is not enough then the final section of this new edition contains Seymour's long essay *The Old Religion*, which many think is *the* finest piece of magical writing this century. A true manual of self-initiation, this essay covers more ground in a few dozen pages than most writers on the topic can manage in a dozen books.

The original working title for the first draft of *Twentieth Century Magic* was "Mistress to Magicians," taken from a couplet in a Cat Stevens song describing someone as a "Mistress to Magicians/ And a Dancer to the Gods." Christine Hartley was so admant that she was *not* going to be described as "mistress" to *anyone*, that *Dancers to the Gods* it became—a title which may have had poetic grace but which consigned the original book to oblivion and everlasting night immediately after its launch.

Christine Hartley died on Michaelmas Day in 1985, only a matter of weeks after it was published. Yet judging from the mail I get from bemused folk who seem to be attuning to her psychically, she is as active after death as she ever was in life.

I ended the introduction to the first edition with a copy of her own words in acknowledging her own debt to Dion Fortune:

In Saecula Seculorum; Shatter the lamp, the light remains.

But as I get older, and simpler, and scornful of such flutterings in a tongue I've never understood anyway, I can't do better than seal my memories of her with the words: *I loved her very much, and miss her still; she was the brightest soul I've ever met.*

Alan Richardson
Wessex, England

1.

The Priestess in the Orchard

In her latter years they called her The Fluff; she liked that. It was a term of affection which threw her back to her youth when life was simpler, and warmer, and all she wanted to do was dance like Isadora Duncan in the free Greek style which was then so attractive and somewhat risqué. She never made it though: her psychism put a stop to that. She discovered the Gods instead. Yet at the end of her life, underneath her illness, underneath her years and obesity, that was how she saw herself at very heart: a piece of fluff, light and floating.

It had all turned inward; the grace and the motion was translated to what she would have termed the inner planes, and the imagery persisted throughout her writing. To her the Gods were like an inward tune with such an insistent and evocative sound that her psyche could not fail to respond in the mysterious kinesis of ritual. Even the love between a man and a woman was to her like an endless dance, "... giving and receiving; accumulating force and discharging it; never still, never stabilized, ever in a state of flux and reflux as shown by the moon and the sea, and the tides of life—ebbing and flowing, waxing and waning, building up and breaking down in the dance of life to the music of the spheres..." To her, mankind was like a gauche youth drawn by music to the edge of the floor in a seedy hall, too self-conscious to join in, yet yearning for the partner, the motion, and the magic that he felt was out there, under the lights, amid the dancing throng. All he needed was the courage to forget himself and surrender to the rhythm, letting the body take over in its movement. Too often, she knew, man spent his time watching and analyzing and tapping his feet, thinking too much and afraid to take the first step that might transform his life.

She understood this; she herself had spent a lifetime dancing in one way or another. She knew the fears and stumbling-points. From the hills of her native Wales and across to her adopted Yorkshire, down to the sandy fastness of the Hampshire barrens and then back into the heart of London, no one could stop her. She danced between the counties and she danced between the worlds, spiraling inward to the heart of the Western Mysteries, and knowing it was through God's will and not by fortune that she did so. She was born to the dance.

Dion Fortune was a contraction of the motto *Deo, non fortuna*. The latter was her true Magical Name, as it is called, and the former an expression of her public persona. In most cases, however, these mottoes were not chosen because they represented high spiritual principles, but because they were traditional to the family. All of the old families had mottoes, and where an occultist had difficulty in this matter he would cast around the names on the distaff side with the aid of a book such as *Elvin's Mottoes* until he found one for himself. The latter book almost provides a roll-call of the Magical Names used within the occult groups. There was a snob value in this sort of thing in that era.

In her public persona, Dion Fortune has come down to us today with the reputation of being one of the most influential occultists of the century, espousing a native Western tradition at a time when most people did not know (or did not want to know) that such a thing existed. At her best she was a superb writer, lucid and stylish; at her worst she was at least on a par with innumerable other teachers in this field who have now sunk without trace.

She was a very good magician, but not as great a one as some would have it; she was highly intelligent, but no scholar; formidable, but by no means all-powerful; exquisitely human, and in no way the quasi-divine changeling that some of her more excitable followers are inclined to suspect. Sometimes, one can almost feel a little sorry for her. Dion's pursuit and exercise of power was, in the final analysis, at the expense of all warmth and simple loving. In her latter years she knew that—which was why she liked the nickname Fluff so much. In her heyday, before the crucial year of 1935, no one would have dared be so intimate

Since her death in 1946 a great deal of misinformation has grown up around her. This is partly her own fault for having written about herself with the sort of tantalizing vagueness that just begs for misinterpretation. This, plus the inevitable myth-making which occurs around any personality like hers, almost compels commentators to offer pure supposition as positive fact, in order to create significant patterns. Magicians, it must be noted, like significant patterns. It is part of their urge to discern how the paths of life are organized. And the pattern they like best is that of the spiral, which will take them into the center of all things or outward to the very edge of the known. To outsiders it all looks very much like a maze, and can give rise to real bewilderment as to why the magicians take very straight and ordinary lines and then bend them to fit into the appropriate curve, in the proper direction. It makes for elegant narratives, but it scarcely does much to rescue the reality of the woman from the heart of the maze.

Major genealogical research is beyond the scope of an introduction like this. The full story of Dion Fortune will never be known. The best that can be done is give the facts clearly while at the same time stating, even to the point of tedium, those areas which are pure and individual speculation.

She deserves no less.

Violet Mary Firth was born on December 6, 1890, at Bryn y Bia in Llandudno. Her father was Arthur Firth, a solicitor. Sarah Jane Smith was her mother's maiden name.

Those are the facts. The myths, however, go something like this:

She was born in Yorkshire in 1891. She was an orphan. Her parents were killed in a tragic crash. She was adopted into the Firth family.

Although she obviously had close relatives in Yorkshire, and always described that as her native county, there is no confirmation in any source yet checked that she was anything other than Arthur and Sarah Firth's own child; and Arthur was still alive in 1927 when he witnessed his daughter's wedding.

This idea that she was orphan, however, seems to have been a later claim on her part. It might well have been no more than a tongue-in-cheek comment made to fob off the younger pupils who were showing an unseemly (and in those days, rather improper) interest in her background. They would have seized upon this in a way that she would never have wanted, for in the idea of such a person being an orphan, we are thrown back into the mythos of the changeling birth, of other-than-human conception and upbringing.

She did allude on more than one occasion to connections with the steel firm in Sheffield, founded by Mark Firth. A clue may lie within the marriage in that city of Edward Harding Firth to Frances Maud Harrison. Born in 1863, this was the fifth son of John Firth, and thus Mark Firth's grandson. It is not known whether Frances had any siblings. The significance of this is possibly in the fact that the motto of the Harrison family, in Yorkshire, is *Deo, non fortuna*. Although a recent compilation of mottoes ascribes this to the Firth family too, at the time of Violet's birth it seems that only the Harrison and Digby families laid claim to it.

This may be near the center of the maze; it may be just another dead end. Ultimately it is unimportant.

She was reportedly brought up as a strict Christian Scientist, forced into a rigid discipline, thus becoming a lonely child who sought refuge in daydreams and fantasy. This led on to psychism, and all those perceptions which alienate a child from an early age.

It rings true but there is no real evidence to support this. The Mother Church of the Christian Scientists could find no records of any Firth family being members at the time in question, and regional inquiries among the local branches of Weston-super-Mare, Bristol, Llandudno, and Sheffield have likewise failed to turn up anything concrete.

However, although she almost certainly was not brought up as a Christian Scientist *per se*, there was certainly a period in her midteens when she was an adherent. In April 1908 a poem by Violet M. Firth appeared in the *Christian Science Journal* entitled "Angels," about the empty tomb in the garden, containing the telling lines: "And thy heart tells thee all things are mortal,/ And frailest of all, thy love!"

She certainly lived in Weston-super-Mare for a time. This is revealed in the May 1905 issue of *Girl's Realm*, which reviewed her first book *Violets* and noted that "wise little Violet Firth works hard at her school at Weston-super-Mare all the term, and reserves versemaking for her holidays!"

Yet there are no records of any Firths living there during that period. She probably attended some now-defunct boarding school.

In 1906 she followed her first volume with the appropriately entitled *More Violets*, subtitled *A child's thoughts on Nature in verse and prose*. This, in contrast, was published in London.

The poems in the books represent solid-intelligent verse-making; but there is nothing precocious there: cleverness, but no genius. They are the sort of books which proud and even doting parents would willingly pay to have published. Which tends to give the lie to the idea that she had a difficult and strict upbringing under the cold eye of unloving parents. And also the assertion that her psychism sprang from the loneliness attendant to such a childhood is also refuted, perhaps, by her own later statement that she was a trained psychic, not a natural one.

It is all very vague, and failing the appearance of some hitherto lost documentation, or diaries, it is unlikely to get much clearer than this.

For the next period there are two main sources of information and disinformation: her novels, which draw upon actual locales and often actual people, plus that literary oddity known as *Psychic Self-Defence*.

The latter is essentially an autobiography which was written when she was forty years old—traditionally one of the stocktaking years in a person's life. In it she writes of her occult training, her mysterious and powerful teacher described simply as "Z," astral journeys, non-humans and the problems they cause, battles between herself and rival magicians on the inner planes, the dangers of Green Ray workings, traumas from past lives, secret lodges, materializations and visions, the philosophy of magic and the nature of evil, sexual vampirism and divine inebriation... and much much more, all interspersed with simple techniques to safeguard the neophyte against every variety of occult attack.

Although her fellow magicians saw it as essentially a "factional" piece, to use a modern term, nevertheless *Psychic Self-Defence* is superbly written, tantalizing in its vagueness, and always enthralling.

A critical analysis is beyond the scope of this chapter, and the main concern is to garner biographical information. There are four sources, therefore, which refer to her early life in one way another.

The Secrets of Dr Taverner—a collection of short stories of varying quality based around the cosmic mastery of "Z."

The Demon Lover—a first novel which oscillates between the sublime and the ludicrous.

The Winged Bull—which describes a magical courtship, possibly her own.

And *Psychic Self-Defence* itself.

The next stage of her life to which we have some definite clue is around the year 1910, when "As a young girl of twenty I entered the employment of a woman who I now know must have had a considerable knowledge of occultism obtained during a long residence in India..." She says no more than that this was an educational institution, and that it was a training-school of some sort. There is nothing in this ambiguity to suggest that she once taught in some residential school, as later commentators have assumed.

Writing in 1927, she gives us clues as to where this institution was. Unless one has unusual talent then a first novel is invariably autobiographical to some extent, so it is worth noting in *The Demon Lover* the several references to the Surrey hills in which her heroine, Veronica Mainwaring, had lived, and also the college where she had studied.

> ... the pupil who stepped out of the dark entry of the business training college into the blazing sunshine was engaged upon the urgent quest of fresh work now that her secretarial course was finished. Only the most rigorous self-denial had enabled her to get through her training; the third term had been one of semi-starvation, and this, added to the strain of the final examinations, had reduced her to an abnormal state in which she floated rather than walked, and saw grey ghosts about her instead of men and women.

She had not been happy there. The novel suggests that part of the problem was caused by the inability of this "sleeping priestess" to fit in with the unfamiliar, and essentially hostile girls of a lower social class.

As to the precise location, tangible directions are given in *The Secrets of Dr Taverner* in the preface of which she mentions a mysterious nursing home where the eponymous Doctor practiced, but which, as will be shown later, did not actually exist. Nevertheless she describes a specific area, giving names, directions, distances, and such geographical asides that the reader can build up a vivid sense of locale. It disposes one to suspect that she was using an actual place for the basis of the nursing home, one which she knew well and could write about from memory after many years. The general location is on Hankley Common, an area of moorland to the north of Hindhead, in Surrey. Taking all the clues and doing a rough triangulation, then there are really only two places on the Common which would fit. One is now a private house that had been run as a children's home from 1900-20 by a Dr. Tanner. His daughter could find no trace of any V. M. Firth having worked there. The other, and more likely, contender has since been demolished but once stood in a triangle of land on the southeastern edge of the Common, fulfilling all the criteria, and bearing the name of the British Colonial Training Institute. Despite extensive research in local records, in the India Office Library, in the Foreign and Commonwealth Office Library, no further details of this have been found.

Whether this is the place or not, Violet was given her first intimation of occult power from the Warden she writes about. This lady, using secrets she had learned in India, would "control staff by means of her knowledge of mind-power, and she had a steady succession of most peculiar breakdowns among the people working under her." The Warden wanted Violet to give evidence in a lawsuit. Despite her own diary record as to events, she found herself eventually agreeing with the older woman in a series of baseless charges against an innocent man.

> As I walked out of the room at the end of the interview I had a curious sensation as if my feet were not in the place I expected them to be. Anyone who has walked across a carpet that is belying up with the under-floor draught will know what I mean. Occultists will recognize it as having to do with the extrusion of the etheric double.

At the final confrontation the Warden used what one can only regard as hypnotic techniques, repeating incessantly the statements that she was incompetent, and had no self-confidence. Needless to say Violet demurred, somewhat, as to this estimate.

> Now there was no doubt that much could be said concerning my competency in my first post at the age of twenty, with a great deal of responsibility on my shoulders, and newly inducted into a disorganized department; but nothing could be said against my self-confidence, except that I had too much of it.

Nevertheless her employer did not argue or abuse her, but kept on with the two statements repeated like the responses of a litany. She entered the room at ten and left it at two. The statements were made several hundreds of times. She entered it a strong healthy girl, and left it a mental and physical wreck, and was ill for three years afterward.

She had only been saved, in fact, from complete psychological destruction by a clairaudient perception in which she distinctly heard an inner voice say: "Pretend you are beaten before you really are. Then she will let up the attack and you will able to get away! What this voice was, she added, she never found out.

In fact it was the voice of her common sense, no more. Had she been less proud, less stubborn, she would have heard it immediately; but she insisted upon this battle of wills and got a nervous breakdown for her pains. It is a testament both to her folly and her unwitting integrity. Had she been two-faced, saying one thing but meaning another, she could have walked out of that establishment with ease. As it was she *made* the Warden's magic effective.

She went away to the country to recuperate, her health being very poor. While there she came across a friend who had been on the spot at the time of her breakdown. To her intense relief, Violet found that here was someone who was not inclined to explain away the experiences but who in fact asked pertinent questions.

> Another new friend became interested in my case and haled me off to the family doctor, who bluntly gave it as his opinion that I had been hypnotized. It was before the days of psycho-therapy, and his ministrations to a mind diseased were limited to patting me on the back and giving me a tonic and bromide. The tonic was useful, but the bromide was not, as it lowered my powers of resistance, and I speedily discarded it, preferring to put up with my discomfort rather than render myself defenceless. For all the time I was obsessed by the fear that this strange force, which had been applied to me so effectually, would be applied again. But although I feared this mysterious power which I now realized was abroad in the world, I cannot tell what a relief it was to me to find that the whole transaction was not an hallucination, but an actual fact that one could rise up and cope with.

This illness would take her up to the year 1914. What she did during this period of recuperation no one will ever know, but following that there is a tradition that she worked for a time as a Land Girl, during the Great War. Clive Harper's research shows this was almost certainly at Monk's Farm, situated just outside Stansted-Mountifichet, which provided the background for *The Goat-Foot God*. An aprocryphal tale from this time goes as follows:

Violet was having a row with the farmers she was working for about the money they owed her and did not pay. She just happened to have the huge bunch of keys for all the various doors on that farm. Eventually she got the cover off the cess-pit and stood on the edge with the keys poised over the poop. She then threatened that if they did not pay forthwith she would hurl them into the faeces and they would have to fish them out after she had left. They paid, and she left in triumph.

It is a good story, and one entirely in keeping with her character. She could not have been there too long, however, for she later described in the *Occult Review* how she had worked as a therapist at what she termed the Medico-Psychological Clinic, claiming to have been the highest paid lay analyst in London, utterly without qualifications but greatly in demand. This was not, as has been supposed, the Tavistock Clinic, for the latter was not established until 1920 and has, in any case, no records for any Firth. Anne Bancroft in her book *Twentieth Century Mystics and Sages* gives it as being the East London Clinic, where she worked after having taken courses at London University. She gives the dates as being in 1918 but Violet herself implied that she worked there some years earlier.

It was around this period that she met her occult teacher. Now this was not, as has been boldly stated in several sources, Aleister Crowley. She certainly corresponded with him, but at that time most young occultists would have done so; he could hardly be avoided, like the dark shadow on some national institution. His secretary for a while, Israel Regardie, wrote that while Dion always spoke very highly of the Great Beast's writings, she gave the distinct impression that she would run a mile rather than actually meet him. There is, for example the apocryphal story that she once wanted to contact the spirit Taphtarthareth, and wrote to Crowley asking how she might set about this. The latter made discreet inquiries to find out what it was that the young lady most disliked. He found out that Miss Firth was allergic to fish. Needless to say he promptly sent her a potent ritual which just happened to involve the eating of fish in quantity and with frequency. After hearing that she had done this and been violently sick as a result, he reportedly dismissed the matter, saying: "Bloody stupid woman!"

It is a good story also, but one that should not have too much weight placed upon it. Magicians tend to be polarized between those who favor Crowley and those who favor Fortune, and each group seeks to gain by either insisting upon a connection between the two, or else denying it completely.

The truth is that Dion's knowledge came not from Crowley, not from the Knowledge Lectures in the Golden Dawn, not from supra-conscious revelations using her own innate vision, but from one man: Dr. Moriarty, "an Adept if ever there was one!"

1. Dr Moriarty

His exact identity has been confused by her own writings, notably *The Secrets of Dr. Taverner*. This was a collection of short stories written between May and October 1922, and published in *The Royal Magazine*, finally issued in volume form in 1926. The stories, with titles such as "Blood Lust," "The Soul That Would Not Be Born" and "The Death Hound," describe how a Dr. Taverner, using the methods of a mysterious occult fraternity, effected cures in the seemingly incurable, and dealt with patients whose troubles had malign magical roots. The collection was preceded by an introduction which reads, in part, as follows:

> "Dr Taverner" will no doubt be recognized by some of my readers; his mysterious nursing home was an actual fact, and infinitely stranger than any fiction could possibly be. It is a curious

thing that the picture of him drawn from fancy by the artist who illustrated these stories for the Royal Magazine, is a recognizable likeness, although that artist has neither seen a photograph nor had a description of him.

To "Dr. Taverner" I owe the greatest debt of my life; without "Dr. Taverner" there would have been no "Dion Fortune" and to him I offer the tribute of these pages.

In fact the nursing home did not exist. She was simply using a literary device common to many authors then and now, in which the writer of an astounding tale would begin by solemnly affirming that all of which followed was perfectly and provably true. Dion being who she was, later generations have taken her words at their face value.

The confusion has been compounded by the fact that there was a Dr. Moriarty living in that area at that time, namely Matthew Denis Moriarty, MD, FRCSI, of "Clonmeen," Epsom Road, Guildford. There is no evidence that this was ever anything else but a private house, and one would be inclined to discount him entirely except for one thing: India. Matthew Moriarity was born at Ventry in Co. Kerry in 1849. He was the son of the Dean of Ardfert, and by 1911 was a retired Colonel in the Indian Medical Service. It was in this Service that a Dr. Burnes founded Freemasonry in India in the 1830s. Burnes was a member of the Grand Lodge of Scotland and soon became Provincial Grand Master for West India. There seems to have been some very close links between the masonic lodges in India and the magically inclined groups in and around London. Colonel Seymour, for example, the third of the trinity of men behind Dion Fortune, was a member of the Grand Lodge of Scotland during his time in India; as was W. E. Butler, who appeared later. The Dr. Moriarty to whom Dion owed such a debt was known to be a prominent mason too, but despite the probability there is no provable link between him and Matthew Moriarty. In fact the former, I have been told, actually changed his name to that for reasons unknown. Matthew Moriarty died of leukemia in 1925. Again, he may be without significance in the history, but the details have been given anyway: at least they lay bare the pseudo-Taverner which has crept into so many people's convictions.

The true object of our interest was also an Irishman, namely Theodore William Carte Moriarty, born around the year 1868, who was given a strict Roman Catholic upbringing before eventually running away from home to join the Merchant Navy. It was here that a kindly ship's officer gave him books to read on philosophy which ignited his interest in such things. He studied at Dublin and also Heidelberg, where he gained his doctorate. Having discovered by this time that he was suffering from advanced TB he went to South Africa on his doctor's orders, worked at road surveying, and for the Customs, and found that the dry climate proved beneficial to his complaint. During this time it is known that he was very active in Freemasonry, with large numbers of students. In 1909 he wrote, with Thomas N. C. Day, the *Freemason's Vade Mecum*, but by 1916 he was back in England lecturing to various small groups.

It was at this period that he met the forceful young woman who would soon come to regard herself as the inheritor of his knowledge.

Violet, as she still was then, probably met him in connection with the Medico-Psychological Clinic, and those stories in *The Secrets of Dr. Taverner* which did have some basis in fact would have been taken from the casework within there. She provides us with a source of information and misinformation in her book *Psychic Self-Defence*, so this should be read with some discrimination. Written in 1930, it describes how she left London to study at an occult college "which was hidden away in the sandy fastness of the Hampshire barrens!" The term "occult college" is a grand one, and rather an overstatement of fact. It was actually a private house named The Orchard, plus an adjoining cottage, in the village of Eversley. It had been bought by a Mrs. Elsie Reeves and her sister Gwen Stafford-Allen to give Moriarty a platform for his lectures and the means of some income.

Eversley lies to the north of the county, almost on the border with Berkshire. It is the village where, in 1863, the Reverend Charles Kingsley wrote what was almost his last book, *The Water Babies*. It is a lovely parable about young Tom the chimney-sweep (who is thus an explorer and cleaner of dark channels) who uses his innocence to explore a strange aquatic world. In the light of the community that would be studying in that village fifty years later, one might be forgiven for looking at that book as somehow prophetic. By this time, though, Moriarty's health had declined once more. It is understandable that this, in connection with his remarkable gifts, tended to bring out the best in his students. In fact they were all devoted to him, the nascent "Dion Fortune" no less than anyone.

She writes at some length about her time in that community, as she termed it. She describes the main building as an old house with a massive front door that was secured at night by two enormous bolts, modern casement windows "of the most gimcrack description," and a place that was sometimes loud with the noise of the ancient creaking stairs. She paints a convincing scene but then she was always something of a novelist-manqué. This said, one must always hold the personal pronouncements of magicians lightly—which is not the same as taking them lightly, or with cynicism, or scorn. Magicians, by the nature of their craft, have an innate self-dramatizing quality. Used properly and kept within themselves, it is this quality which ignites their inner flame and enables them to alter consciousness towards other than the purely mundane levels of function. Sometimes, when the magicians in question are writers or raconteurs, this self-dramatization slips out and tends to lead them, and those who follow them, back into the dead-ends within the maze again. The yarns of all such must be held lightly therefore, for the magical material has its own weight and gravity and will in due course thin itself out into golden threads—which can lead us somewhere.

The other people in the community saw the young Miss Firth as just one of the pupils, no one exceptional. There were others there with greater insight, larger gifts. Had the woman in question not been keen to write a good and luminous story (at which she succeeds admirably), she would have been prompt to concede this.

One of her first visits there was in the company of one whom she describes as Miss L., an ultra clean and ultra-sensitive woman who was verging on a breakdown and was anxious to escape the city for the balm of the countryside. On getting out of the ancient fly, in which they had been driven from the station, the decrepit horse which pulled them bolted at Miss L.'s friendly pat, nearly turning the equipage into the ditch.

The phenomena did not stop there. The community had nightmares. Inhabitants were afflicted by similar dreams, and a pervasive sense of evil. On one occasion during the night Violet "distinctly saw the head of Miss L., in the air at the foot of my bed, and snapping its teeth at me." At first she was inclined to blame it all on the local baker, as it was known even then that when rye got infected with ergot the bread consumed had hallucinogenic properties. This was some years before they could define it more precisely as a crude but potent form of LSD. It all came to a head however when the older woman attacked Violet with a knife. This was partly because Miss L. had developed a "crush" for her, and Violet, having "a constitutional repulsion for crushes," had given her overtures scant politeness, causing Miss L. to complain bitterly of her lack of responsiveness. The incident occurred in the kitchen, and at one point Violet found herself fending off the attacks with a hot sooty saucepan full of freshly boiled greens, dancing around the kitchen table while Miss L. slashed at her with a large carving knife.

Moriarty came in then. He took in the situation at a glance and scolded them both impartially for the noise, telling them to get on with the work. Later, dealing with the magical basis of the problem, he filled an ordinary soap-dish with water, consecrated this liquid, and drew a pentagram upon the threshold of Miss L.'s room to stop her leaving it until such time as he was ready to deal with her properly. When he did so he discovered that the root of the problem was black magic: she had practiced it in previous lives. Miss L. herself said that this had been confirmed by several independent psychics. With the wise handling of Dr. Moriarty she ceased to become a menace to anyone, and Violet ends the chapter with the point behind the story that "a case of well-marked insanity was cleared up by occult methods."

This was one of her recurrent concerns: the maladies and pathologies of the present life having karmic origins. Often the recovery of such "far memories" would have a therapeutic effect comparable to psychoanalytic counseling. In those days it was a radical idea. Such therapies which utilized the concept, however, tended to be influenced by an era which saw black magicians behind every curtain, just as a later generation would find Reds under the beds. In the occult field personal aberrations, minor idiosyncracies, or divergences of opinion from the accepted canons of thought, would be ascribed to the work of black magicians. Although in fairness there were a lot of these about. Violet came along at the fag-end of a time in which that state of consciousness known as Bohemia still sent echoes around the staid corridors of rationalist thought. It was almost *de rigeur* for artists (especially in France) to be thought of as vaguely satanic. The practices of art and self-styled black magic coexisted very happily. Cyril Connolly made the most acidly perceptive comment about Crowley, for example, when he described him as the man who bridged the gap between Oscar Wilde and Adolf

Hitler.

Nevertheless, even taking this spirit of the times into account, Violet *was* a good seer, and she did have some acute insight into the human condition. If one can accept the influence of karma on the physical and psychological health of an individual, then Violet was as good an authority as anyone for discerning it. And Moriarty was an even better one.

During his time at Eversley his tuberculosis seems to have re-asserted itself. This is a disease which has always had a peculiar association with the more visionary members of the artistic society. It has been speculated that the very nature of the disease releases toxins into the bloodstreams which can produce an intensified vision of life. Being who and what he was, TB in Moriarty's case produced some rather bizarre side-effects.

In discussing the mechanism of the extrusion of the etheric double she remarked how the doctor was able to perform this operation. He would go into deep trance, after a few convulsive movements, and would then lose about two thirds of his weight. She noted that when he was in this state he weighed little more than a child. She described what actually became of this missing weight too, for on one occasion when he was going through delirium, his ectoplasmic body found its way into her bedroom, presumably because it was she who had had the lion's share of the nursing—particularly the night work.

> He was plainly visible in the moonlight, clad apparently in his dressing gown, or so I took the muffling folds of material to be that swathed him about. Both his face and wrapping appeared grey and colourless in the moonlight, but there was no question in my mind as to his solidarity, for not only could I see him, but I could feel his weight resting upon my feet. But at the moment I moved, he vanished, and I was left staring in amazement at the smooth fold of the blankets over the end of the little camp-bed on which I lay. It was then, and only then, that I realized he had appeared all grey and colourless, more like a shaded pencil sketch than a human being of flesh and blood.

The community was at Eversley in 1920. For some reason it then moved to Hertfordshire where it functioned under the title of the Science, Arts and Crafts Society, and comprised some twenty souls who listened to him lecture several times a week. Unlike the community at the Orchard, this was not instrinsically residential. At least one member had been directed to the group by the venerable educational placement service, Gabbitas Thring Ltd., and believed that she was going to study gardening. The extraordinary nature of the man who ran the course (which lasted four years and involved written exams) affected her so much that fifty years later she was still actively cultivating the seeds he had planted within her psyche.

The exoteric teachings within his curriculum are divided into four sections under the headings of Evolution, Anthropology, Psychology, and Comparative Religion. Individual lectures were on such themes as: the Evolution of Matter; the Root Races of Atlantis; Structure and Mechanism of the Mind; Evolution of Physical Man from Primordial Spirit Matter; the Thread of Ariadne and the Laws.

These were his basic lectures for public consumption, yet it is obvious from the transcripts that his was a formidable intellect indeed. For his more advanced students there were his lectures that were collected and published under the title *Aphorisms of Creation and Cosmic Principles*. It is here that we find the true genesis of Dion's cosmology. The Aphorisms themselves are worth quoting in full:

1. The Eternal Parent was wrapped in the sleep of cosmic night,
   And nothing existed in manifestation either real or apparent.
   Light there was not; for the flame of spirit had not been rekindled.
   Time there was not; for change had not yet re-begun.
   Things there were not; for Form had not yet re-presented itself.
   Action there was not; for there were no things to act.
   Polarity there was not; for there were no things to manifest opposites.
   The Eternal Parent, causeless, indivisible, changeless, infinite, rested in unconscious dreamless sleep,
   And other than the Eternal Parent there was naught, either real or apparent.

2. The Germ within the Cosmic Egg takes unto itself Form.
   The Flame is re-kindled.
   A Thing exists. Time begins.
   The Pairs of Opposites spring into being.
   The World Soul is born and awakens into manifestation.
   The first rays of the new cosmic day break over the horizon.

3. The One became Two,
   The Neuter became bi-sexual.
   Two-in-One evolved from the Neuter.
   Generation began.

4. The One becomes many,
   The Unity becomes diversity,
   The Identical becomes Variety.
   Yet the many remains the One.
   Diversity remains Unity,
   Variety remains Identical.

5. The One is the Flame of Life,
   The Many are the sparks in the Flame.
   The Fire, once kindled, kindles everything within its sphere;
   The Fire is in everything and everywhere.
   And there is nothing dark or cold within its sphere.

6. As Life is the essence of Spirit,
   So Consciousness is the essence of Life.
   Spirit is one, yet it manifests in many forms of Life.
   Life is one, yet it manifests in many forms of Consciousness.
   All Consciousness manifests on seven planes.

7. From the subliminal to the transcendental,
   From that which is, to that which was,
   And God requireth that which was.

8. For the All is One and all are part,
   And not apart as they seem to be.
   And the blood of life has a single heart,
   Beating through God, and clod, and thee.

All of this lies at the very nub of Dion Fortune's philosophies.

The anonymous students who compiled these lectures in volume form note in the foreword that the origin of the Aphorisms was never given, but that they bore a strong resemblance to the Stanzas of Dzyan, and that it was not unlikely they are "another interpretation of the symbols which were the original fountainhead of the Stanzas." There is more than a hint of the pristine days of Madam Blavastsky here, although Moriarty's last surviving student insists that he did not belong to the Theosophical Society or anything else beyond Freemasonry.

Within the aphorisms there are references to the seven planes of consciousness whereon the Flame of Life is in function, namely:

The seventh or Upper Spiritual Plane
The sixth or Lower Spiritual Plane
The fifth or Upper Mental Plane
The fourth or Lower Mental Plane

The third or Upper Desire Plane
The second or Lower Desire Plane
The First or Physical Plane

Furthermore he lists the seven cosmic principles "without which the world of manifestation could not exist as manifestation" as:

The Principle of Correspondence
The Principle of Law and Order
The Principle of Vibration
The Principle of Rhythm
The Principle of Cyclicity
The Principle of Polarity
The Principle of Sex

Afficionados of Dion Fortune's writings will note the obvious and immediate resemblance. Also, within the terse analyses and comment which accompany each aphorism, several statements take the eye:

> The Christ is essentially the Power, Love and Wisdom of the Son (the Sun) made manifest...

> ...and thus from the initial aspect of the Eternal Principle ever unmanifest and the Logos in duality comes a threefold aspect, the Three-in-One. This Initiatory Three itself comes into manifestation as three Powers—called in this philosophy the Lords of Form, Flame and Mind, the Lords of Form and Mind being the reflection of the duality and the Lord of Flame the reflection of the entitial three of the highest level.

> The law of Correspondence is briefly summed up in the ancient Canaic saying of the Order of Melchisadeck—"From one, know all..."

We shall learn more of the significance of these in due course.

One philosophy which Moriarty did not teach in any depth, however, although he was clearly familiar with it, was that of the Qabalah. What his pupil seems to have done was to take his teachings and look at them through the lens of the various spheres upon the Qabalah's Tree of Life. This last she would have got from the Golden Dawn.

It is impossible in a single chapter to do justice to the breadth and depth of Moriarty's work, but suffice to say that he was the first of the trinity of men who would influence her direction in magic, and without him Violet may not have become *Deo, non fortuna* at all, taking her talents into less demanding psychic labyrinths than those of Hermeticism.

The secrets behind Moriarty are now well lost within occult Freemasonry, in lodges which were allied in sympathy at least with the more esoteric brands of Theosophy, and the more masonic branches of the Golden Dawn. It is significant that when Violet Firth was finally initiated into a magical group *per se* it was in 1919 by J. W. Brodie-Innes, who was himself a prominent mason. Perhaps she had been passed on by Moriarty. No one will ever know.

Theodore Moriarty died of angina pectoris in the Duke's Head Hotel, King's Lynn, August 18th, 1923. He was remembered by his students as an unpredictable but affectionate and approachable man, though not one to suffer fools of any sort. He vehemently refused to have anyone call him "Master" as was sometimes the fashion in those days, and wanted to be regarded as no more than an ordinary man making a sometimes lonely way toward the center of things. If he could sum up his philosophy in one sentence it was this: Love is the fulfilling of the Law. Which was the one area in which Dion could never really follow.

She described her initiation as like coming into a harbor after a storm. The ritual drama finally sealed up the rent in her aura that the Warden of the training college had made all those years before. She no longer leaked prana, to use her own words. It is another way of saying that by this time she was completely recovered from her nervous breakdown, and was able to enjoy reasonable health on all levels.

The temple she joined was the Alpha et Omega, as run by Brodie-Innes. She described it "the Southern branch of the Scottish section of the Order." After a short time she transferred to a temple known as the Stella Matutina, under a Mr. and Mrs. Hughes, but whose ultimate head was Moina Mathers. The former temple, she felt, had become effete, the rites without power, the province of "widows and grey-bearded ancients." The Stella Matutina at least had an air of potency about it.

All this, be it noted, running concurrently with her visits to Hertfordshire for her real source of inspiration.

In 1922 she decided that she was sufficiently advanced along the path to form her own group. This was originally known as the "Christian Mystic Lodge of the Theosophical Society." Francis King, in his excellent study of the time, opined that it acted as an outer court to the Golden Dawn system, which would offer public lecturers, magazines, etc., to entice new recruits to the parent body.

After 1924 when she published *The Esoteric Philosophy of Love and Marriage*, Mrs Mathers expelled her for allegedly betraying inner secrets of the Order. Magical battles followed in which Dion, as she was now invariably called, prevailed. From that time on she was her own mage and no one else's.

When a magician leaves his fraternity with the intention of setting up a group of his own, it means that he (or she) has made contact of his own with discarnate sources of power and intelligence—in short, the so-called Secret Chiefs.

We might define these as discarnate entities of high status who have what is essentially an evolutionary interest in humanity. Occultists have failed to agree on any one term for these beings because each one has tainted associations. Mathers caused some embarrassment when he insisted that he had met his Secret Chiefs, in the flesh, in Paris. The term Masters had such unpleasant connotations with all the various Blavatsky scandals that it gradually lost favor. The eminently descriptive term Spirit Guide was never favored by magicians because it smacked of what they saw as the inferior techniques and maudlin communications of the generally (and unfairly) despised Spiritualist movement. This is an example of the inherent elitism of many magicians: they regard themselves as on a higher intellectual plane than mere mediums. For all practical purposes we might simply use the term "contact," for that is their very essence. Whatever these entities really are, to the magicians they provide a point of contact between the worlds and levels of consciousness.

A high level contact, therefore, would give each magician a charter to form his own group and express his magic in his own way. Thus Dion would have made her contact in 1922, and the question is: just who or what gave her this inward authority?

The answer is almost certainly Melchizedek of Salem.

It is important not to confuse the issue here with psychological jargon. It is meant quite literally. Senior magicians within Dion's group (and presumably Moriarty too, judging from the previously quoted reference) believed themselves in direct psychic contact with an entity who had once been known on earth as Melchizedek.

It is a name which appears in many of her books, almost as though she were bursting to tell us all about this contact she had made. In *Training and Work of an Initiate*, for example, written in

1930, she writes: "In the same way the archetypal ideas were brought to mankind by the Manu Melchizedek, who was a Lord of the Flame and also of Mind ... and therefore it is that the highest of our Initiates are referred to as 'High Priests after the Order of Melchizedek', that is to say, they trace their spiritual lineage back to a primordial initiation." It is thus he who acts as something like a master co-ordinator behind the various Orders, and who in his most ancient role was the Being who had first come to earth from Venus, bringing with him the elements of Wheat, Honey and Asbestos. These are symbols peculiar to the system Dion used, representing on one level certain qualities of self-creation that were held in common with the Master of Magicians. They are not necessarily accepted or even respected by other magical groups with different sources of illumination.

Melchizedek then, was regarded as the contact behind the contacts, and the one which validated the authority of the group which she was then calling the Christian Mystic Lodge of the Theosophical Society.

This is a curious title which was calculated to appeal to an extremely broad spectrum. The Theosophical Society as such was in a lively state at that time: there were the first stirrings of the "Back to Blavatsky" movement by those who were tired of the dubious seership of Messrs. Leadbeater and Besant; there were moves to align the esoteric section of the TS with the ritual marvels of masonry; Co-masonry was becoming a force. Just being known as a lodge of the TS would cover a wide variety of occult styles.

Dion's Christian Mysticism however, at least in the early years, was rather more than the rapt ultra-pure adoration of the Lamb that such a title often conjures up. The tone of her own approach is best summed up in the words of her teacher, Moriarty, who said:

> The Gospels we know were esoteric allegories, compilations of the Chasidim and other Christian Hermetists, and their authors, as well as their hero, are, by some, thought to be mythical and allegorical not historical personages. The truths set forth in these God-spells, as teachings of the Christ are Gnostic verities, and although they are, for the most part, veiled in allegory, they are the communications of the Word, the eternal Christ principle. There is no doubt that Gnosticism was early Christianity and the early Christian Fathers and writers are all initiated Gnostics. The Gospel of John, for example, is pure Gnosticism.

The Christian mythos constructed out of Egyptian and Hellenic Hermeticisms, Indian, Magian and Hebrew theosophies, far from being the teaching of a few uneducated Hebrews, was in all probability the carefully planned system of the Neo-Hermetic secret conclave composed of the stricter sect of the Chasidim and the initiated Gnostics.

Gnostic Christianity, which reached its best and most numerous expression in Alexandria, was essentially knowledge through revelation. Sometimes the individual revelation took the seer a long way from the modes of expression and belief he had used until then. It is the sort of Christianity which could happily countenance and embrace the philosophies of pagan beliefs. This, therefore, provided her lodge with its tone.

But if her primary contact was Melchizedek, whose influence was filtered out through her own exotic version of Christianity, she actually relied upon a pendant trinity of contacts which gave her lodge its stability and immediate energy. In effect these created a perfected microcosm of the universal mind—as they understood it. The initiation of each adept within the lodge could be likened to the awakening of new cells within the inward and occult cerebral matrix, creating a symbiosis between differing kinds of consciousness.

This trinity of contacts (echoing Moriarty once more) were held to express the qualities of Power, Wisdom, and Love. This is the sacred triangle. (A positive force, a negative force, and the reconciliation between them.) The entities filled these angles, in a manner of speaking, and in so doing gave the lodge an energy which could be tapped, a two-way feed.

Studying the magical diaries which comprise the most important part of this book, one can hazard a very good guess as to whom these contacts were, and how they fit into the triangle. It will be at least a substantially accurate if debatable reconstruction of the system that was once used by her group. (The present day Society of the Inner Light, it should be emphasized uses a very different set of contacts.)

The first of these was the High Priest of Ptah, known as Kha'm uast (various spellings); he was son of Rameses II, an overlord of all the magico/religious ceremonies within Egypt. His own center was in Memphis, and he lived from about 1300 to 1246 B.C. His mother was the Queen Isit-nefert. In his youth he had been a soldier; later he became a priest and a great scholar. He died some ten years before his father; had he not, he would probably have become Pharoah.

From the folklore that survives today, collected in the *Stories of the High Priest of Memphis* by F. L. Griffiths, he is shown very much as a Merlin figure, potent and ambivalent, neither good nor evil—or beyond both. Kha'm uast related, one presumes, to the angle of Power. Sometimes this angle was referred to as Strength.

2. *Kha'm uast, the High Priest of Ptah*

Next, at the angle of Wisdom (also known as Knowledge), was the being who had once been known as Cleomenes (or Klemenes), a Spartan king from the house of Agiad who lived from 235 to 222 B.C. A vigorous and ultimately maddened man, he had defeated the Achaean league at Ladoceia in 227, and then instituted the cancellation of all debts, the redivision of land, and the return to the old Spartan training. He curtailed the powers of the council and introduced the board of six elders. He was defeated in battle in 222 by the Macedonian king Dosun, whence he fled to the sanctuary offered by Ptolemy Euergetes in Egypt. Imprisoned by the latter's successor, Cleomenes broke out in 219, and, having failed to raise a revolt in Alexandria among his fellow Gnostics, he took his own life. It was this entity which gave the lodge in those days its serious, strict, and determined air—the Spartan quality to do the work and battle on without complaint.

Here we must take another speculative leap.

It was stated that *The Cosmic Doctrine* had been "received" from the inner planes in 1923/4, and that it had been communicated by a Greater Master. Within that text we read about the Lords of Flame, Form, Mind—and Humanity too; of the different laws of form and force, attractions and limitations; of impactation and epigenesis. This is, in fact, the philosophy of Moriarty writ large. Although we have only the *Aphorisms* to compare with, a former pupil of his told me that there was little essential difference between *The Cosmic Doctrine* and the extended, esoteric analyses of the good doctor.

There are three explanations, one of which is cynical enough to be discounted, leaving:

Either Dion and Moriarty shared the same content, the same Greater Master. Or that Moriarty was the Greater Master in question.

Furthermore, in a piece of pure guesswork, I would submit the possibility that Moriarty and Cleomenes were in fact one and the same, and that his discarnate consciousness was functioning through the persona of a previous and more dominant incarnation. Similar things were happening fifty years later, with the revenants who contacted Arthur Guirdham.

That Moriarty/Cleomenes was at the angle of Knowledge is interesting. Nominally a Christian, his Christianity as we have noted was essentially Gnostic in origin. It had dark, glittering, and arcane aspects. Not for him the formula of the Lamb, the milk and water. His was the Christianity of Ambrosius in one of Dion's novels: there was a goat-foot background to it.

These two contacts in fact gave real expression to the paganism inherent in Dion's psyche. They were probably the first to go when she began to lose this side of herself.

They were completed in the triangle by what was at least for that period the chief of the lodge, the reconciler, the Love aspect. This was Lord Eldon, called simply Lord E, or more often "Himself." Eldon was born as plain John Scott, in Love Lane, Newcastle upon Tyne, on June 4, 1751. Genealogical conjecture has sought to connect his family with the Scotts of Balwearie, and he himself made vague claims of being related to Michael Scot, the wizard-scholar,

3. Lord Eldon

who lived roughly from 1175-1234. His father was a fairly wealthy man who owned several keel-boats, a pub, and was involved in coal mining. John was originally intended for the church but to his eternal credit he sacrificed that by eloping with Elizabeth Surtees. They eventually had ten children. He was a lawyer, whose maxim was to live like a hermit and work like a horse; he became Lord Chief Justice, and was then created Baron Eldon of Eldon, in County Durham. Politically he was what we would now call reactionary, but there is no doubt that as Chancellor under both George III and IV he held the country together through his work behind the scenes. Both kings came to adore him, and if there was one personal quality upon which everyone was agreed, it was the extraordinary degree of charm and sheer fascination that he was able to exert. That is the giveaway. The sign of a real mage is in his magnetism: sometimes it repels, sometimes it attracts, depending upon one's own polarity at the time, but it is magnetism nonetheless. It is something—everything—to do with the contacts behind him. Physically he was middle height, active, regular features, keen, sparkling eyes and luxuriant hair—almost the ideal of manly beauty. He shunned intellectual society and not unwisely, it was said, for he was ill-read, untravelled, and without either knowledge of or taste for the fine arts. He was a great drinker, with an inexhaustible fund of witty anecdotes, a good landlord, quietly charitable and a devoted husband. If he was described as a buttress of the church it was partly in jest because he spent so little time actually in church. He died on January 13, 1838, and was buried near his Encombe estate in the graveyard of the weirdly atmospheric Kingston Chapel in the Isle of Purbeck. Despite his poor attendance in places of worship he was a deeply religious man, as evidenced by his biographer, Horace Twiss. He wrote many poems in Latin for his own amusement, one of which is worth looking at for an insight into his true nature, a translation of which reads:

> Let him, who shall desire it, stand in power
> On the slippery height of the mansion:
> Me let sweet quiet satisfy.
> Placed in an obscure situation
> May I fully enjoy mild leisure.
> Noted by none of the Romans
> Through silence may my age flow on:
> Thus, when my days shall have passed
> Without noise,

> May I die a plebeian old man.
> On him death presses heavily
> Who, too well known to the world,
> Dies to himself unknown.

For reasons that will be given later Dion probably did not make the Eldon contact until after December 8th, 1923; but if Moriarty had a Greek antecedent, then John Scott had even more ancient origins; he was a high priest in the Temple of the Sun in the City of the Golden Gates in lost Atlantis. Or so they earnestly believed. He stayed behind while the island sank, but his last act had been to bid farewell to the young priestess Morgan, the old priest Merlin, and a seasoned warrior to protect them, who thence sailed on a great billow to the shores of Lyonesse.*

The theme of Atlantis is omnipresent in Dion's works. She regarded it as her alma mater in the same way that other magi looked toward Karnak, Delphos, Alexandria, or Anglesey. She presents the basic threads of the story again and again, reaching almost poetic levels of intensity in her novel *The Sea Priestess*, but summed up most succinctly in *Avalon of the Heart* where she writes:

> There was a great civilization built up with the help of the gods who then dwelt among men. There was built the City of the Golden Gates, concerning which the folk-lore of all races has a tradition. This city, so we are told, was built upon the flanks of an extinct volcano on the sea-coast of this ancient land. Behind it was a plain stretching back to the inland mountain ranges. It was an isolated pyramidal hill, shaped like a truncated cone, with one side, the inland side, sheered off into a precipice. At its base there was a vast concourse of wattle huts in which dwelt the bearers of burdens. On the shoulder of the mountain dwelt the merchant and craftsman castes, and upon its flat top were the palaces and colleges of the sacred clan, which was divided into two branches, the military caste, and the priesthood.
>
> This sacred clan was most carefully segregated from the rest of the population, and its breeding was carried out under the supervision of the priests... The maidens of the sacred stock were guarded with the greatest care, and were given in marriage to priests or soldiers according to their lineage and temperament. So was the heritage of the Sacred Clan kept pure, and a carefully selected stock bred for the development of those rarer powers of

---

* Later Adepts within the F.I.L. had never heard of Kleomenes, and always believed that DNF's contact was one Lord Erskine. There are obviously many strands of magic involved here, perhaps of a schismatic nature.

the mind so highly esteemed among the ancients and so little understood among ourselves.

Is there any possibility that Avalon, with its undercurrent of pagan legend, was originally an Atlantean colony? Is it possible that Merlin was an Atlantean—a priest-initiate; and in presiding at the birth of Arthur he was carrying out the Atlantean custom of kings bred for wisdom? In order to bring the higher consciousness of the evolved Atlantean race into the Celtic tribes of the colonized island, did Merlin, in defiance of the strict laws of the sacred clan, and in pursuit of ends of his own, cross the Atlantean stock on the Celt, and so breed Arthur? And was Morgan le Fay, the half-sister of Arthur...a pure-bred Atlantean, the British-born daughter of the sea-people?

As will be shown, however, she did not necessarily identify herself with Morgan—a name which in fact means "sea-borne"—but recognized her as a vital figure who is something of a Celtic equivalent to Isis, in her bright and dark aspects, and certainly equates directly with the triple goddess scheme that runs through Western mythology (her sisters were Morgause and Elaine).

This trinity of Kha'm uast, Cleomenes and Lord Eldon was a representation of three great traditions: the Egyptian, the Greek, and the British. They even suggest a chronological progression from the near-forgotten depths of post-Atlantean Egypt, through the Hellenic flowerings, up until the burgeoning days of Empire, when something very vital was aflow within the Western psyche.

They were not rigidly held to each angle. Contact with the consciousness at one angle automatically aligned one, metaphorically speaking, with the qualities of the other two. For ritual purposes the magus would tend to specialize, however, and the triangle was completed by his or her co-workers. In the early days Dion took the Knowledge aspect. This was a measure of her attachment to Moriarty and the energies he was pouring into the lodge.

When necessary, she was also more than happy to bring through the Power. She could never really work the Love aspect. Although her adepts came and went, the most enduring trinity comprised herself, a Mr. Loveday who filled the Love aspect, appropriately enough, and Thomas Penry Evans who most surely manifested the Power. These three worked together for more than a decade during the most productive period of the lodge.

Loveday has suffered to some extent by being identified as Raoul Loveday, Crowley's excellent and most willing pupil. Yet

Raoul died in Cefalu in the late 20s and certainly bore no semblance to the lean old bachelor Thomas Loveday who ran what was essentially the Outer Court of the lodge, known as the Guild of the Master Jesus. It was a devotional group which expressed Esoteric Christianity as interpreted by Dion. It took its charter from psychic contact with one of those entities "known to estotericists as the Watchers of Avalon." Perhaps she meant one of Bligh Bond's spirits, for she knew him quite well. The services used the same form of Eucharist as the Church of England, and although anyone could join the Guild as an associate, membership required completion of the Junior Study Course.

In practice, the Guild, for all its earnest sentiments, was no more than a dumping ground for those unable to cope with the intellectual demands and self-discipline needed for the full magical curriculum. Dion regarded it privately as something of a sop to her less able neophytes. Mr. Loveday, in contrast, took it all most seriously. It was his child. He was an aesthete, an intellectual, with the sort of gentility that comes from a lack of inward virility. Many of the seniors found it all very dreary.

Nevertheless, Dion did write some of the prayers. Fragments of these survive in a privately published leaflet which contains her Morning Hymn and Evening Hymn, the first verses of which are, respectively:

> Father Divine, the sunrise gloweth bright;
>   I rise to do Thy will.
> The love that kept me through the passing night
>   Can guide and keep me still.

and

> Father Divine, the daylight now is gone;
>   I rest in Thee.
> Teach me Thy will, that I may be at one
>   With Love and Harmony.

It is not very good. It is scarcely more accomplished than the verses she wrote for *Violets* at the age of thirteen. Her Christian expressions were fervent enough, but they never achieved the ringing magnificence of the invocations she made to the ancient gods and goddesses.

The third member of the trinity appeared in 1924 although she undoubtedly met him earlier than this. It was said quite openly that

Loveday had seen his especial qualities and helped pay his way through medical school. This was Thomas Penry Evans, named after the charismatic Welsh evangelist, and son of Kercy Evans who was a shearer in the local tin-works. He was born on September 27, 1892 at an address given simply as "Farmer's Field," Pontardulais. No one knows precisely how or where they met. It might have been in connection with Moriarty, for Evans' speciality as a doctor was in the treatment of tuberculosis. He qualified in 1924 and was renting a room in 3 QT (3 Queensborough Terrace) the following year, while working at Charing Cross Hospital.

Coming from a simple working class home and with a common name he had nothing in the way of family tradition to fall back upon for a magical motto. Yet they all knew he was a bit special; more than that in fact. And so they gave him the most exalted name of all: they called him Merlin.

Within the group however he was always known as Merl, or Doctor Evans, depending upon how close one got. Dion simply called him Penry. He was a vital, virile and unsophisticated man, a real Welsh Prince despite his lack of polish. Dion believed that he was one of those who had come from Atlantis before it sank, carrying the seed of the Sacred Clan's knowledge with him. Some of the juniors were rather afraid of the power he seemed to emanate at times.

They got married on April 7, 1927. Arthur Firth and Merl's sister Hazel were witnesses. Dion showed a very human touch on the wedding certificate by lying about her age, giving it as 35 instead of nearly 37.

As the new Violet Evans she stayed with Tom's parents on several uneasy occasions. The Evanses did not know quite what to make of their new daughter-in-law. Few people did. Back within the security of 3 QT, Dion confessed to the almost unbridgeable social gap that existed between her and her in-laws. Soon, she stopped going.

Outsiders have speculated on the marriage and on Tom himself, because Dion had always been aware of an inherent mannishness in her personality. She confronts this in several places within *Psychic Self-Defence*, which is as much a study of her own occult (in the literal sense) pathologies as it is that of the fraternities. She patiently explains that where a leader of a magical group is a woman then that person will get a lot of unstable people of her own sex acting out their passions for her, and noted that: "I was accused of being a man in disguise and attempting to seduce the complainant, and the charge found believers." It has also been implied that she may have had a lesbian relationship with Maiya Tranchell-Hayes, who had been a superior within the Golden Dawn. But the former is not the confession of a closet lesbian, or of anyone who had anything like that to hide. Dion was aware to an extraordinary degree that we are all two-sexed beings. No intelligent person would be unaware of this today, but at that time it was a stimulating concept. She knew that it was part of the ancient Mysteries to look for the woman within the man and the man within the woman. Had anyone dared press her to describe her orientation, she would have just inferred that she had found more of the opposite sex within herself than most. As she wrote in *The Sea Priestess*: "But the ancients did not concern themselves with anomalies, but said that the soul was bisexual, and that as one or the other aspect manifested in the world of form, the alternative aspect was latent in the world of spirit."

4. *Thomas Penry Evans*

It is not likely, either, that Merl married her to get on in the world. He quickly made a successful career for himself with his own skills, becoming an authority on tuberculosis and smallpox, and latterly the Medical Officer of Health for Arnersham, Beaconsfield and Chesham, among other responsibilities. Their marriage lasted some dozen years. No small achievement for two such formidable people.

Merl in fact *was* the magician within the lodge. He was better at magic than his illustrious wife—who took great care to vet the women he would work with, ensuring that he rarely had the chance to perform magic with them alone. Her cosmic visions were not inconsistent with a very human jealousy. In her own cold, magical, and essentially sterile way—despite her disclaimers—she loved him dearly.

Disclaimers. She told several of her senior female adepts that she had married him for the Work, not for love. In *The Demon Lover;* written the year before she married, she wrote: "The mating of an occultist is much more than an ordinary marrying." At its best this is true. But also, often, the mating of an occultist becomes much less than an ordinary marrying, too. Something has to be sacrificed, usually: physically, emotionally, mentally, or spiritually. The tension engendered by the lack of one or more of these enables the magic to move. Dion and her husband-mage had no children; toward the end they rowed with an awesome intensity.

Merl's magical aptitude was not confined to himself alone. His sister Hazel, a nurse, came to rent a room at 3 QT as well, where she met and soon married one of the other students, the old Etonian Edward Maltby, an officer in the Royal Corps of Signals.

The house in Queensborough Terrace was by this time a real community. It was a return to the lovely days at Eversley. The basement contained the kitchen and communal breakfast room. The ground floor had the administrative offices where Loveday attended to such matters as the correspondence and the production of the magazine. The first floor had two large rooms that were used for rituals and public lectures, where J. F. C. Fuller once came to hear her speak. (He was the Colonel described in *Psychic Self-Defence* who dealt with the mysterious Indian adept who was attempting to influence the British group psyche.) The floor above was where the Evanses lived and had small bed-sits for paying students. They also had a set of rooms next door at 2 that came be used almost exclusively by Charles Seymour. The whole place was only a short walk from Sinclair Road, where Moriarty had once lived.

By 1926 the first advertisement had appeared in the *Occult Review* which stated discreetly that Dion Fortune, author of *The Esoteric Philosophy of Love and Marriage*, would be giving lectures during the Winter. It added that "In accordance with Esoteric Tradition no charge is made for admission and all contributions are voluntary." Those interested were directed to write to a Mr. E. Homan for further particulars.

The next year her group was now openly advertised as the Christian Mystic Lodge of the Theosophical Society, and jostled for space with the Brotherhood of Light in Penge, and enticements for the talismanic jewelry of W. T. Pavitt of Hanover Square. It stated that the President, Dion Fortune, would be giving public lectures on Mondays at 5:30 and 8:15, and that the latter was a study group conducted by the President herself. The transactions of the lodge were also for sale at 31/- per annum post free, and these were in the form of a monthly magazine dealing with Esoteric Christianity.

June 1928 saw a significant change, however. It was now the Community of the Inner Light, and Dion Fortune was the Warden, rather than President. The group now saw itself as "a fraternity whose purpose it is to pursue the study of Mysticism and Esoteric Science. Its ideals are Christian and its methods are Western. It maintains a Lecture Centre and Library in London...Public lectures are given on Mondays 8:15 p.m. by Dion Fortune throughout each term."

Note the new title. The Christian aspects which had been emphasized in large letters and heavy print in preceding advertisements were less prominent now. This was probably due to the increasing influence of Merl. If anyone had ever thrilled with the "lissome lust of the light" from the goat-footed one it was he. His force, his energy, deflected the direction of the lodge. Although the ideals were still essentially Christian the power that was now being tapped came from a pre-Christian era. It came from Merl, working the Kha'm uast aspect, bringing through energies she had never known before. It was the best time of her life.

In one sense the year following her marriage was her *annus mirabilis*. During this time she formed what she then called The Chalice Orchard Club, at Glastonbury. This was open to the general public from Whitsuntide to Michaelmas as a hostel and pilgrimage center, and the terms were from £2 12s 6d per week, although the

34 / 20th Century Magic

5. Dion in Chalice Orchard

accommodation was in what had once been a forty-foot Army hut that had been given to her and which eventually found rest at the foot of the Tor. The price of the magazine had doubled too, and it was now called *The Inner Light*, and dealt with the familiar themes of Mystical Christianity, Esoteric Science, and the Psychology of Super-consciousness. Apart from the number of stimulating articles in the *Occult Review* she still had her book on love and marriage to her name (for which Mrs. Mathers had expelled her from the Stella Matutina), the collected short stories of her Dr. Taverner character, and her first novel *The Demon Lover*. And Merl.

The Glastonbury aspect is an important one. Here in one spot was a tangible resolution of the dichotomy she had always felt between her pagan and Christian sides. The windy heights of the Tor satisfied one side of herself, the ruined serenity of the Abbey catered for the other. She was always at her best here, and the only surviving photograph of her with Merl was taken in the Chalice Orchard containing the sacred well that was peculiarly associated with Morgan le Fay. Here on the physical plane was a center which she felt resolved the antagonisms between the magic of the standing stones and the mysticism of the Cross. She soon made it part of her will that no matter where she died she was to be buried here, in the "holyest erthe in England," in the graveyard of the Church of St. Michael, that angel associated with hilltops and the conversion of pagan places.

The image of the orchard is interesting too. The very name Avalon is *Ynys Afallon*, or Isle of Apples, and the magical tradition links Avalon with the secret Garden of Hesperides where the sacred apples grew, watched over by nine fair maidens. These nine maidens, wrote Christine Hartley, represent the triple divisions of the triple Goddess, herself the original triplicity of the One, and the Muses are but her various aspects. Dion was thus linked in her turn as one of these Muses, a priestess of the orchard, of the Great Goddess herself.

Within the town itself she always made a clear distinction between the Avalonians, of whom she counted herself one, and those who merely lived in Glastonbury. Avalonians, it was to be understood, inhabited a world that was not entirely physical.

After John Cowper Powys brought out his great work, *A Glastonbury Romance*, she used her own book, *Avalon of the Heart*, to make a brief but dignified defense of the people and all their little pecadillos. Yet ironically, had she been able to take her mask off and step aside, she would have seen that Powys was a far greater mystic than herself, one of the real Earth-mages of Britain, who could make the land talk in sibilant, erotic whispers, whose very nickname among his peers was The Old Earth Man. Dion was never in the same league as him.

The following decade was the period of her greatest creativity. During this decade she wrote:

Esoteric Orders and their Work	1928
Sane Occultism	1929
Training and Work of an Initiate	1930
Mystical Medications on the Collects	1930
Psychic Self-Defence	1930
Spiritualism in the Light of Occult Science	1931
Practical Occultism in Daily Life	1935
The Mystical Qabalah	1935
The Winged Bull	1935
The Goat-Foot God	1936
The Sea Priestess	1938

She also wrote for light relief, three detective novels under the name V.M. Steele. These were:

The Scarred Wrists	1935
Hunters of Humans	1936
Beloved of Ishmael	1937

They were competent novels at the time, but are now dated in the extreme.

It is said that magical rituals attract entities from the Otherworld like moths to a flame. In this case 3 QT was a lighthouse on a lonely shore. People flocked to it in increasing numbers. On Monday evenings upward of 30 people would sit in the larger of the two lecture rooms and sit spellbound as this tall handsome woman walked up and down before them, talking in her resonant, accentless voice, clad in bright red or blue kaftans which contrasted so pleasingly with the drabness of the fashions at the time—a sorceress enchanting, her neophytes entranced. Bohemia brought unto the Bayswater Road. Kenneth Grant gives an accurate description of her in his *Magical Revival*:

> ...rich jewels beneath a flowing cloak, and, on the rare occasions when she went out, a black broad brimmed hat from which her sun-glinting hair sometimes strayed and fluffed about her head like a golden nimbus. Her personality contained more than a streak of exhibitionism, strongly reminiscent of Crowley, and towards the end of her life she collected about her an odd assortment of talismans and magical impedimenta; she burned strange perfumes in curiously chased basins of glittering metals. Her afternoon stroll in Hyde Park was undertaken in

the voluminous cloak which recalled the advertisement for Sandeman's Port. She describes the heroine of *Moon Magic* as similarly dressed as she paces the misty Thames embankment...she imagined that she passed unnoticed on these strolls!

Except that he is misleading in his assertion that she imagined no one saw her: she just did not care. And the British in any case have long had a talent for refusing to give any outré dresser the satisfaction of being stared at.

It was this burning personality and what she seemed to promise behind it that attracted so many. Apart from Christine Campbell Thomson and Charles Seymour, there was W. K. Creasy and Bernard Bromage, Paula Trevanion and Mary Gilmore, Margaret Wilson and the Maltbys. Another, who joined later, was Walter Ernest Butler who would come to write one excellent and several indifferent books about magic.

He had served in the Army in India where he had attempted to join a magically orientated group there, comprising Europeans and Indians. He was refused entry and told that this was not the group for him, but that he was to go back to England and find "the lady with the red roses." Back in London he heard for the first time about a certain woman in Glastonbury. He cycled there. As he turned, exhausted, into the little lane which led to the chalets, he saw a striking woman with a bunch of freshly picked roses in her arms. "I've been waiting for you," said Dion.

Another member for a brief spell was Israel Regudy, who by this time had anglicized his name to Francis Israel Regardie, and was regarded as something of a notoriety for publishing the rituals of the Golden Dawn. He had done so because he felt that the once-splendid Order had grown effete, little more than a pompous friendly society filled with incompetent adepts. It was an opinion with which Dion heartily concurred. Regardie, contrary to what most assumed, did not make a single farthing out of the venture, having deliberately foregone any royalties. He gave a full justification of his deed in his book *My Rosicrucian Adventure*, and while there are few people today who are not thankful that he did so, at that time he was rather *persona non grata* in many occult fields. Dion, who had attended his initiation in the Stella Matutina, freely offered him sanctuary. He stayed with the group for only a short time before going to live in the Welsh Borders and thence, ultimately, to the psycho-therapeutic vales of America, where he remained for the rest of his life.

There were many others, of course, but not everyone who claimed membership of the fraternity was an adept. Most never got beyond the first year, or outside the Guild.

It was in 1935 that her masterpiece was published. This was *The Mystical Qabalah*. She submitted it a portion at a time to Christine Campbell Thomson, her literary agent, using that lady as a sounding board with the wry comment that if she could understand it, then anyone could. She told her intimates, too, that in writing this book she would almost certainly lose her contacts. This would be the penalty for breaking her initiation oaths. Nevertheless, she said, it was better for one person to suffer than a whole nation. She said it casually enough, but meant it.

To magicians the idea of losing one's contacts can provoke horror. It is a calamity akin to castration—the removal of one's very *raison d'etre*. Without her contacts she would be like a light bulb in which the electricity has suddenly been shut off: a gradually fading warmth, an after-image on someone's retina. The usual solution is to cease active magical work entirely for a number of years—usually seven or eight—and then start again from scratch and see Who or What turns up this time. If anything.

The Mystical Qabalah is still the finest exposition of that philosophy ever written. Attempts by modern writers to supersede it have failed through sheer unoriginality or impenetrable style. It is lucid, informative, and never flags. She writes with authority and never lapses into the morass of occult sermonizing which marred some of her earlier work. Crowley had a far greater technical knowledge of the Qabalah than she; Regardie had a genius for the presentation of his own material; but nowhere had anyone presented such a clear and comprehensive sphere by sphere guide to the Tree of Life upon which so much of the Western magical system was based. It might not have been pure Qabalah by the standards of those pundits who favored the *Sepher ha Zohar* or *Sepher Yetsirah*, but it was the Qabalah that the magicians used, adapted for the peculiarities and prejudices of Western and Judaeo-Christian man. If she was a physically sterile woman, as might be inferred from one of her novels, then this was her child. The knowledge contained within this had once been bound into her psyche by the oaths taken in the Golden Dawn. It was a cellular part of her inner self, a living thing. In cutting apart her oaths and plucking this knowledge from out of herself before casting it adrift within the coracle of her public image like Moses or Mordred or a hundred other miscegenated magicians, she was losing a part of herself. Or giving birth to something greater.

1935 is the year upon which all interpretations of Dion Fortune hinge. This is when interpretations diverge:

She went onward, ever upward.
She slowly began to decline.
She stayed at the same level but turned aside, took another path.

Whatever the ultimate truth might be—if there is such a thing—then one thing is at least certain: she never stood still.

The original thesis of this chapter was that from this year onward, until about 1940, the Kha'm uast and Cleomenes contacts which gave her her pagan/Gnostic orientation, slowly began to withdraw. After a flat period she made new contacts to replace them, and contacts that she felt were more in keeping with the original direction of the lodge before Merl appeared. In this thesis, the onus of withdrawal is upon the contacts themselves. It tends to imply, also, that Dion went "wrong" and that she was chastised by the same entities which had so recently given her real power.

The alternative thesis is this: from 1935 onwards, disenchanted with the direction of the lodge, disenchanted with Merl, and seeking to become truer to her own essentially Christian self, she deliberately began to relinquish the pagan side of her magic, deliberately withdrawing the links with those two entities. She might have ossified had she not.

No one will ever know the truth of it. We can only dream the myth and get it to work for us. The essence of each life is never clear cut when we look at someone from the outside. We might interpret their motion as blind gropings, when in actual fact they are moving with ritual certainty. Sometimes, as a priestess's real power grows and her knowledge widens, the way she can follow grows ever narrower; until at last she chooses nothing, but does only and wholly what she must do.

What is certain is that from 1935 onward the bulk of her public work was fictional. For the rest it consisted of articles in the Fraternity's magazine which showed an increasingly Christian tone, which accelerated after 1940. The only possible exception was the ominously entitled *Though the Gates of Death* which was originally published privately, without a date given, and not re-issued until 1957. Apart from the detective novels she wrote:

The Winged Bull
The Goat-Foot God
The Sea Priestess
Moon Magic

There were rumors that a fifth had been planned and even completed, entitled *Sun Magic*, but no trace of this has been found.

It is in these novels that we can learn the most about her but there is no space for an extended analysis here. Besides which it is in the sphere of literary criticism that personal interests are most easily evoked. The images she wrote with are like crystals; each man sees his own Dion Fortune therein, although there is nothing intrinsically there. Yet what can be said is this:

Her novels were all, without exception, about sex magic. It is genteel and sanitized compared with the explicitness of today; it is elegant and often poignant; it is safely parcelled up in the arcane images of the remote past with nary a hint of genitalia, or even Freudian allusion—but it is sex magic nonetheless. A Western tantra. It is here that we have the center of the maze just around the next turning, where the half-beast, half-human roars.

In these novels we can see a range of castrated, ineffectual men achieving superb consummations on magical levels when they yield to the inherent (if sometimes unconscious) superiority of the woman. Of them all it is *The Winged Bull* which is the *roman-à-clef*. That her heroine Ursula Brangwyn shares the same name of the female protagonist in D. H. Lawrence's *The Rainbow* and *Women in Love* is no coincidence; it is both parody and tribute. The characters are as follows: Ursula = Dion; Murchison = Merl; Colonel Brangwyn = Colonel Seymour; Astley = Crowley; and Fouldes? No one knows.

The danger here is that we must not project our modern sexual attitudes upon her and her era. Compared with today Dion comes across as a woman driven by the clash between her spiritual and physical natures, and there is a tendency to condescend towards her in consequence. Yet in the 20s and 30s many people, if not most people in British society, were struggling with just such a dilemma, but without any of Dion's insight and daring. Her books were barely acceptable in terms of contemporary morality, and if she had had the skill and the time, then in due course she might have written novels that would have ranked alongside some of the better (and proscribed) writers of the century. She was heading in that direction when she wrote *Moon Magic*. If she had gone on from there, or rather devoted her life to the novel in the first place... who knows?

At a time when sex was still the great numinosom, then she was enlightened; as avant-garde for her era as any of the ithyphallic magi rampaging through the circles and covens of today. She herself wrote: "I decided to produce novels that should come as near an initiation ceremony as possible; that is to say, that should produce in receptive persons something of the same results as are produced by the experience of going through a ritual initiation." By and large she succeeded admirably. And her last two novels *The Sea Priestess* and *Moon Magic* are arguably the finest novels on real magic ever written. Looking around at what has been offered to us since, one is inclined to say that they are the *only* novels on real magic ever written.

The war, of course, interrupted everyone's life. She and Merl separated at about this time. Her senior magicians were either called away to do their bit for king and country or else they just ceased coming, disillusioned with the way they thought the lodge was beginning to go, complaining of a sense of deadness about the place and their teacher. Perhaps it was no more than their own dissatisfaction projected into the group: powerful personalities can never mix for long; they seek ways to separate. In any case members were no longer able to meet as before. Links were thus maintained by regular newsletters and esoteric discourses, as well as the equivalent of a Silent Minute in which each member would attune him- or herself to the group-mind at the same given time. By concerted meditations they aspired to influence the course of the war, working without national bias, invoking purely spiritual principles which would filter downwards. Sometimes they would place themselves, in their imaginations, in the Hill of Vision, or Glastonbury Tor itself, wherein they would commune with the Masters. They mediated purely spiritual qualities which would in due course, in a proper manner, filter downward, affecting all men.

This new Dion Fortune, with her new Masters and her rosy

workings with the Cross, was a far cry from the young woman who had once engaged in tooth-and-claw combat on the inner planes with Mrs. Mathers. Perhaps it was a case of being older and wiser by this time.

She and others insisted that this type of magic worked, that it had observable effects upon the outer planes. Yet some magicians knew her during this period said that she was a mere shadow a mage and more a spiritualist medium. Others who met her the first time during the war said that she was indeed a formidable figure, brimming with magic undiminished.

Around, around; turning and turning...

The temple was bombed. Magicians gave each other Significant looks. Dion moved to rooms at 21b Queensborough Terrace. Here she was attended by W. K. Creasy, an intense and apparently narrow man who had succeeded Seymour within the group, and one of the few seniors to stay loyal from her early days. A Christian Mysticky sort of person, he might well have helped to get it all back in the original direction, away from the ruined but still potent altars of forgotten worships, and back toward Calvary again. He was helped in his ministrations by a group of women in whose eyes Dion could do no wrong, who bore nicknames like Healer and Dragon—the latter being a Miss Lathbury who now ran the office and guarded what was left of the threshold.

Dion was dying by this time, of leukemia. Some people thought this was a direct expression of the dichotomy between her two natures. She finally died in the Middlesex Hospital on January 8, 1946.

After her death it was rumored that Dion still continued to lead the group from the inner planes. Loveday for one definitely maintained a psychic contact with her, but the onus of transmitting her messages fell upon Margaret Lumley-Brown, whose special interest was in the Arthurian Tradition which Dion had made portentous noises about but which was developed and interpreted by others.

Francis King in his study *Ritual Magic* opines that the change in the tone of the lodge came about in the 50s, and ascribes that to the influence of the present-day contacts. This may be so, but it is likely that they were made in Dion's own lifetime. What she left behind, in essence, was a group which continues to function along its own lines, its own Christian Mystic lines, just as she had intended all along, before Merl appeared. After all, this was inevitable to her way of thinking. She had even presaged it in *The Demon Lover* when she wrote:

> The country curate who dabs some lukewarm water upon the little form in his arms sets a seal that takes a very great deal of breaking, as all who deal in the hidden side of things are well aware.

As *she* was well aware.

Quite what happens behind the doors of the Fraternity of the Inner Light today is a secret known only to their initiates and their gods. Being the society it is, more people have probably applied for admission out of fascination for the mysterious Dion Fortune than out of interest in the Mysteries as such. The group seems to have evolved, out of necessity, an unusually high and even stern standard of admission, and it is stated that the training given is "of benefit only to those who are natural inheritors of the cultural traditions of the British Isles and neighboring Europe." It insists upon regular attendance at their rituals, and warns that prospective candidates for supervised teaching must fulfill all obligations to work, family and society at large before they can even be considered. Wisely, they refuse to initiate anyone below the age of twenty-five. Their system has undoubtedly gone through many changes as they have endeavored to bring it up to date with the modern era. This would be laudable in an individual, but for some reason they have come under frequent attack as a group from those who took it as an affront to the Work of the founder. Yet, abhorring the cult of the personality, all it apparently wants to do is to get on quietly with its own system, aiming at the regeneration of the individual and the nation as a whole. It works, it survives, it attracts new members. It has lasted, to date, over sixty years. Some of the much vaunted and loudly praised temples of the Golden Dawn had effective lives of mere months.

Failing treachery in the lodge, it will never be known when their present-day contacts were originally made. Indulging once more in pure speculation it could well have been that Dion fell back at last into the Guild of the Master Jesus, making new contacts there which were developed and expanded by Loveday and Creasy. Such details are, in any case, just ornate patterns around the doorway. They frame the exit and entrance to the maze, the alpha and omega. It is the path inside which counts.

It was rumored that Dion ruled the group from the inner planes for thirteen years. Which takes us to 1959. It was that year, on

August 30, that Merl died.

Perhaps she remained earthbound waiting for him. Maybe he came to take her away.

Thomas Penry Evans had taken her from the altars of lost gods, down strange druid tracks by the light of forgotten constellations, through the echoing temples of Egypt and Greece, far far from the path she had wanted to go as a girl, which was toward Bethlehem and the Saints. His magic was like a straight rod of light through the darkness of infinite space. In taking Dion and the group in his own direction he took us all. Someday he will return, the once and future mage.

In the last analysis the glories of the original Inner Light were as much due to him as to his wife. And the name of the house in which he died in Weedon Lane, Amersham, just about says it all. The name of his house was:

Pan.

2

The Dancers to the Gods

Magicians, like royalty, need heirs. The passing on of papers, secrets, ritual equipment does not come into it. What they need is someone to link into the same circuit and bring through energy of a subtly different sort, so that the Work might progress. Usually, the choice of heir is made by the inner contacts rather than the hierophant.

Crowley used the term "magical son" to express much the same thing. In his case he had Frater Achad, a brilliant man and excellent writer who was once jailed for indecent exposure after he had opened his raincoat and cried out to the indifferent citizens of Vancouver that he had stripped away the veils of illusion. Indeed.

Yet Dion was never motherly enough to look for a magical son or daughter, she just wanted to pass on the power to whoever was best suited. It was not a matter of giving that person 3 QT and all therein. There was no financial gain. It was a matter of keeping the flame alight and shining in the right direction. There is always a great danger involved here. And it is something to do with masks, and power. Unless a mage earths the power at the right time—just *before* he reaches his peak—then there is the likelihood that it will come to scour him out, leave him empty. He might look the same on the outside, he might have a residue of wisdom left, but in truth he is a hollow man. The exaltation that Power brings often blinds the mage to nothing else but himself. In many of the ancient Mysteries the priests wore masks; this had the side-effect of being a safety device. The ritual over, the mask off, he was merely a man again. No person would associate the everyday man with the priest in power.

Unfortunately in the present century professional occultists are finding that their masks are getting stuck to their faces. Merl could avoid that, he had other roles in the outside world. Poor Dion, however, had been hounded into a cul-de-sac, stuck within her own maze. She was no longer called Violet even by her husband, and if she escaped into V. M. Steele for a while it was not very effective, because no one much knew or cared about those novels anyway.

Of course any fool can be wise with hindsight. What we have to remember is that Dion was in the forefront. Although Merl was behind her, pushing her into his own precise directions, she was the one taking the brunt of all the collisions on the way. She made it easy for the rest of us. She was used by the gods just as much as she was used (unwittingly) by her pupils. Generations later it is easy to score points by knocking her down. This happens to every public figure What we must never forget is that she heard the music, she devised the steps, and she led the way into the spiral dance in the first place. We must not make the mistake of thinking purely in terms of power, and creating a league table of potencies. In her system magic expressed itself through Power, Wisdom, and Love, and these were different in kind, rather than degree. Those who came after her, using her system, were neither greater nor more insightful, but just different rhythms in the same tune, using different steps.

This is the account of two who followed closely behind her, linking hands, circling in from Atlantis, across to Egypt and Babylon, up to Scandinavia and around to Ireland, taking in the Languedoc, before eventually ending up at a precise and prosaic location just off the Bayswater Road in London, where time, space and events were all resolved in one central point...

Christine Campbell Thomson was born in London at 11:30 a.m. on May 3l, 1897. Her mother was a jewel of Victorian narrowness, the sort who counted imagination as a vice to be suppressed. In her home, and over her two daughters, two rules prevailed: When in doubt don't do it; and Never make yourself conspicuous. These were like the halves of an Iron Maiden: outwardly the very image of true womanhood; but inwardly, the spikes. Her father was a man apart, however, H. Campbell Thomson MD, FRCP, a noted neurologist whose book on the nervous system remained a standard text for many years. Both he and his father-in-law, Robert Temple, were dominant figures within the early years of the Middlesex Hospital, where Dion would later go to die.

Here was what might be called an Empire childhood, of Queen Anne Street elegance, nannies and butlers, glimpses of Queen Victoria, streets that rang with the noises of horses and the sound of servants standing in their doorways blowing shrill whistles to summon carriages. Paul Dukas was writing *The Sorcerer's Apprentice* in that year, Wells *The Invisible Man*; Havelock Ellis began shocking people with his *Studies in Psychology of Sex*, while Pickering, using photographic techniques, found the nine moons of Saturn a short while later. She was a child in an important family growing up in the most powerful nation on earth. Unlike Dion, there was no mystery about her childhood, no angel poetry. It was the world of *pur sang*, good form, and servant problems. And she was not very happy with it at all, thanks to her mother's approach.

Today, it seems no more than apt that a woman whose mother chose to suppress the imaginative faculty, and whose father explored the hidden structures of the brain, should one day use her visionary talents to explore lost areas of the psyche in ways that have influenced us all.

Her first job was with the literary agency of Curtis-Brown and Co. She started a secretary but quickly had some say within the workings of the business. Before long she left to form her own agency which still thrives today as Campbell Thomson & Laughlin Ltd. Those are the bare details of her professional career.

She describes this time at length in her memoirs *I Am a Literary Agent* written in 1951. It is a book which is crammed with names, dead names, like some literary necronomicon: names which have an almost incantatory ring to the modern ear, evoking half-remembered spirits from forgotten times. Everyone from T. E. Lawrence and George Moore, through the originals of Secker and Heinemann and Gollancz (and all the authors they published), the child stars Noel Coward and Esmé Wynne, Max Freedom Long and Paul Tabori up until her very great friend Nicholas Monsarrat, whom she once bet she would outlive—and did. They are not deliberately dropped for effect but offered almost with embarrassment, the necessary details of a crowded life. Throughout the book she acts like the medium she could be, channelling through the souls, giving their shells a last spark of energy. And ending with the words:

> Many of those who read this book will wonder at omission of all reference to people whom they know have influenced me, or to whom I have been devoted: my response is that this is not an ex-

> position of myself: it is a book of memories culled from the past and there are some things too precious to be printed.

Some things indeed. Like the fact that in the previous twenty years she had operated on equal terms with some of the most powerful magicians of the century. The nearest she comes is a reference to the "throb of recognition" she felt on first glimpsing Africa from Gibraltar in 1923; plus another brief description of how a friend cajoled her into doing dream interpretations for a weekly woman's paper for twopence a dream. She wanted to use the pseudonym "Serpent of the Old Nile," but was made to settle for Madame Mascotte instead. She never came any closer than that to revealing the hidden side. Two decades of magical work were pushed firmly beyond the pylon gates into that Otherworld to which she had a key.

It might be said the she had transformed her mother's command—Never make yourself conspicuous—into the fourth of the magical maxims: Know, Will, Dare, and *be Silent*.

The role of the literary agent is curiously analogous to that of the magician: their job is to mediate between the creative and formative worlds and forge a link between the artist and those who need his vision. In this sense, she herself was a contact. She began in an era when, far more so than today, writers were felt in some way to be front-runners in the evolutionary march, their deeds steeped with unspecifiable import. They were a strange breed, writers. Punch made jokes about them as it would about faddists of any sort today. To the establishment they were, on the whole, vaguely immoral—the avant-garde ones, that is. They were vaguely threatening. And for their part they had powers to shock and cause outrage that are largely lost to the writers today.

Christine was necessarily a part of it all. Energies went both ways.

Once again we are talking about the magnetism that adepts have. A real teacher does not actually need to utter a single word to pass on his power. It is done purely by his presence. Verbal precepts are ultimately just so much noise. It is what goes on at inner levels that is important. It is only this which gets us anywhere. The tremendous changes of consciousness that took place as a direct result of the major writers' visions had effects upon Christine and her ilk; and at the same time her clients and associates were picking up something from her, and thus from the contacts behind her. Though she would have been the first to demur as to this.

Nevertheless, it was a writer who first glimpsed her inner potential. This was John William Brodie-Innes who was born on March 10, 1848 at Downe in Kent, graduated from Oxbridge and entered the legal profession at Lincoln's Inn. The latter part of his life was spent in the Scotland of his ancestors, becoming Chancellor of the Diocese of Argyll and factor to the Duke of Argyll. Brodie-Innes is chiefly known to us today as a minor novelist, a student of Scottish lore—especially witchcraft—and a man at the center of various political machinations within the Golden Dawn. He came to Christine just after the Great War with the manuscript of *The Golden Rope*, which was to be his last published novel. A dry, wry man he was also at this time the head of the Alpha and Omega Temple in London, using the motto *Sub Spe* (Under Hope). It was he who eventually did an about-turn and came to support Mathers in his belief in the "Third Order" behind the Golden Dawn which boasted a supernatural authority. Although he agreed to differ with Mathers as to the precise nature of this authority, he came to feel that this was the very essence of magic.

6. *J. W. Brodie-Innes*

He had undoubtedly changed his mind in Mathers' favor because he had made a real contact of his own. Too often magic stops short at stately rituals backed up by complex psychologizing. Every once in a while the practitioner finds, to his astonishment, that there is a further stage in which verbalizations fail, and that there really is some indefinable substance to those beings that had hitherto been thought of as poetic images only, mere metaphors.

B. I., as she called him, was the first to suggest that Christine might have an aptitude for study along "certain occult lines." He might have seen the marks in her aura from initiations in previous lives.

Magicians claim to be able to do that, and some of them really can. In fact magic, one might speculate, is almost tribal in nature. The shamanic totems and the contacts of the magi are not dissimilar. Western magical tribes are scattered in the geographical sense, but the members all have a subtle feel for their own, and every now and again groups will gather under the aegis and impulse of the same contact. Moriarty, who had closely studied the Bushmen, recognized this. B. I., who had lived in the primitive communities of the Highlands and Islands, knew it too.

One thing we should remember: No matter that he acted on several occasions within the political battles of the Golden Dawn with an apparent lack of acumen: to those who worked with him, Brodie-Innes had real power. On inner levels he was one of the great magicians.

In his excellent book *The Golden Dawn: Twilight of the Magicians*, R. A. Gilbert notes: "Brodie-Innes also was supposed to have had contact with the Sun Masters but there is no evidence, except—perhaps—on the astral plane, that there ever was a Sun Temple in Edinburgh." Now although occultists from that era were insistent that such a temple *did* exist on the physical plane, the more likely explanation is that the whispers got twisted in the telling. The connection is through *the* Sun Temple, on Atlantis, via Lord Eldon again.

The obvious assumption is that B. I. had made the Eldon contact too. This would make sense. (More so if it was Eldon who "communicated" the Cosmic Doctrine as most of the pupils assumed within the Inner Light, although it was never spoken of, or asked about.) But when Christine went through the whole system of Dion's group and made her own contact with Lord Eldon she recognized him immediately as an old friend; she was quite sure that

Lord E and B. I. were one and the same.

And it gets more complex yet.

Brodie-lnnes had confided to several of his intimates, Dion among them, that in a previous life he had been Michael Scot. We have already noted that Eldon opined as to a family connection with that man. Thus: Michael Scot, John Scott, and John William Brodie-Innes were all the same entity.

Yet there is—or might be—a fourth link in the chain.

When discussing all this with Christine in her flat in Hampshire she listened as gracefully as she always did. Blinded by cataracts at this time but all the more aware because of it, she "went away" briefly, as psychics do. That is the only way I can explain it. When she came back she gave me one more name: Dr John Dee. So that the chain now reads: Michael Scot, John Dee, John Scott, John William Brodie-Innes.

7. Christine Campbell Thomson at Michael Scot's tomb

52 / 20th Century Magic

Michael Scot, in brief, lived from approximately 1175 to 1234. Although the good people of Kirkcaldy claim him as one of their own, through the Scots of Balwearie, he was probably from the Borders. After graduating from Oxford and then Paris, he served for some time within the court of Frederick II in Sicily. In due course he was patronized by both Emperors and Popes. Later, living in Toledo, he learned Arabic and translated many hitherto inaccessible

8. Dr, John Dee

works on natural history and mathematics—particularly those of Aristotle. He helped to revive the ancient learning and bring it West. In his time he was a prominent figure. Roger Bacon seems to have been jealous of him; Dante and Boccaccio both described him as a magus of great renown. Certainly he made accurate prophecies for kings. Later in life he came back to the Borders, where he died from food-poisoning it is said, from drinking broth of a sow in heat.

John Dee was born, by his reckoning, on July 13, 1527. He graduated from Cambridge, Trinity College and although he never rose higher than an MA, he claimed a doctorate in law from studies on the Continent. The man certainly had one of the finest minds of the age; he was what we would now call a polymath. He excelled in all fields of knowledge. He was also an extremely effective spy who made full use of his genius for cryptography, Today he is chiefly known for his studies within the crystal, his contacts with the angels, and his creation of the Enochian system of converse with them, via the mediumship of several scryers, notably Edward Kelly. He was not by any means the witless dupe of the latter that Meric Casaubon's writings stated. Dee was no one's fool. Throughout his life he remained a formidable personality, a lovely, lively and pleasantly eccentric man. He died some time in December 1608.

Perhaps it should be noted here that Christine was a direct descendant of his through the female line, from the Welsh background common to both.

This then, is the reincarnational pattern of identities for one Being. It is the product of one woman's psychism. And like all psychism it is subject to the same vagaries as purely intellectual speculation. That is to say it might be wrong. Although it would be folly to accept these details without question, it would also be lunatic to reject them off-hand.

Personally, having been subject to a wide range of what might archly be called synchronistic experiences during the research and study of all these personalities, I am, on the whole, rather inclined to accept them. B. I. died on December 8, 1923. Dion would have had to make the Eldon contact some time after that. At least it is psychically possible.

To get back to Christine, however, she was not ready for Brodie-Innes' offer to teach her magic. She was what might be called a Sleeper. Besides which the High Church element was still very strong indeed within her. In some ways it never lessened. Toward the end of her life her Christianity co-existed quite happily with her paganism. That might be ascribed to the Geminian qualities within her natal chart. While on the other hand, in the outer world, she was busy getting on with her first marriage, to Oscar Cook, and the birth of her only child, Gervis, whom she also outlived.

It was not until 1927 that she met the woman who would one day lead her in vision through the now-drowned temples at Philae. Violet Firth dropped the manuscript of *The Problem of Purity* on her desk and asked if she could do anything with it. It is not a good book, even for that era. Christine didn't like it much at all but did manage to get it placed the following year.

From her point of view nothing of any significance passed between them on the first encounter. There was no sudden empathy or antipathy as is said to occur when meeting someone from a past life On those occasions when great upsurges of emotions do occur it is usually between members of the opposite sex and is more to do with the libido than karmic links. Magicians can be as blind as anyone during brief meetings like this one between Dion and her new agent.

It was not until 1932 that the older woman came back into the agency offices and asked simply if Christine would be interested in attending a lecture on Ceremonial Magic. She was. She went.

And that was the start of it all. At this time she was thirty-five years old, a petite and attractive woman with blue eyes, dark hair, and the tip-tilted nose that was the family trademark. Astrology of the zodiac (as opposed to that of the planets) is a dubious art, the natal chart being as empty of anything real as the crystal of a scryer, but nevertheless capable of yielding something of value when used properly. So we can say that she had the finely developed sense of intuition ascribed to Geminians, capable of registering all sorts of things at a non-rational level. And also, in the analysis of Liz Greene "... a sense of the eternal, of the secret currents at work in the fabric of life." An ascendant of Virgo, moreover, gave her the figure of Isis Rising, whose Celtic manifestation is through Morgan le Fay. Greene also notes that the ultimate goal of Virgo is "nothing less than the self-possessed psyche, the person who is integrated within himself and can therefore give freely because he need not fear losing himself in another." Which anticipates rather neatly the magical work she would come to do with Seymour.

She was a woman of great warmth and charm, but behind it a

9. Christine at the time of her entry into the Fraternity of the Inner Light.

certain *noli me tangere* quality to all but her intimates. She could be hard when necessary. The Guild of the Master Jesus, for example, held no attractions for her, despite her own Christian inclinations. Loveday, she felt, was a darling in his own way but the atmosphere of the Guild was too dainty and twee for her own needs. She was never capable of the spiritualized lovingness and watery compassion that lay behind it. No one who had ever worked in Fleet Street could be.

Like many people who can muster great outward charm, the sword of Geburah was always a second option.

To an extent she was a diminutive version of Dion herself in her early days—the Dion who would lock herself in occult combat with her antagonists. The difference was that she started later in the day, and still had things to shake off. Never at any time did she lose her own individuality within the enveloping flares of her teacher's magnetism, and in many ways they complemented each other: Dion could write with brilliance but often lacked control of her subject matter and over-wrote; whereas Christine could write with no more than skill, but knew exactly where to use the red pen. Christine had learning and an inherent quiet wisdom; but Dion had the Knowledge and the will to present it with flamboyance. They were equally charismatic women in their own solar and lunar ways.

One of the first people to see her enter 3 QT was Merl. The silvan mage was heard to comment: "At last, we've got a priestess of Isis in the house." And he should know: he had brought her from Atlantis to Lyonesse in the first place.

Oscar Cook joined the group at the same time as his wife. He did so because he wanted power. With power he could get on in the world. It is the same attraction that most people have for magic. They look to it for a short cut, and are invariably sad and often neurotic people. The Junior Study Course proved too much for him though: he left well within its limits. Which is the same for most people, when they find that magic—real magic—is the sternest of disciplines.

Christine failed the first part of the course. Part of the trouble was to do with her marital difficulties; part of it to do with the woman who ran that course, a Claudia Brine, who had a most beautiful individuality as they all said, but—they always added "but"—a most hateful personality.

At a second attempt she passed the exam and thereupon

adopted the Magical Name *Frere Ayme Frere* from her mother's name. But this was rarely used. She came to be known almost exclusively as CCT, or simply Chris.

The first part of the course related, roughly, to Malkuth on the Tree of Life. It lasted nine months, the traditional gestation period in magical groups. It consisted of basic occult teachings, the reading of recommended texts (namely all of Dion's) and groundwork on the Cosmic Doctrine. At that time this was not a completed text but duplicated chapters handed out one at a time when the students proved they had understood the foregoing.

The second part of the course was run by Teddy Maltby who had some real talent for magic as well as a typically military style of delivery. This involved basic visualization work, meditations, information on the planets and the occult anatomy of man, breathing techniques, esoteric histories, etc. On top of this the weekly lectures that Dion gave were open to everyone.

It was all a tribal gathering, a homecoming, a meeting of people who had known each other and worked together in many previous lives. Yet there were no prima-donnas, no place for loud spiritual athletes. No one would have dared with Dion or Merl around. There are no loud exultant claims about discovering past lives; no excited hubbub in the corridors about new occult revelations. Dammit but they were British after all, such a thing was just not on! Which is an influence on style which should never be underestimated. As long as one did not overstep the bounds of magical decency, 3 QT was a place of freethinkers, a sanctuary for individual vision. Christine wrote:

> There is an undoubted effect produced from time to time in a closely knit magical group where the advancement of one member can effect the evolution of the rest—a theory borne out by St Paul's words, "Where one member is honoured, all are honoured..." indicating the sharing of the advancement.

Imagine a brain, a huge portion of its cells never used. As each magician achieved some degree of personal illumination within the lodge it became analogous to new cells being awakened within the brain, the collective consciousness of the group.

The first two parts of the study course were, by and large, theoretical, and corresponded to Malkuth and then Yesod. It was only on the next level, at the sphere of Hod, that the student was allowed to participate in ritual work.

Each person was given a large and shapeless black hooded cloak which they wore over their everyday clothes. There were no grandiose robes in splendid colors or anything, on the outer planes, to distinguish the seniors from the juniors. Felt slippers were also compulsory as it was felt that outdoor shoes would bring unwanted influences into the temple in the way of street dirt—not necessarily of the physical variety. And most important of all they wore pieces which covered the face too. So that the rituals comprised a group of psychically linked people who were utterly without personality and were instead Presences.

The modern era with its indulgence in projected two-dimensional entertainment, electric lighting, double-glazed and centrally-heated lives has forgotten the impact of the great rites which were once part of our heritage. We have forgotten the effect of candlelight and shadow, chanting, incense, ritual and invocation, when each member is unknown, a pair of glittering eyes, an expression of Power in a throbbing room. Used to the cult of the personality we have forgotten the awe that such obliteration of the face can bring, forgotten the way that we ourselves when cloaked in anonymity can become something other than our normal selves, momentarily greater, immeasurably truer to our higher natures, no longer tied down by physique and physiognomy, but pure expressions of light even though clothed in black in a darkened room. What bears light more surely than darkness? In such rites each man becomes a true lightbearer, and stands in an energy field of almost tangible weight, feeling as though his mind is peeling open like a bud, revealing the glowing jewel within, glowing with the Spiritus Mundi that dwells inside, awaiting its call. We have forgotten how to make this call. We have forgotten so much.

All of this took place within the 2° of the curriculum which took in group work in ritual and taught the elements of Nature worship too, the so-called Green Ray workings.

It is interesting that the actual framework of the major rites was essentially masonic. There was an Officer of the South, at the Love—sometimes called Beauty—aspect. The juniors began here. The Officer of the West mediated the Power, or Strength. The students progressed to this point. At the East, the place of Wisdom, the seniors gathered—only the seniors. The North was empty. People might sit there, but there was no Officer; there would always be a gap of some sort. This was the dark and mysterious place from whence the Masters would come. Only in the lower degree Elemental magic would there be an Officer for the North.

Apart from this Dion did much work with smaller groups in her own rooms. Christine was often allowed to watch from the sidelines, clairvoyantly, while Dion, Merl, and Colonel Seymour would perform their Egyptian rites.

In due course she became a 3° herself, which relates to the sphere of Tiphereth, and was the highest degree offered within the lodge. The 3° was only attained when the magician had made his or her own contact with the entities behind the group.

Tiphereth was, in fact, her favorite place, the Sun, where she favored the vital lion-magic that had been given to her by Sekhmet herself and which captures the very essence of the British psyche, even if this is somewhat tired now, the roar muted. Once, arriving early in the lecture room, she passed the time until the others turned up by assuming the powers of that goddess and projecting a vivified phantasm of a lion onto each chair in the room. It is the sort of thing that magicians do in their early days, testing their powers. She achieved her intention and saw the beasts sitting there, proud and sleek expressions of the energy within her subconscious. Dion had done much the same thing herself, years before, when she had extruded the great wolf Fenris as described in *Psychic Self Defence.* When the others came into the room the mage in charge, Seymour, immediately "saw" what Christine had done and ordered her to get rid of them before the workings could take place as planned. She did so, but found that the banishing caused more problems than the evocation. The manifestations of power are like that.

Yet it was by no means a happy time. A magical apprenticeship rarely is. Security and happiness are usually the first things which go. There is an old saying that when you knock upon the gates of heaven it is the gates of hell which open first. In fact, the budding mage is tested in the very sphere in which he would hope to operate. Someone aiming for the mysteries of Mars, for example, might find himself reduced by circumstances to positions of great personal weakness and moral impotence. Someone wanting to move along the path between the Moon and Venus, of sex and passion, might find herself trapped in a sexless and cool relationship. It is the only way to learn; and the moment that the mage thinks those lessons are fully learned, that is the moment that he becomes due for some more. These are the only *real* initiations. The wand of the magus symbolizes less occult force and more the standards and qualities one can build up and cling onto, hauling ourselves from our knees to our feet, and giving us support as we stride a hard path.

Christine's life became very difficult on many levels. There was the day to day management of her agency, struggling to make ends meet and find the new talent necessary to the success of all such enterprises. While in another sphere her marriage had started going downhill with great and ruinous speed. On top of this she had a child to bring up. No easy matter. At one point the stress became so obvious that Dion took her into her private rooms and went into full trance, bringing through a message from "on high" to the effect that her pupil must either stay in the schoolroom or else go on to better things.

It was the kind of message which, while trite to anyone else, triggers off the surge or relief which comes when one is told the right thing at the right time. Only the recipient of such a message can understand the profound and liberating effect such a thing can have—something infinitely beyond the mere sense of the words. The younger woman heeded the advice of the eminent being that Dion had allowed into her body and felt emboldened to make the final separation from her husband. It was something she never regretted.

There is something oddly touching about that: a woman of power going into a shaman trance for the sake of someone in torment. Few self-styled magicians actually put their powers on display like this; they tend instead to hide behind the tricks, comments and brittle philosophies which make being a guru the easiest act of all. So rarely do they lay their talents bare. And on another level, on later occasions when Oscar Cook would ring his wife up at 3 QT or even go around to make a scene, there was always Dion's formidable presence acting as a buffer this time, instead of a channel, protecting her small priestess until such a time as she could cope for herself.

Among so many other things Christine would always remember one: that during a hard and troubled time Dion Fortune helped her along with a degree of grace and wisdom that was unparalleled.

It was inevitable that she became her agent. It was a job that she did very well. During long lunches in the Strand Palace Hotel or in the Chinese restaurant which had just opened in Piccadilly they worked at putting Dion's novels into shape, at one point cutting almost 40,000 words from the beginning of *The Goat-Foot God* in which

Paston meandered on about his marriage, and doing similar for the two Atlantean novels *The Sea Priestess* and *Moon Magic*. They wrangled over the pseudonym to be used for the detective novels: Christine urging her to use Violet Orchard, but Dion finally deciding upon V. M. Steele. One of the aforementioned, *The Sea Priestess*, was privately published in Guernsey in 1938, owing to something of a paper shortage on the mainland. Bearing the imprint DF on the spine, Christine's own first edition is autographed "To CCT Ltd., from DNF Unlimited, 20/9/38." This original version contains two extra, if subsidiary, characters and makes Molly a far more complete figure, as well as detailing her peculiar relationship with the Moon Priest. Later editions have been skillfully edited by still other hands to cut out the dated idiom, but at the expense of these aspects. After Fortune's death her successor, Mr. Chichester, decided that the firm of Christine Campbell Thomson should no longer handle the books in question.

By 1937 her training period was over. She had learned the art of "conscious mediumship" in which

> ...you must withdraw consciously from the world around you without losing consciousness. Gradually you still your roving thoughts, your active mental brain; you refuse to admit the sounds you hear, not by sending them away from you but by withdrawing from them, and gradually you will be able to see yourself standing within the envelope of your body but able to leave it with your mind.

Nowadays it is known as mediation.

All she needed now was the right priest to direct the power that she was increasingly able to bring through. Merl would have been ideal but Dion kept them well apart. Instead she was put into the hands of a man whom she detested, Colonel Seymour, who at that time held the place of Power, in the West. He had seen her written account of a lunar meditation, using a crumpled ball of tissue that she had made to look like the pockled moon using a violet backcloth, candlelight, and imagination. "How refreshing it is," he then wrote, "to find someone willing to do some real practical work on the subject." He had worked out a magical technique, he confided, for which he thought she might be suitable. It would probably require months of work before achieving anything tangible. Would she be willing to try?

She demurred at first. The plain truth was that she just did not like the man. But in due course she agreed to become his pupil, his priestess. And July 13, 1937 marked the start of a relationship that was already ancient.

Charles Richard Foster Seymour was born in Ireland on April 9, 1880. He thought of himself as a Galway boy but in fact his family seat, as one of the landed gentry, was at Killagally Park on the border of Galway and what is now County Offaly. His father was a J. P. and had been a lieutenant in the Connaught Rangers. His mother was the daughter of a Hampshire rector. Charles had one brother and four sisters, all younger than him. The family motto was *Foy pour Devoir* which, literally translated, means "faith for duty." Or "my faith is my duty." On a few occasions he even extended it to read "I desire to know in order to Serve." The large and rambling house had a bush growing out of its structure which was said to flower every time a Seymour was about to die.

An Anglo-Irishman and fiercely proud of it, the one goddess could never escape nor would ever want to escape, was Erin. Knowing that no man of his nature can ever, really, return home, he took the spirit of Killagally with him wherever he went. He was never far from the Sidhe, or the Tuatha de Danaan.

Born in Ferbane, and receiving his second level education at Dungannon, he entered Trinity College Dublin where he studied Russian. He graduated at the age of 19. (He gained his M.A. in 1929 after retiring from the Army.) On graduating he came to England and joined the Hampshire Regiment, specializing in what was still called musketry. That alone, to the modern ear, gives him an almost medieval air. He took part in the Boer War, fighting in operations in the Orange Free State and later the Transvaal. In 1900 he served in the Orange River Colony. For all of this he received the Queen's South Africa Medal with four clasps. It was then, in 1902, that he was appointed to the Indian Army and the 13th Rajputs, which wore a splendid uniform of scarlet with blue facings. During the First World War he served in German East Africa and was wounded. After this he took part in "police" operations in Iraq, during the years 1920-21, and was mentioned in dispatches.

He held, also, a number of interpreter appointments and acted in this capacity on a diplomatic mission to Moscow, in 1917.

His last rank was Lieutenant Colonel.

These are the bare bones of a long and quietly illustrious career which also fitted in studies at the Staff College, in Quetta, and time with the Rangoon Volunteer Rifles and also the Burma Rifles. Straight and simple details such as these do not begin to express the nature of the man or begin to explain that he was a hard, sad, scholarly, respected and a very brave fighter. To later generations who have had some inkling of his importance to Dion Fortune he is remembered simply as Colonel Seymour. To many people who have not had a military background, however, such a title in civilian life conjured up a Colonel Blimpish image of gouty, peppery and essentially laughable period-pieces. But if he retained his rank after retirement he never spoke about his personal or military background. People knew no more than that he had done something in India, at some time. They also knew not to cross him.

Of the three great magicians in Dion's life—Moriarty, Merl, and Colonel Seymour—the same phrase crops up in describing each of them: they did not suffer fools gladly. Seymour did not suffer them at all.

Which meant that no one ever liked him much at first meeting. A fact which worried him not at all. Fighting men of his rank and prowess were not put upon this earth to fret over social niceties. Yet those whom he gradually allowed close almost idolized him. They knew him as Kim, "little friend of all the world." This was a truer picture of him.

Dion and Merl, for their part, called him Griffin, or Griff. They felt that the image of a winged lion's body with eagle head was a peculiarly apt symbol for his inner nature. The winged lion and Merl the winged bull had a mutual respect for each other, though they never got too close.

Seymour's background in occult work was masonic. He was a member of the Grand Lodge of Scotland and managed to remain active in this work during his army travels by means of the regimental lodges which had charters to move from place to place.

It is quite possible that he knew Moriarty during his time in Africa. Quite possible that he knew Brodie-Innes. Dion certainly knew *him* when he first appeared at 3 QT, but precisely what or who drew him there no one will know.

There is a curious reference in his diaries which reads "Working with Volens in the Museum Chambers." Volens is obviously a magical name of some now unidentifiable adept, but the whole statement calls to mind the old tradition that a temple of the Golden Dawn once worked magic in the British Museum with the sanction and cooperation of E. A. Wallis Budge, the eminent Egyptologist. He might well have had preliminary magical experience with one of the Golden Dawn temples, even though this entry was dated for 1937 by which time he was already a 3° adept within the Inner Light.

He joined the latter some time around 1932. The Junior Study Course proved no obstacle to his progress and *The Cosmic Doctrine* no hindrance. Before very long he was editing the monthly magazine and writing many of the articles himself either under his own name or signed with the initials of his magical name, F. P. D.

No photograph has yet been traced with Seymour on it but there is an accurate word-picture of him in *The Winged Bull* where Colonel Brangwyn is transparently based upon Seymour: "He was a tall, slight, dark-skinned man; and his black hair, brushed straight back from the forehead, was greying over the ears and receding over the temples." It is an accurate description except that Seymour was not a tall man, although he had the sort of bearing which suggested that he was. One person who worked with him at the time described him as being of medium height, ostensibly an unassuming man, but with something inside of him that was utterly, utterly powerful.

His articles represented the very best outpouring from the lodge. His vision was in no way dependent upon Dion's. Beyond anyone else within the group he had a real scholarly knowledge of ancient religions, history and literature. All of which he wore lightly, only really showing his knowledge in print. Dion, in many ways, drew heavily upon this, as well as upon his priestly qualities. He was her co-worker for the original Isis Rites which were written up in fictional form in *Moon Magic*. Seymour himself stopped these, and there is an equally telling note in his diary saying: "Self fit but very fed up with the Belfry Isis Rites."

This comment refers to an interesting tributary from Dion's torrential flow through life.

The Belfry is one of those rare buildings which seems to have a life of its own, independent of the occupants. Its radically different style of architecture makes it stand out like a beacon in West Halkin Street, off Belgrave Square, and it was in fact built in 1830 as a Scottish Presbyterian Church. It was the time of the early Reform Bills and the church's first customers were the down and outs of a colorful community described in contemporary reports as "proverbial for rioting and disorder, for drunkenness and ignorance." By 1923 however it had been taken over by a Mrs. Zoe Oakley Maund, who later became known as Lady Caillard, and who used it as her own private spiritualist temple.

Lady Caillard died in 1935, and it was around this time that Dion rented the place from her, using it as her own retreat, and where she performed the Isis Rites that were described at length in *Moon Magic*. The Belfry is clearly the original of the building which forms the *mise-en-scéne* of that novel, although Dion never managed to renovate it as completely or as satisfactorily as its fictional counterpart. For one thing she had an elevator installed. Except that it was not a passenger elevator as such, but more nearly one of those platforms which lurk beneath theaters, and which can silently bring up the Demon King into the center of the stage. Except that in her case she used it to bring herself into the center of her temple, so that she could quite literally rise before her priest's magical gaze like Isis. It is easy to laugh at such *Deus ex machina* toys, but the fact is that it worked.

The retreat did not last long. This was partly because neither Seymour nor Merl were particularly happy in their priestly relationships with Dion at this time, but largely because she could not afford the upkeep of this on top of both 3 QT and the sanctuary at Glastonbury.

(The Belfry, however, continued to assume its own life, and in 1954 it was transformed into an exclusive dining club by Joseph Vecchi. When the present owners took it over in 1981 the very first thing they did, before completely redecorating it to its present superb style, was to have the whole place blessed—"a fitting remembrance of its original sacred ancestry" as they put it in their leaflet. Dion would have liked that.)

Seymour by this time was feeling that his superior was demanding too much of his inward self, and the estrangement began to accelerate from then on. He who had appeared in *The Sea Priestess* as the lean and ascetic-faced Priest of the Moon began to move further away. But unlike so many adepts whose visions are as cosmic in scope as their treachery, he kept his feelings to himself, and quietly, simply got on with the Work. More than anything else, Seymour was a gentleman.

The Welsh poet David Annwn was shown the handwritten pages of the Colonel's records and made the following graphological analysis. Those still alive who knew the man pronounced it as an accurate summary of his character. It reads as follows:

> Warm, artistic handwriting. The upper sector is emphasized which shows great imagination and idealism. The ability to use and channel imagination and dreams is pronounced and associated consciously with the person's conception of himself. He is proud but not arrogant, and, though the writing shows compassion, he is level-headed, practical and not given to indulging fools.
>
> A double burden in life seems to be (a) some great depression which resulted from emotional pain (intense!), and (b) a hate of certain routine he finds himself part of. The emotional disaster was of a sexual character and gave him no little inhibition about some aspects of sex. He is basically warm but, because of sadness, has learned to be self protective and not to wear his heart upon his sleeve. He can keep his own counsel. Some illness or instability is shown from time to time but the life-force in this hand is considerable. The real obstacle to his achieving his dreams is an irksome "rut" he gets himself into. He can be swamped by depression but has found that the way out of this (and to reach other people) is through utilizing his imagination. Sadly his affections tend to be *very exclusive* and part of the reason that he finds himself isolated at times is that he is very particular about choosing friends and confidantes. The hand is meticulous and even scholarly—capable of all kinds of writing and speaking.
>
> The basic opposition in this writing is the conflict between a person who was disappointed (even mocked) early in life and grew disenchanted, perhaps bitter tongued with people of lesser intellect. Set against this is a visionary and warm personality which loves to be expansive and friendly. This person would charm you after a certain initial iciness and superficial aloofness fades. An extremely good and loyal friend, he protects those he loves and has not a fickle bone in his body. Paradoxically (after reading the Avebury Vision) he does *not* live in the past. He is still hopeful but knows that he has obstacles in his way. Frailty depresses him and he feels it entering his system at times. When he musters it, he has tremendous will-power.

Part of the emotional pain he felt was surely due to his marriage. In 1917 he had taken his wife and child with him into Russia where he was acting as an interpreter on some untraceable mission. The child died but the mother conceived again almost immediately. As often happens when a new child appears before the mother can come to terms with the grief of losing a previous one, Zoe Seymour was precipitated into grief and recurrent depressions from which she never quite recovered. Seymour could at least take solace in his belief that the same soul had reincarnated immediately, but his wife abhorred the occult in any shape or form. Dion would later tell the story of how the poor wretch would appear outside 3 QT at unexpected times and scream up to the windows for Charles to come out, quite certain that the bemused and imperturbable Mrs. Evans was his mistress. Even allowing for the latter's natural hyperbole in telling anecdotes, her listeners felt it to be a true description of events.

Nowadays he is the forgotten mage; then he was a sad one. Like Dion, like Christine, he eventually separated from his spouse. Again there is a telling phrase in his diary. After a particularly potent piece of magic working with his new priestess, Christine Campbell Thomson (CCT), he concluded: "I worshipped—for the first time for a very long time with a real intensity of purpose." The rite had involved the descent of the goddess Isis into CCT, who then gave the priest Her blessing. The energy filled this hitherto wearied man almost to bursting point. He was left with a wonderful sense of peace and fulfillment. At another point in the early days of this relationship he noted that he was now filled with a new sense of reality and importance of the work he had to do. These are the comments of a man who was coming out of the darkness after a long time.

One further clue as to his emotional state is given in his long essay "Children of the Great Mother," written in 1938. This essay is an excursion into myth, within which he takes us around from theme to theme enwrapping us in coils of imagery, writing at times with an almost hypnotic effect yet without stating clearly what he means. He describes the blue-robed Merlin in his Moon Cave with the silver and white priestesses at his shoulder, the crescent moon and star at their heads; he describes the affair of Connla and the otherworld maiden; he talks about the crystal boat of the Lord Anubis. And just when one begins to tire and wonder where it all leads he adds, significantly, that we are not meant to understand these pictures that he evokes. If we understand them then he, the writer, has failed in his purpose. These myths, we are told, are meant to be incubated in the depths of the unconscious mind, and he goes on to add: "Some day, perhaps under the stress of some great emotional strain of love or hate, or possibly in the adoration of the ALL which is both love and hate—the inner fountains of your subliminal life will be broken up. These universal images that have worked long and silently in the darkness will spring full grown and powerful for better or for worse into your conscious life. Will you, as Lord of the Moon Wisdom... use them, or will they abuse you?"

No man with a happy life could have written that. One can imagine this quiet scholar compensating for his unhappy marriage through study of his lost gods, and finding their psychic realities at the same time as he reached the emotional nadir of his life.

It is possible too that the first contacts he made on his own account were those he described in the same essay, the Egyptian priests Setne Kha'm uast and Ne Nefer Ka Ptah. This latter was a priest of Anubis, and the entity referred to throughout the Magical Record. He notes in the essay that the excellent statue of Kha'm uast in the British Museum has an undoubted magnetism which can be used, and tapped, and that by this one can make direct contact with the minds of the greatest of magicians in Ancient Egypt, namely the two aforementioned.

Much of the magic within the lodge used the technique of creative imagination that had been pioneered by Ignatius Loyola. There are obvious dangers in this method and Seymour confessed that in the early stages of such work it is almost impossible to distinguish between fancy and the results obtained by the imagination trained magically. However, as a result of years of experience a system of cross-checking grew up and a reasonable degree of probability was obtained.

He summed it up like this: the magician must learn to act *as if* the images are real, and *as if* the gods really are what they seem to be. "If you can do this you need not worry about the whys and wherefores of the human reasoning mind; gone are the bogies of the ancient superstitions; gone are the semi-sacred tabus of the superstitious past. You are free, for now has begun the Age of Aquarius, the Airy sign of the free man who strides across the wide firmament of the boundless realms of the Great Mother, carrying his own burden upon his shoulders."

That was Seymour's way. He believed that in the new Age man would learn not to depend upon a Redeemer who would absolve all sins, alleviate all burdens. Having waded through fields knee deep with corpses, having seen rivers red with blood, having killed and taught to kill, and almost been killed himself, he had had enough of Christianity to last him several lifetimes. He turned to the Great

Mother; he carried his own burden toward Her. There was not a shred of complaint or self-pity within him.

It was this formula of acting *as if* which held the key to his magic, to all magic He added also "A magician is *what* he believes himself to be; a magician is *where* he believes himself to be."

Although he knew the dangers of this method, and knew that even his system of cross-checking was not necessarily effective on all occasions, it was his contact with Lord Eldon which summed up the validity of the work. After he and CCT had both had visions relating to La Pucelle, the Maid, Eldon appeared and they asked him if they were accurate. "Old Bags," as he had once been affectionately known, smiled and said, "Substantially." This is important. It is perhaps crucial to the validation of magic.

To a great extent psychic researchers suffer because a different and unfair set of criteria are applied to them. For example, if a noted intellectual were asked his opinions as to the outcome of, say, a political conference, no one would think any the less of him if his purely intellectual predictions were absolutely wrong. Or if that same man were to change his mind about any given topic then his reputation would not suffer in the least. If a psychic wrote his own visions as to the outcome of any forthcoming event then even if he were only 40 percent wrong his reputation would suffer out of all proportion. The fact that he was largely accurate is not counted. Likewise he is never allowed to change his vision in the same way that another is allowed to change his mind.

Academic researchers will no doubt be able to find apparent errors within the visions of the remote past contained in the Magical Record. But I believe that they are *substantially* accurate.

That a man can have visions at all is interesting.

That he can have visions of the past is noteworthy.

That these visions are for the large part accurate is astonishing.

And even were they not then as Seymour says: A magician is *what* he believes himself to be; a magician is *where* he believes himself to be. With this formula he became a very wise and influential man, one much loved by those he allowed near. The same cannot always be said about those scientifically oriented critics who do not so much prune the magical roses as tear the bushes out by the roots in their urge to get at what they believe is the truth. Throughout his life Seymour continued to grow. That was his triumph, and the glory of his magic.

Juniors within the lodge speculated that he was the man that Dion should have married. They saw in him an alternative version of Merl with all the strength and drive that Dion would have wanted in a husband, but without Merl's rough edges and from an impeccable social background. Yet the modesty and self-effacement he used in respect of his peers was of the sort that only the really strong can express. He would have proved just as intractable as the Welshman, just as resistant to her dominance.

Nevertheless, Dion must surely have seen within him something of her own late teacher, Moriarty. They were both well-travelled older men, both hailing from Ireland, both of similar religious background and soaked through with masonic experience.

If Seymour replaced Merl for a time as her priest then it was less congenial to him than to Dion. As he went deeper and deeper in his magical work with CCT and also Paula Trevanion, his "wise child," we see brief entries in his diary about the increasing antagonism he was beginning to sense from Dion. We can put what interpretation upon that we want.

In fact DNF gradually disappears from the diaries completely from the time that this trinity began working together regularly and with effect. He had formed his own triangle of Power, Love and Wisdom and had little need for the large rites of the lodge, even if he did discharge his obligations and commitments therein diligently and often. If the Fraternity was a microcosm of the universe then the small groups that he favored were microcosms of the Fraternity. Most of his work was done in the rooms next door, at 2 QT, through the adjoining walls of which they could often hear the Evanses having the most explosive rows.

One can understand Dion taking exception to this. The parent organization of the Golden Dawn had suffered because of the innumerable splinter groups that had formed. Yet it was never the Colonel's intention to create internal rivalries. It was simply that he preferred working in small cells. This is symbolized by his favorite tarot card The Hermit: a lonely and venerable figure on a mountaintop holding out his light to those willing to make the climb after him.

There was during this time in his life a definite John Dee-ish air about him. Both were formidable linguists and wide-ranging scholars; both favored working behind the scenes; both were connected with Intelligence work; and both were devoted to scrying although neither was innately psychic.

Contacts have a way of calling their own. In the last analysis (if there will ever be such a thing) they will probably prove to be somewhat different in essence to what the magicians believe. It is perhaps more accurate to think of them as pulsations of energy at a particular wavelength and frequency, the tuning into which can be achieved through means of the outward physical image. What these contacts have to say in verbal terms often bears a suspicious resemblance to what the magicians themselves would say, at their best. But the real value of the contact is not in the supposed information it puts across but in the peculiar energy of which the mage can avail himself. Like plugging into an electric circuit. Dee would have been drawn to Seymour (and vice-versa) because they were on the same frequency. Seymour would have become overshadowed by him.

This idea (or variations on the theme) is one of the explanations as to why so many honest and serious people all claim at the same time to be reincarnations of the same historical personage. It is not simply a matter of neurosis. Had each budding adept been less obsessed with gaining an occult pedigree—for which who can blame them?—the impressions and apparent memories of a previous life might well tail off and leave them with a genuine contact capable of giving across power. It has to be borne in mind that this may well be a truer explanation behind the Scott/Dee/Eldon/Brodie-Innes chain of identities than the suggestion they are all the same entity.

One craggy old sorcerer told me that he distrusted all contacts as a matter of principle—especially his own, whose names he didn't even know and wouldn't have believed if they had told him! He was a man who wrestled with his gods as all magi should do from time to time.

If Dee needed his Edward Kelly to bring through visions from the crystal then the colonel wanted for nothing but a priestess. As already described he found her in 1937, in the shape of Christine. Though neither of them knew it, their magical work began on July 13, exactly 410 years after Dee's birth. That CCT had not come to his attention much before is clear from the Magical Record. In the first couple of entries she is referred to rather impersonally as the priestess, or CTC. He was confused about her name because she was still legally Christine Mary Cook. It is only gradually that he warms to her and they begin to see that their relationship had its real roots back in the Temple of the Sun, on Atlantis.

For her part there is an interesting comment at the end of one of their first rites, before it became clear to her that this was not just a brief working relationship: "I would one day like to do this kind of magic without people who might be disturbed because I always get a strong desire to get up and dance and it is so difficult to hold on to my personality enough to remember I must not move." The dance again. She was hearing the same tune that Dion had heard. She began to follow the same musicians. Sometimes it was reed pipes that she heard.

Seymour came to regard himself and his co-worker as separate parts of a whole There are references to their auras joining. In a working for November 1940, during the blitz, he uses the term *syzygy* to describe his other half, which might be defined as the conjunction of two organisms without loss of identity.

The working explores the Atlantean seaport of Ys, on the Breton coast, where Seymour (FPD) enters a temple shaped like a low truncated pyramid built of very large stones, dedicated to the worship of a serpent cult. After making contact with the priest of that temple he writes: "I knew that as an initiate of the Serpent Wisdom I had to share this power with my syzygy. And turning to the priestly adept who gave me this initiation I saw that he, as an adept, was himself his own syzygy. He had polarized the higher and the lower natures, and so was a complete self-polarizing entity." At the end of the rite they came back to the present, in Latymer Court, where they were somewhat disturbed by the gunfire outside. The idea of the adept as a self-polarizing entity was by this time constant to his conception of magic's aim. Like Dion had expressed in her novels, he deliberately sought this unity with the help of another soul in a different sex. It brought him into situations in which he and his priestess were, as they put it in those days, "sailing into the wind," although to the modern perspective nothing remiss took place at all. They were not, to forestall the immediate assumptions of a salacious era, lovers. No sex occurred between them. "Although," as CCT told Dolores Ashcroft-Nowicki, "that does not mean that sex was not involved."

What *was* involved was an exchange of energies on magical levels for which physical intercourse is but a lower analog. "I *drove* the energy over to her," wrote Seymour, "And she *drew* it from me." On emotional levels his attitude was never less than grandfatherly and protective, even though the age difference was only seventeen years. He had stated with some pleasure on more than one occasion that he had been her grandfather in Ancient Egypt, and that was how he always conducted himself toward her. It is an attitude that is recurrent throughout the far memories of the Magical Record. He is almost always older, always a protector: a father, brother, or guardian of some sort. Never did he overstep the bounds of propriety. Never did either of them feel remotely inclined to do so.

The *modus operandi* of their work was simple. Wearing their voluminous cloaks to shut out worldly influences, they sat down on the chairs before the gas fire in 2 QT, held hands, closed eyes, and projected their consciousness beyond the pylon gates into the Otherworld. Often they would use ritual techniques such as the chanting of simple mantras or else spontaneous invocations to whatever power was concerned; often, too, they would work at building certain images into the psycho-spiritual centers known as chakras.

Seymour knew that the great magicians had no need for wands: a pointed finger was just as effective. They had no need for elaborate chalices: the cupped hands did the same work.

And so his magic was simple. All they did was hold hands.

Theirs was a very dignified dance; no matter the intricacy of the steps and tune they kept their balance, they kept their places.

It is apparent from the Record that by 1937 they had each made their own contacts with "Himself" because there is no surprise or mystery when he appears. For the rest of it too it is clear from Seymour's visions that he had been to the astral temples of Egypt before, with DNF, while there are still echoes of wonderment in the accounts of Christine.

Seymour's system of cross-checking involved correlation of his visions with those of fellow-workers. Usually, apart from CCT, there was a third present to act as observer and scribe. In the early days this was Paula Trevanion, but later it was Margaret Irene "Weeny" Wilson who took over the role and became a clairvoyant Watcher in the same way that CCT had been for Dion and Merl. (It is from these points of reference that the tentative correspondences between the inner chiefs and the points of the Power/Love/Wisdom triangle have been suggested. It is an area which is still very much open to discussion.)

With the help of these, "the subtle and profound females," he was able to project himself in all but body back into the time-drowned temples along the Nile where he had been at his happiest, most effective. If, for example, Arthur Guirdham's Cathar incarnation had been his most dominant, then it was as Nefer-su, priest of Ptah, that the Colonel was most exquisitely himself.

Yet his relationship with CCT hearkened back to Atlantean times. They had left that island just before it sank and had been carried on a great rolling wave to the shore of Lyonesse where the young woman in his charge had been hailed as Morgan, the sea-borne priestess.

Those who tend to deify Dion will not like that. It was the role she had always seemed to appropriate for herself. There will be arguments as to whether Seymour's visions suggested Dion's story *The Sea Priestess*, or whether in fact Dion's discussions of the plot had worked their way into CCT's subsconscious and re-emerged as vision. Christine has always maintained, however, that Morgan, Merlin and Arthur were initiatic titles, and that several functioning units of magicians had left Atlantis by this manner at about the same time. Furthermore she thought it unlikely that Dion, with all her great Knowledge, would have to use their visions to provide the theme of that novel. On the other hand the memory of those prehistoric events was still fresh within her, she could still see herself with the long, black hair and widow's peak, and was so seen by others. After almost fifty magic-filled years, her times with Dion were by now only an interesting, if important, portion of her life and hardly the *ne plus ultra* of her existence; she could not recall the precise details. It was not important to her. She never saw herself as any sort of rival, never sought to score points against her. These memories and others were a valuable part of her life but of the sort that one tends to put away in the attic after a while, to be dusted off now and again, like curious heirlooms.

One dull life occurred in what CCT described as Arabia where they were both empty and unintelligent wretches, she the mother of an illegitimate child and he an old fighting man who was looking after her. They were together in a way along the Roman Wall where she was a hostage and Seymour her captor, being a senior officer fighting off barbarians. They had harrowing memories of being burnt as Cathars at Avignon, recorded some thirty years before Dr. Guirdham became involved in his own extraordinary and well documented saga. (Oddly enough when Christine was doing magical work with H. A. Hartley and gaining an amplification of her earlier Cather visions, the same Dr. Guirdham came to CCT's offices with his novels *These Paid* and *The Lights are Going Out*, which she tried, but failed, to get placed for him. This was many years before the revenants appeared in his own life and he had no inkling of his agent's peculiar interests in that or any other field.)

The very fragmentary nature of these visions helps to convince. There was no manic attempt to get a cradle-to-grave existence appear to their inner perceptions. She might have achieved this with trance, or hypnosis, but was wary of both techniques. Besides which, their records were never intended for public consumption. There was no urge to satisfy anyone but themselves. All in all the far memories were just not that important to either of them.

At this time Seymour assumed responsibility for teaching the Celtic aspects of the magical curriculum in 3 QT. These he knew well. In connection with this he wrote what they all referred to as "Kim's Book," a long essay which CCT typed up and made four copies of, which later found its way into print as *The Old Religion*.

This was—is—virtually a manual of self-initiation into the Celtic Mysteries through which the reader could take himself in controlled fantasy into the Otherworld, into the realms of the Sidhe, the Bright Ones. It is an essay that is studded with magical techniques, psychological comment, and some quite beautiful and evocative writing aimed at taking the neophyte a few more steps toward the heart of the Celts' inner landscape. It had been written round the results of experiments in group meditation upon the use of ancient Pagan symbols. "These experiments had for their objective the linking up of memories dormant in the subconscious minds of the members of those meditation groups with ancient cult memories that still live in the subconscious mind of the Great Mother of all-that-exists on this planet." He goes on to add that most of the members of these groups have, in the past, served at the altars of pagan religions, and that if any one of the members had had a strong contact with a particular cult at a certain period, then that individual could communicate these memories to others, and could link them with the cult memories that still lie within the Earth memories of Isis as the Lady of Nature.

Seymour, in his heart of hearts, was a matriarch, one of the last torchbearers of the Celtic Twilight that had been initiated by Yeats, AE, William Sharp (Fiona Macleod) and the rest.

He shows within this essay the lodge's obsession with the symbolism of the triangle, although he came to apply it in different ways to Dion. He wrote: "In the Old Religion the priest who stands at the altar as mediator between the Great World Mother and her devotees is also in his inner aspect a child of the Two Moon Mothers. For he is the focussing point for the consciously directed powers of Nephthys and Isis as energizing negative and positive cosmic factors." He goes on to tell us that a man has within his soul his Isis and his Nephthys, while a woman has her equivalents in Osiris and Set. Perhaps thinking of Zoe he writes further, " 'Hell,' it is said, 'knows no fury like a woman scorned,' a saying easy to understand when Set as the Red Lord of the dark moon phases becomes the ruler of a woman's inner emotional life—for is not Set the slayer of Osiris?' " Even in the working the relating to Ys, already mentioned, there is a third soul there with them in the Temple of the Serpent Wisdom, but it is not clear whether it is Paula Trevanion or indeed Lord Eldon who guided them there.

He gives lists of the trinities we might use.

(a) **Male**
Shiva—Vishnu—Brahman
Set—Horus—Osiris (as moon-gods)
Ptah - Sokar—Ausar (as the primeval creative power and darkness, the Dweller in the secret place)
Ptah—Seker—Temu (the lord of the Hidden Place)
Balor—Bress—Tethra (the three aspects of Buar-Ainech who is Cernunnos as the wearer of the horned moon)

(b) **Female**
Hathor—Nephthys—The Green Isis (Aspects of Isis)
The Three Bridgets as aspects of Dana
The Three Bridgets (Bride) as aspects of Anu
Aphrodite—Persephone—Hecate

(c) **Combined**
Ptah—Neer-Tem—Sekhet (Sekhmet)
Horus—Set—Isis
Sinn—Merodach—Ningala
Nannar—Bel-enlil—Ishtar
Tammuz—Belit-sheri—Ishtar
Tanmuz—(Eresh-Ki-gal)—Ishtar (Allatu)

Osiris—Isis—Nephthys
Shiva—Kali—Durga
Adam—Eve—Lilith

He also adds with something of an afterthought the trinity of Jesus, Martha and Mary, but the Christianity within Seymour's heart paid heed to Columba rather than Paul, to Iona rather than Rome.

"These trinities," he writes, "have nothing to do with the father-mother-child combinations so delightfully explained by some students of comparative religion and folklore. There *are* divine forms for use in magical rituals. They are still potent and can be unpleasant and dangerous if used unskillfully by those who fail to balance Wisdom and Power in Harmony."

The essay goes on to give precise details of how to use this symbolism to call down the gods and also awaken analogous psychological factors in the soul. In many ways it is a piece of writing which is years ahead of its time, prefiguring many of the trends in magic today.

More importantly instead of the vague and dreamy approach to the lost traditions of the Western—especially Celtic—mythology he was giving out instead hard information, unmistakable techniques. It had all been learned as he himself practiced the moon magic in another dimension, the Celtic world of Tir-na-noge.

The precise nature of his importance is this:

Dion formed an organization which she hoped would awaken the glories of the Western Magical Tradition. She wanted to show that the East has nothing to teach us, that we are not dependent upon their methods.

Although the Western Magical Tradition can happily embrace Christianity it was Merl who deflected the direction of the lodge into pagan areas of research.

If Merl brought into the lodge raw energy that was given shape and popular appeal by Dion, then it was Seymour who used his scholarship to bring precise definitions to the Work in hand. As an essayist he could stand comparison with anyone writing in that era. As a man he continued to give Dion her direction in the years when Merl began to withdraw from the lodge. She was a great woman but she needed her direction; and it just so happened that Kim and Merl were going in essentially the same way.

Seymour, far more than anyone else, was the great mage of Western magic. By that he aimed not so much for the pylon gates of the ancient Mystery centers around the Mediterranean but for the moon gates of the Celtic Otherworld. In that he gave the lodge a new dimension. It seems odd that it should have been a grizzled old warlord who did so, but Seymour gave the lodge its access to the world of faëry. He was concerned not so much with Glastonbury, which was the focus of Dion's aspirations in this realm, but with Tara, the home of the High Kings of Ireland, and all the other holy places in the West.

As any student of racial migrations can testify, the links between the Ireland of the Goddess Dana and the Greece of Merl's beloved Pan are manifold and profound. For a long time he stood on the westernmost peaks of the world, a dark shadow before the setting sun. It is only now that we are beginning to get close to him.

On the outer levels, in previous lives, he and his priestess had lives in which they expressed this peculiarly British magic. There is the final and superb vision in the Magical Record, at Avebury, where Dion and Christine had been the sacrificial priests and he the willing victim, their sexes reversed on this occasion. Not included in that document Seymour had a vision of his own in which he had been the witch of Wookey Hole in Somerset, and CCT his young child. Again his sex was reversed. (Christine herself had no memory of this incarnation. Interestingly, people whose psychism I respect have picked up strong echoes of the man at this place, even though they had no knowledge of the foregoing; while on the other hand magicians of what I would deem equal efficacy, knowing from me of this link, picked up nothing at all. It is a testament to honesty and accuracy all round.) From his own work with Dion he had grown into the certainty that he had once been a sacrifice within Chalice Well, and described with casual and chilling detail how he had bubbled his life away within that other sacred hole.

It was around 1939 that the Colonel began to get seriously disenchanted with the group, and with its leader. It was obviously entirely mutual. His opinions were less and less sought after, his priestcraft less in demand. There were probably too many adepts clustered around the cauldron for Dion to be as pre-eminent as she would have liked. That is one of the downfalls of the successful magical group: it creates adepts who are by definition complete and strong individuals. 3 QT just could not hold them all.

There is the question too, of whether Seymour was becoming less and less enamoured of the particular type and tone of Christianity that Dion was now espousing. He had no time for any peurile form of Christianity. He truly revered the Christ, but in his more acid moments would have agreed with Nietzsche that the last Christian died upon the Cross.

It was probably a relief for him when the War came. He could leave the group with dignity. In fact he was called up to become temporary head of a section of the Censorship board, in Liverpool, which was involved in keeping a check on the various occult and secret societies in Britain to ensure that none of them had links with the enemy.

It was not very productive work, one assumes, because he was back before long and took a blissfully humble post in the Local Defence Volunteers, later reorganized as the Home Guard. He was given one stripe and put in charge of filling all the inkwells, a task which he discharged with amused delight. On magical levels however he was as active as before, although by this time he felt that he was a bit too old, too ill, to be able to handle the levels of power that CCT was increasingly able to bring through. Accordingly he rang her up one day to tell her, with some excitement, that he had found her a new priest, a younger man, who would be ideal for the Work in hand. This alone betokens Seymour's true status in magic, for the right channeling of power was more important to him than whatever thrills he might personally derive from it.

Seymour, Christine, the young priest "J," and a handful of others were by this time all members of a group which was nominally run by William Elliot Carnegie Dickson and his wife Edith who were working the traditional Golden Dawn system from a makeshift temple in a room of his house in Upper Harley Street. The war tended everything in those days toward the makeshift.

In 1910 Dr. Dickson had been active with Brodie-Innes in the setting up of the Amen-Ra temple in Edinburgh, and as a prominent freemason. It is likely that the Colonel had known him for some time Once more they were back within the realms of Egypt, wearing robes and the striped nemyss on their heads. Christine declines to name the temple in question, but it may well have been a remnant of the Stella Matutina. Whatever, it was certainly moribund when Kim joined it. They set about creating their Group Mind, as we would call it, and making their contacts. According to notes for that group a "troublesome and undesirable entity appeared which looked very like Socrates," which they firmly banished before going on to "work under the aegis of Merlin" and eventually consolidate inward links with their old friend Kha'm uast, Brodie-Innes in his own form, a certain F. M., and also, interestingly, S. R. M. D., which was Mathers.

At one point in 1942 the group came under magical attack from various malign entities. These were dealt with summarily. J's comment on the matter was:

> The awakening of the Forces against us is due to the fact that the Lodge has suddenly become militant and active: while it was merely passive, religious and intellectual it was not worth powder and shot. Now that K[im] has woken it up and the ranks have been swelled by active members it is becoming a danger to the Black Forces—especially in view of K's work. Primarily it is K they want. He has been too careful for them in his personal work and has guarded the rest of us too carefully.

If Seymour's ability to handle power at raw magical levels was waning because of illness, it is clear from the records of this period that CCT had by now perfected her own seership. The following is a precis of a detailed working dated 4/8/42, beginning: "Prepared for anything; contacted B. I. who gave his one-sided smile and then granted J's wish to 'see how it all began.'" The seers involved were CCT, J, plus a mother and daughter whom we shall simply call M and D respectively. There is some preliminary description of Atlantis as seen from the small boat they were on, pointing out the Sun Temple on the peak, and the cliffs which went sheer down to the water. M and J were about seventeen, CCT and D perhaps two years less than that. M was already a priestess, CCT expecting to become one. J and CCT were regarded as prospective mates within the Mysteries. They saw a shallow stream running into the sea, which they decided to explore...

> We pulled up the stream, which was little more than a backwater, and through a tunnel and came out at the little beach where the Death Ship of the High Priest is launched. There was a sharp bend in the water there and though I had been down once to the launching, I had never seen that backwater. All I knew was the swiftly flowing stream under the tunnel where the Death Ship went. The devil entered into all of us...and we agreed to take the boat down the sacred stream. The current here was pretty swift and we went down at a good pace: sud-

denly M said she heard falling water; we listened and there was the sound of a very deep waterfall. We did not like it at all. Our little boat swept around the bend and we could see the stream falling over the lip of a tremendous chasm and then we knew what happened to the dead High Priest in his barge. J took command; he saw something in the shape of the guardian of the waterfall, and he knew also at that moment that that was the most sacred place of all, where the new High Priest took over the Apostolic Succession just as his predecessor went over the fall. There was a chain fixed across the river which, catching under the flat-bottomed barge, swung it round and tipped the sacred burden into the depths. J was instructed by someone on the other side that we were to jump for it to a little ledge on the left hand bank. We scrambled ashore somehow... but we all got very wet and managed to save our lives by hanging onto the chain. The pressure of the water was terrific and of course the boat went over like a stone. D kept complaining how wet she was (she wasn't any wetter than anyone else) and we struggled up footholds in the cliff-side—seemed to be metal footholds, like steep steps. As we went I knew where we here coming out and didn't like it at all. We came to a door in the rock and opened it... We went up a more regular staircase, up and up and round and round in the rock. There was a door at the top and I knew that it led into the Priests' room at the temple—a very "grown-up" place... We were all very wet and cross and very frightened of the consequences. Even M's bouyancy and continual remarks that it had been worth it, seemed to have dried up a bit.

We opened the door and filed in. As we expected the room was not empty. It was a circular room and at a desk or table in the middle was Kim. He was one of the Senior Priests. He looked at us and never said anything and we seemed to grow smaller and smaller. Then he told us to go and get dry clothes and then to report back...

A little later we found ourselves back in the Round Room. There were three or four senior priests there as well as K. The whole thing was so horrible that it is difficult to get it into words because it was so much on the astral and it was so much in a sense a moral scolding... We had our sashes taken away and we were shut off from all our magical contacts for an unspecified period while the Elders considered what to do with us. We went out on the terrace and I started kicking stones about and D hung over the wall and fingered the roses and M started to be bright and helpful about occupations, and J went off to the priests' quarters in a furious temper. I know I hung over the wall with D and said that as we are shut out of the Temple Working nothing mattered and why shouldn't we go down the mountain and explore the soldiers' and craftsmen's quarters on the second shoulder, as nothing could be worse than what we were going through... The picture got a little blotted at intervals.

After a time (weeks, I think) I was sent for myself and had to interview the High Priest... I got the biggest dressing-down I have ever had because the worst of the fault was mine. I was of the Blood, I was supposed to be growing-up and on the point of taking the priestess estate and I had helped to lead D into committing sacrilege—that was our crime and the only thing that really saved us was that (a) it was not deliberate, and (b) the Powers had saved us and therefore the Priests felt that it was intended that we should live because otherwise we should have been swept over the abyss.

Eventually we were told to appear before the full Council of Priests and we arrived—very nervous and very ashamed. I think I had been working in the Priests' quarters all the time for there seemed to be no contact between us and we reckoned the time as about three months. The roses on the wall were dead and the wind seemed colder. D says that she thinks we were put on to some sort of fatigues but I can't remember—nothing mattered when one was cut off from the magic power. There was a very grave homily from the High Priests... the gist of it being that M was to be sent to the other island to do new work there and that D and I were to be reinstated at the next Zodiacal transit (in a day or two) but that we would probably have to work it out in some form of Karma—this certainly for me, if not for her. J was I think to be sterilized so that he could not function as a High Priest in the fullness of the mating.

There was a very unhappy meeting on the terrace; M was heartbroken at leaving us (incidentally she had a short vision of her own during the interview, when she went down into the bowels of the mountains in the astral and saw pain and suffering spread before her—it must have been something to do with her new work). J and I were not really on speaking terms—only on spitting terms. D who seemed to be curiously plump and placid, was making the best of things philosophically.

Then I took the matter into my own hands and I demanded an interview with the High Priest. Why I got it I don't quite know but I did. I marched in with my chin up and seemed to tell him that if I could not be mated with J I wouldn't carry on as a High Priestess... that it was both of us or neither and that I was as responsible as he, if not more so. He had been sent for and was standing there, saying he would rather undergo anything than be mated with me. The High Priest just sat there at the table with his chin on his hand and looked at me with a crinkle of amusement. I remember stamping my foot (which shook J a bit) and generally carrying on magnificently. I think the High Priest was a little amused; I seem to remember his saying to J that he thought probably the worst punishment he could inflict would be the fact that he would have to have me throughout the ages as his opposite number and that we should have to sort out our Karmas together. I know he agreed to what I demanded and waved us away.

When we got into the courtyard J boxed my ears in public and flew into a frightful temper, saying he would never go through with it. I dashed into our room and told D who was sitting by the dressing-table I know she was irritatingly mild and cool about it all and I threw my gold sandals at her and hit her twice. That was when she got up and flung me down on the bed and refused to put up with it any longer. I remember drumming my heels on the bed with temper... I think I was rather proud of having stood up to the High Priest and got my way and didn't at all see why I shouldn't be pleased. Besides, it was most unflattering.

I am not sure what happened to him because it was then that the picture started to break up.

Obviously, from this working alone, her capacity for vision had come a long way from the tentative Atlantean memories she gained when she first started working with the Colonel. By now, 1942, she was a mature priestess whose talents were on the upward climb; when the diaries which comprise the main part of this book were written, she was just learning her craft.

In the 1938 workings which picked up Atlantis, Seymour was a soldier; in these later ones he was High Priest. One would assume they both had several lives on Atlantis before they finally left. It must be stated, however, that not all magicians believe in the existence of that continent. Some of them, men and women of undoubted inner attainment with contacts of their own, are openly scornful of the classical beliefs about a great land that once existed somewhere within the present-day Atlantic ocean. Possessing formidable psychic talents and practicing all the techniques that would have been practiced by Dion and her pupils, nevertheless these people can find no room within their own cosmologies for the types of island or the Sacred Clan described here. It does not matter. The truth about Atlantis is this. Whatever the physical realities, Atlantis exists within the psychic geography of that tribe of magicians which centered itself around Dion Fortune. It is fully explorable.

Yet despite the intensity of the workings within that new group, involving much more than simple far memories, Christine told me that her *real* work at this period was with the Colonel alone. Under his direction, and with all the knowledge he had given her as to defensive techniques, she had gone "into the crystal" to deliberately seek out and fight the Black Magicians they perceived as being behind Hitler's regime. It is an extraordinary thought, that, and a far cry from the passive meditational work that Dion was doing at this time. They were details which slipped out during my affectionate but devious questioning, and although she proclaimed that as the most important of all the magic she had done, she would say no more of it than that. Perhaps the full story will emerge at a later date.

In 1941 a new influence appeared within Seymour's life. While in Liverpool he had as one of his staff a Mrs. Lilian Yates, who was a senior member of Co-Masonry. It was through her that he came to join the lodge in Notting Hill Gate. Although he could not take much of an active part because of his failing health he did manage to get CCT admitted shortly afterward, on his nomination. More than forty years later she is still active in it, still working magic even though by her own admission she is reduced to a relatively "small magic" these days because of her age.

In occult terms it is Co-Masonry which proved to be the great and enduring influence upon her life, far more so than the decade she spent within Dion's group. It is one reason why she has been able to look back at the latter with a remarkably dispassionate attitude and one which is (as far as humanly possible) devoid of self-interest.

By 1943 the Colonel had worked out a magical curriculum for CCT for the next seven years, going deeper into the Celtic and Arthurian mysteries with special reference to the Welsh traditions. Long before it became fashionable, he wanted to show how these were still vital and alive today, and how they could be used to transform the consciousness not only of the magical group, but of the nation as a whole. She had the Welsh blood which he felt would equip her for the task. And, believing he had seven years left to live, he wanted everything completed by that time.

Adepts know such things.

He also said that he would return again (and soon) as a Chinese doctor. Perhaps it was for this reason that he began to collect statues of the Buddha and Kwan Yin, one of which, he told Paula and Christine, would call to him during the night, whereupon he would go down and talk to it. They gave each other long glances at that. It did not sound healthy at all.

Taking a charitable view, though, such apparent abberations are often the end result of a lifetime working with power. The person concerned would simply think his behavior beyond mundane logic and laws, the onlookers grossly misunderstanding the sublimity and spiritual significance of the behavior. That may be true. On the other hand Yeats came to see Mathers as "half a lunatic half a knave," while that poet himself occasionally caused people to snigger at parties by attempting to demonstrate his occult powers and failing miserably. To everyone's perceptions but his own. Crowley, who was burned out by power handled at high level while still comparatively young, was said to have sacrificed the love aspect of his potential in order to gain knowledge and power. The apparent idiosyncracies of the advanced magicians are one of the consequences of the work they do, when this is not made stable by a solid and supportive outer life. The older Seymour got and the nearer he approached to his gods, the lonelier he became.

In the June of that year, 1943, he came to CCT and told her that his sister Emily was about to die. He knew this because the bush had flowered in the grounds of Killagally which only did so when a Seymour was about to die. He felt sad, he was fond of Emily. Then, on the 24th of June he died, not Emily. He had had a cerebral hemorrhage brought on by essential hypertension. His vision had failed him at the last.

His compatriots were stunned. No matter how much time they spend in the Otherworld or exploring previous lives, magicians are as prone to sorrow as anyone else when their loved ones die. Their only advantage is that their recovery time is quicker than the rest of us. The funeral was rushed through and kept private to the immediate family only. Christine, for her part, had some difficulty extracting her documents and records from the Colonel's executors, hence the Record of this book is by no means complete.

Determined to do something she and a co-worker held a ceremonial burning of such magical equipment of his that they possessed, which included the lamen that he had made as an adept, plus some masonic regalia. They made a Fire of Vision of the sort described by Dion in *The Sea Priestess*, of juniper boughs with cedar and sandalwood mingled, built into a pyramid. The magical side of him, the best part, danced into a cloudless Norfolk sky as so many particles of smoke. The forgotten mage went finally into the Otherworld he knew so well.

Yet the story of his and Christine's magic is not entirely finished.

Although she had by this time formally left the Inner Light, CCT got a phone call from Dion one day asking her to go around. Why, she never really understood. The sight of her former mentor dismayed her: a burned-out woman with suspicious disciples at her elbow and feet. She was quite certain that Dion's contacts had gone completely. After a few desultory pleasantries she left, and was glad to do so. It was the last time she ever saw her.

If that part of her life had ended completely a new one began with the arrival of Henry Alexander "Dair" Hartley. An electronics engineer, it was communication over an impressive little book that he had written called *The Science of Astrology* which brought them together. A Northumbrian of Scots background, he confessed to having a strong psychic link with Michael Scot, an entity whom Christine knew well in other guises. Before too long, after she had received her decree absolute, they celebrated a mystical marriage in the grounds of Melrose Abbey, taking their vows over Michael Scot's tomb while the sky almost became dark at noon, and that ancient soul assumed a near tangible presence.

Being both now almost fifty they made up for lost time, doing the grand tour of the Mystery centers in Europe and Africa before coming back to buy their large and beautiful cottage in the village of Exton, in Hampshire. Two people very much of a kind, they matched on all levels; they matched so well that real magical work was not feasible for they lacked the necessary tension.

Nevertheless some things were possible, and these she describes in *A Case for Reincarnation*, written at the age of seventy-five. They include more Cathar memories, more Egyptian memories, including the almost apologetic statement that she had been the priestess Merit-aten, sister-in-law to Tutankhamen. In that young prince's tomb, Merit-aten's writing equipment had been found between the paws of Anubis, the Guardian, with whose priest Seymour had been so powerfully contacted. Plainly there was no getting away from him.

This apart, over a period of years she compiled several anthologies of stories on the supernatural, wrote a series of light romances under the name Dair Alexander, a book of children's names, and a slim guide to the unusual water closets she had encountered on her travels, including the one in Chalice Orchard where the brambles pushed through the open window with all the cunning of triffids. But 1968 was the year of her *magnum opus*. It was then that she wrote, at the direct if discarnate bidding of the Colonel, a book called *The Western Mystery Tradition*. Parts of it were dictated by the Colonel himself, she mediating his words with pen in hand in a New York hotel.

It is a learned and neglected work which draws together the strands of Celtic mythology and ties them with occult lore and clairvoyant insight. She takes the themes of the native British myths and shows that they can be made to live, that they are remnants of a once potent system. She avers that Arthur, Merlin and Morgan were initiatic titles rather than personal names of historical entities; she writes about the Druids and the Isles of the Blessed; Atlantis and Hy Brasil; the Wild Hunt and the Hosting of the Sidhe; fairy marriages and ancient rites. She speaks with the authority of someone who has in some way been to these places, seen these things. As indeed she has.

Throughout the book we can see the stamp of the Inner Light at its best, in writing that comprises three qualities: personal statement, academic detail, and inspired mytho-poetic fantasy. Unlike Dion in her *Avalon of the Heart* she does not try to substitute purple "inspired" prose for hard information—a mistake made by most occult writers—and as a result gives the book a more lasting sort of beauty. In it she went a long way to suggesting a completely British system of magic, one that did not depend upon the Hebrew of the Qabalah. And she dealt with the Arthurian traditions in a way that Dion had only toyed with. It is the sort of book which is packed with information, dense with knowledge, thirteen chapters like the stones of a circle, witches in a coven; no matter how many times one turns to it there is still something new to be found.

Like all magical tomes it can be opened at random and produce something of value. Doing just this I find a section dealing with a Breton poem in which Merlin, the swineherd, speaks of a wonderful orchard containing the secrets of the earth and planetary revolution. In this instance the comment is more pertinent than the actual poem:

> This wonderful orchard was guarded by two dusky birds who each wore a yolk of gold. These birds correspond to the Ravens of Odin and to the two horns which Moses wore upon his forehead. In other words they were the two wings or petals seen by a clairvoyant spectator when the clairvoyant eye is being used by

the seer. They are of course the immediate information that the orchard is not to be found on this plane but is only in the inner vision.

The Ravens are the representation of the pupils in the Mystery School, who helped to guard the orchard and acted as assistants to the priests. The whole of the poem from which this short quotation is taken goes on to tell the loss of these clairvoyant powers as the intellect took over from the intuition during the course of evolution.

In some ways that has summarized the whole of the foregoing book. Like everything else within the Celtic tradition it can be read on several levels.

What she presented, in retrospect, was a curriculum that might have become the very essence of the Fraternity had she stayed, and if the war had not broken up her and Kim's progress in this direction. The Christian element is strong within the book but then again it is the Celtic Christian element which could coast with paganism in most of its forms. This is the way that Dion Fortune could have gone. And, as is always the case with front-runners like her, there is someone to one side of her path indicating with some ire and exasperation that theirs was the way she *should* have gone.

In terms of occult literature, the only precedent for *The Western Mystery Tradition* was Eleanor C. Merry's *The Flaming Door*, a beautiful work of anthroposophically oriented vision upon which CCT occasionally drew, with full acknowledgement. Although the latter managed to maintain a nebulous existence, the former came on the market and sank without trace, as surely as Atlantis itself.

No one at that time was very much interested in our heritage, or in doing anything with it magically. It was the era in which the gratuitous grace of LSD-inspired visions was preferred to sheer hard work and training. It was the period when holy places only existed in the Eastern hemisphere and the clamor was for mantras and koans, gurus and dhotis, joss-sticks and sitars; and besides which everyone knew that Arthur was no more than a sweaty Romano-British warlord, that's all. We knew everything in that decade.

By the same token a generation had appeared who had never heard of Seymour, knew that Christine Hartley was something to do with Dion Fortune, and found that the Tradition they represented made too many demands upon them for their liking.

Those were the years when we had few magicians, merely apologists. And Christine Hartley was so far ahead upon the road that she looked small.

Now, mercifully, people are beginning to re-adjust their perspective, and the work that was done by FPD, CCT, and DNF is bearing fruit once more.

At the time this was originally written, Christine was alive and well and as formidably alert and intellectual as anyone of any age. With gathering speed, and in most unusual ways, the pattern of magic that was broken up in 1940 seemed to be reconstructing itself. While on inner levels the Colonel seems to be rampant, somehow. There are those who aver that he has recently incarnated; others who insist that they have potent psychic contact with him, and so cannot accept this. Once again, it does not matter. Seymour (as well as Merl, Dion and all the rest of the tribe) is a symbol and spark for a peculiar type of energy aflame within the Western psyche.

Christine watched it all with quiet pleasure and some amusement. Here was a small woman who had seen the Hosting of the Sidhe, who had been with her priest to Aurd-na-Rea, the High Place of the Moon, who had talked to gods and been possessed by goddesses, who had known Brodie-Innes on both outer and inner levels, who had shared past lives with Dion Fortune, and who had come to these isles in the first place, thrown onto them by a rolling billow from a sunken land. When I suggested that there was a new generation who would be fascinated by her Magical Records, she demurred for some time, thinking them unimportant, rather passé; and also deeply suspicious that I might be overly fulsome in anything I might write about her. If this has been the case then I make no apologies. Someday, when the rest of the material is released, someone will write a more objective book about it all.

It was my original thesis that the world at large lost something when she and the Colonel left the Fraternity, driven out by circumstance and personal conflict. But it has all been made well by the very nature of Christine's longevity. She remained to see it come full circle, the dance back in fashion and the tune renewed.

More than half a century after Dion had come into those offices in search of her natural heir, I would suggest at risk of Christine's displeasure that she had now become so, in ways that neither would have envisioned.

So here, after a brief analytical section, is the record of her magic, a small portion of her magic. She kept it for us all this time.

The circle is now unbroken.

3

The Magical Record

The Shadows Under the Tree

It was the novelist E.M. Forster, whom CCT knew, who penned the famous words "Only connect...," which he saw would go some way to healing some of the social, emotional, and psychological ailments of the times. They are words which in many ways sum up the essence of the Magical task: we must learn to connect our mundane consciousness with something greater; we must learn to join the worlds. Although FPD and CCT achieved this in the simple act of holding hands, they were like swans, really, as they glided along the river of consciousness: under the surface, furious and powerful muscles were exerting themselves.

By the time that they sat down before the hearth in 2 QT and held hands, they were already familiar with astrology, geomancy, scrying in the crystal, the art of making talismans, the evocation of spirits and the banishing of same, basic Theosophical doctrine with special reference to the occult constitution of Man, and Esoteric Christianity as well as all the pantheons of the Celtic, Egyptian and Norse religions and much much more.

It was a daunting but by no means impossible body of knowledge that they found themselves working with. If we can, like cannibals, throw all this meat into the pot and boil it down to the bare bones, then the skeleton which will remain has to be that of the Qabalah.

The word is derived from the Hebrew QBL, a verb which means "to receive." It is a reference to those esoteric teachings passed on "from mouth to ear," whispered secrets which no non-initiate must hear.

Qabalah is the more usual transliteration, but Cabala and Kabbalah are both acceptable.

The QBL, then, was an esoteric doctrine passed on from initiate to initiate, a mystic lore that was said to be capable of explaining the secrets of the heavens above and the earth beneath. It was supposed to have been transmitted from God, through the angelic orders to Adam, Noah, Moses, David, Solomon, and finally to Rabbi Simeon ben Yohai, who wrote the teachings down during the second century of the Christian Era.

Its main books were the *Sepher Yetzirah*, or "Book of Creation," and the *Zohar*, or "Book of Splendour," which was written in Spain by Moses de Leon in the 13th Century.

The theoretical Qabalah contains elements from ancient Egyptian, Babylonian and Greek philosophies, spiced up with the mysticism of Philo and the early Christian Gnostics, with the doctrines of reincarnation, transmigration, and the enduring realities of Good and Evil, Light and Darkness thrown into the mix.

If the theoretical Qabalah proved irresistible to the mystics, then the practical Qabalah proved itself a manna to the magicians. And it is that diagram known as the Otz Chaim, or Tree of Life, which provided the framework upon which all else was hung. One commentator described it as the "Mighty and All-embracing glyph of the Universe and the soul of Man." Surprisingly, despite the bombast, it is exactly that.

Dion Fortune wrote what is still the best book on the topic in *The Mystical Qabalah*, although this is almost matched by William Gray's *Ladder of Lights*, which more than lives up to its subtitle of *Kabbalah Renovata*. Those readers who demand an in-depth analysis of this philsophy can do no better than study these. Those, however, who can manage quite happily with a grossly simplified thumbnail sketch might care to read on...

According to the revelation, all life preceded via a series of emanations beginning from *Ain Soph*, which we might describe as Absolute Nothingness. This was the condition of the universe before Man, before God, before anything. From that Absolute Nothingness came the single point of pure white light known as Kether, which is that state of consciousness that we might crudely (very crudely) describe as God.

It was from this first sphere, or sephirah, that the universe be-

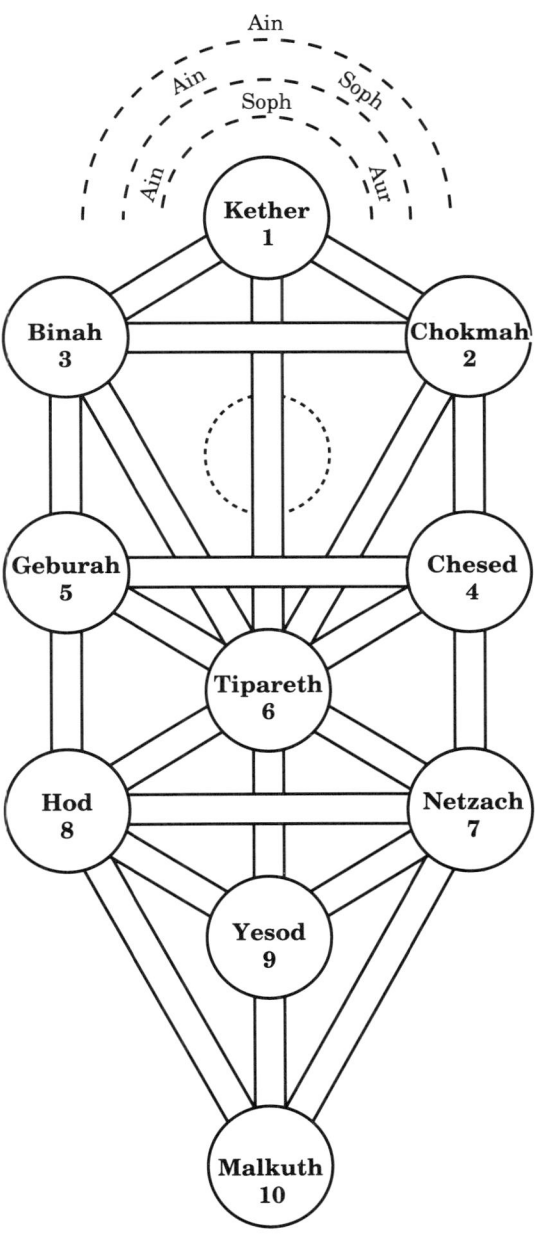

Tree of Life

gan to manifest itself in the numerical sequence shown, so that Kether (1) is at the level of absolute spirit, and Malkuth (10) is the realm of densest matter. It is in Malkuth, the earth-sphere, that we find ourselves. The Tree provides us with a ladder by which we can attempt to climb back up to our Source.

The spheres themselves are clearly arranged on three columns known as Pillars. All the positive, upbuilding energies in the universe are linked with the right-hand column, and all the negative, breaking-down forces placed on the left. In this sense, however, "negative" was never regarded as evil in itself, any more than it is evil to knock down buildings (or psychological edifices) which are dangerously decayed. It is wrong to associate Good with positive and Evil with Negative. Being always positive, always saying "yes," can create just as much evil within the world as its unbalanced opposite. The balance, then, is represented by the middle pillar.

Within these columns we can resolve the universe for ourselves, if we are uncompromising enough: Yes/No/Maybe, White/Black/Gray. Sometimes, as all magicians know, the best way to deal with the world is to retreat into these basics and nothing else.

By analyzing the spheres, however, we can add some subtleties to the way that these three qualities express themselves.

We can best imagine the Tree as a kind of filing system which is divided into ten compartments, and into which everything—*everything*—can be placed. Our initial problem is simply that of having the exact nature of this system explained to us, because after that it begins to explain itself.

Had there been 26 compartments then this would present no problem at all, for it would be based upon the alphabet. Into the compartment "L," for example, would go leopards, lemurs, light, locusts and love. While it would be simplicity itself to store such data the exercise would be meaningless on any spiritual level: it is no good looking for love and finding lice, lugworms and loquaciousness. That won't teach us anything. But with the system used by the Tree we can not only store away our own experiences in a particular area—intellectual, emotional or spiritual—but we can use to it to lead us on into the collective experience of mankind as a whole.

Each of the spheres upon the Tree has some basic attributions. These are known as the Correspondences. The major ones are given in the chart on the following page.

Sphere	Archangel	Divine Name	Color	Magical Image
Kether	Metatron	Eheieh	Brilliance	Face of an Old Man, in profile
Chockmah	Ratziel	Jehovah	Brilliance	Masculine, bearded face, full-on
Binah	Tzaphkiel	Jehovah Elohim	Blackness	A mature woman
Chesed	Tsadkiel	El	Blue	A wise king, on his throne
Geburah	Khamael	Elohim Gibor	Red	A warrior king, on his chariot
Tiphereth	Michael	Jehovah Eloah va Daath	Rose-pink	A child, priest-king, sacrificed god
Netzach	Auriel	JHVH Tzavoos	Emerald	A beautiful naked woman
Hod	Raphael	Elohim Tzavoos	Orange	An hermaphrodite
Yesod	Gabriel	Shaddai El Chai	Violet	A naked man, very strong
Malkuth	Sandalphon	Adonai ha Aretz	Olive	Mother Nature, on her throne

To understand how we can use each of these as keys into areas of consciousness, we need to look at each one in sequence

KETHER

The Crown. The Point within the Circle. Instead of visualizing God as some omnipotent deity in human form, visualize him as an all pervasive radiance, underlying all and everything. Then go a stage further and imagine that light concentrating itself into an intense pinpoint which hangs within the absolute nothingness and complete blackness of the unmanifest universe, *before* The Beginning. This, then, is Kether: a pinpoint of pure white light which contains All. This is the universe before the Big Bang. This is the Essence.

CHOCKMAH

Wisdom. When Kether became aware of itself it exploded outward in what we might describe as the first Cosmic Laugh. This is Chockmah, which represents the archetypal male and is the sphere of all the outrushing, thrusting and forceful energies as they emerge from the Source. One of its images is that of an upright pole, which should speak for itself in phallic terms. All phallic symbolism, therefore, can find an ultimate placement in this second sphere.

BINAH

Understanding. If Chockmah is the sphere of pure and dynamic *force* on archetypal levels, then Binah balances it with the archetypal female qualities of pure and receptive *form*. It is the sphere associated with the black-robed Great Mother, the planet Saturn, and that revelation known as Sorrow, in its spiritual sense: "All life is suffering" as Buddha said, but through that (through Binah) we can begin to understand the deepest parts of life's mystery.

These three spheres are known as the Supernal Triad. They represent the innermost essence of all that which we find in denser levels of manifestation. All of us have qualities of positive and negative within us. How we use these qualities, as opposed to over-indulging in them, determines how much Wisdom (Chockmah) or Understanding (Binah) we have. It is nothing to do with what sex a person may be. Men can be Binah figures just as women can relate to Chockmah.

CHESED

Mercy. The planet is Jupiter. It is the sphere of benevolence, generosity, philanthropy, and all those energies which go toward the creation of stable, peaceful civilizations.

GEBURAH

Justice. Its planet being Mars, it is the natural balance to the sphere of Chesed. It is that energy which ensures that anything effete, corrupt and putrid (however this manifests) is regularly scoured, purified, or swept away completely. Although its traditional symbol is that of the pentagram, the modern image of a surgeon's knife is more indicative.

TIPHERETH

Beauty. Both Chesed and Geburah resolve themselves within Tiphereth, the sphere of the Sun. It is the sphere of all those Sacrificed Gods who abound in major religions, and who bring harmony to the world by dying for our sakes. Harmony is, in fact, one of its titles. Not the placid and often pathetic harmony of, say, an English vicar, but that radiant harmony achieved by the nuclear forces reacting within the sun itself, with its power to heal or destroy depending upon where we are placed at the time.

This trinity of Chesed/Geburah/Tiphereth is known as the Ethical Triad. They represent those qualities which lift us above mere self-absorption toward a consideration of life and humanity as a whole.

NETZACH

Victory, or Achievement. This is the sphere of Venus, with all those quickening impulses which might loosely be termed "romantic," and find expression in the arts generally, and in our emotional behavior personally.

HOD

Glory, or Splendor. This is the sphere of Mercury, whose qualities of pure intellect neatly balance the raw emotion of Netzach, and which find expression every time we act rationally, and logically, or indulge ourselves in the sciences.

YESOD

Foundation. The place of the Moon, and the unconscious mind, and what we might think of as the instincts, upon which so much of our existence depends. It is also the realm of the astral plane, the "treasure-house of images," and because of the use made of this by magicians, this particular trinity of Netzach/Hod/Yesod is known as the Magical Triad,

MALKUTH

Kingdom. The material world on which we all live and find expression. All of the above spheres "pour down" into it. Malkuth contains them just as our physical body contains our mind, soul and spirit. It is related to the four elements of Earth, Water, Air and Fire, which we might think of as Solids, Liquids, Gases and Radiations.

There is an eleventh sphere also, known as DAATH, or Knowledge,where Malkuth used to be before the "Fall," but that needn't concern us here.

As we can see from the diagram, the spheres of the Tree are joined by paths, which might be regarded as the blending points. Thus the path between Yesod and Netzach represents that area within our consciousness which rises from pure blind instinct and leads into the glow of more romantic considerations: where having sex turns into making love. Or else we can study that path connecting Hod and Netzach and make the careful balance that we must all strike sometimes between soulless intellect and brainless passion.

So we can begin to see how this unique filing system of the Tree of Life can work. Like a novice secretary, the neophyte will handle the system clumsily at first, often putting things into the wrong holes; but with rapidly increasing assurance the peculiar patterns and interrelationships between the spheres will begin to teach of their own accord.

For example, all those gods related to the intellectual "hermetic" arts would be equated with the sphere of Hod: Thoth, Hermes, Merlin, etc., while all those with figures of romance and enchantment will go into Netzach: Nimue, Nephthys, Freya, and so on.

There is no dogma attached to this: militant feminists are quite welcome to reverse the polarities and adapt them to their own peculiar vision of the universe. As long as the neophyte makes his or her own efforts in determining the Correspondences for each sphere, that process known as "Building the Tree in the Aura" will take place. It is when this happens that the filing system starts to become more akin to a super-computer of spiritual possibility.

In fact the magicians of the Golden Dawn and the Fraternity of the Inner Light would have done exactly that—building the Tree into the aura (i.e., fixing it in the unconscious) by visualizing it as shown on the following page. They would ritualize it by touching the top of the head (the crown) and intoning the word *Eheieh*, while attempting to experience the qualities of Kether, or the "pure white light," within. Then to the right temple, and the left, and so on, down the body in the order of manifestation, doing all of the above while also visualising each sphere in its associated color. In time—in a surprisingly short time—the magician will have a very marked sense of the reality of these spheres. It is as though the amorphous mass of his psyche has been molded into a particular pattern, and highly specific areas of his consciousness begin to inter-react in the same way as the spheres upon the Tree. When he comes to work on his Correspondences (which involves no more than associating items of experience, symbols, impulses, etc., etc., with the patterns of the spheres) then he will find links, parallels and suggestions springing into his mind which will be altogether surprising, and never less than illuminating.

Then come the simple rituals.

A magician who feels that he has been unfairly dealt with

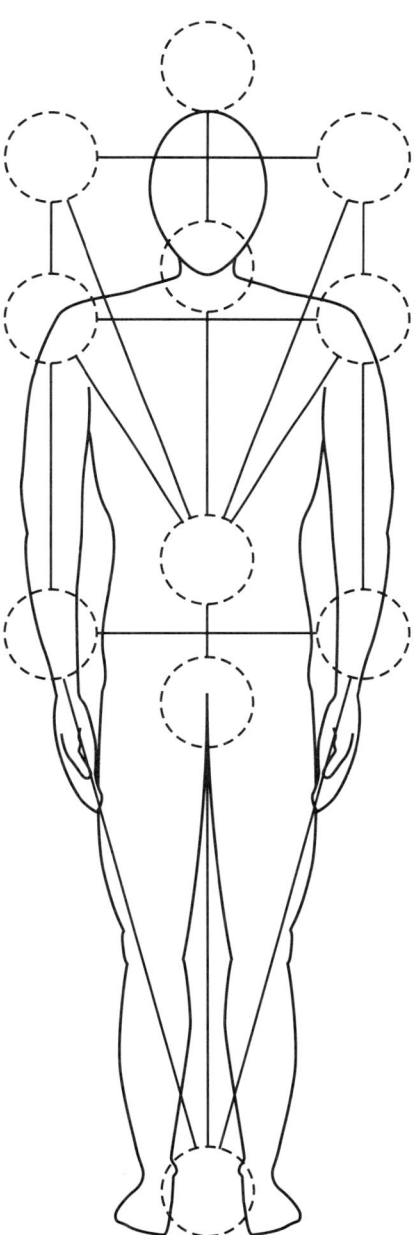

The Tree of Life in the Aura

might use Qabalistic magic to seek Justice. He would wear red clothes, light five red candles, intone the words *Elohim Gibor* in a fivefold rhythm, and even *think* red, before addressing his complaint to the Archangel Khamael, visualized as a great, winged, darkly red figure wielding a flaming sword and wearing a pentagram upon his chest,

This would not, however, be any kind of "revenge magic." Geburah cannot be used for that. His plea to Geburah would be: "If these events are right and proper, if it is part of my karma to suffer this, then so be it. But if it is *not*, and I am being unfairly treated then please redress the balance, bring justice back into my life."

The actual words are less important than the intention, of course, but the supplicant should be very strong in his belief that he *is* being wronged, for if such suffering is part of his karma, or nothing more or less than his own stupid fault, then the effect of such an invocation is to bring all the energies to a head, sooner than usual, with all the intensified suffering that might ensue. On the other hand, he may well find that balances *are* made in his favor, and ways made smooth, and burdens lifted.

The forces on the Tree are all perfectly balanced with one another. It is impossible to "trick" these energies into giving something for nothing. There are always prices to be paid, harmonies which will be maintained. And when the Tree is built into the aura it becomes a device which enables us to connect our own limited consciousness with the *un*limited consciousness of the universe. Whatever changes we effect within ourselves ultimately affect the whole of existence. We become part of the great cosmic balancing act and must accept a grave responsibility for an inward kind of decency and honesty.

But in purely magical terms it means that in time, with regular study and practice, the magician will be able to pick up one symbol—an ankh, for example—and that single glyph will give him access not only to the huge store of his own ideas, but also to the infinite experience of the collective unconscious. By lifting this simple device from his altar of his conscious mind, with ritualistic intent, he is potentially in touch with the experiences of every Egyptian worshipper of Isis, every latter-day hippie, every astrologer who has ever marvelled at Venus, and every Roman who has ever adored that goddess as she rose frown the sea.

Potentially, that is. As FPD writes in *The Old Religion*, it is a matter of the would-be magus asking himself at the end of the day: "Has my brow been wet with mental sweat?" No sweat, no achievement. No effort, no progress. There never has been an easy path in *true* Magic.

When Aleister Crowley was first initiated into the Golden Dawn he complained that the great secrets he had been expecting to receive amounted to no more than a few attributions of the sort that we have already given here. Yet in truth that is all that *can* be given. Power and wisdom only come when the student begins to make his own symbols work, and forges his own links between this world and benign, evolutionary intelligences in the next. No one can do this for him,

The Tree of Life, then, is just one means of enabling a person to make a connection between the worlds of the kind described in the following diaries, It becomes simpler with practice: like driving a car, or handling complex machinery, it becomes almost automatic. In time, you can forget about it all with your conscious mind because it propels you inward from unconscious levels. And then, like FPD and CCT did in those bleak years before the War, you can sit down in some quiet place, summon up your Gods, Goddesses or Guides, and perform the most effective magic of your life by doing no more than reaching out, and connecting.

The Magical Record

Charles Seymour:

July 12th, 1937

Monday evening rite with CTC in the West. I built the Black and Silver Hall of the Sphinxes and conducted the worshippers there. Then, in silence, for I said nothing more until closing, I and the P of A.[1] went to the cave taking a priestess with us.

In the cave we worshipped the Black lsis with fire and sacrifice upon the altar. The power was so great that I felt the priestess had had enough so I closed.

Afterwards CTC told me that she was all out when I stopped. I did not banish but left the power there in hopes of giving Judy something to go on to with tomorrow night. Needless to say in vain!

Note: CTC says she was badly knocked out next day. Her reaction came about 24 hours later and left her absolutely devitalized.

Griff

Christine Hartley:
Rite worked July 13th, 1937

Moon: Third Quarter
Weather: Clearing after heavy day

Personal emotions:
Materialistic, commonplace.
Health: Perfect.

After instruction went upstairs without any particular excitement or uplift. Horribly bothered because my shoes squeaked on the floor and spoilt the atmosphere. Started in a watching, passive state. Aware of power almost at once. In the invocation as the Figure was built behind me, I began to prickle all over, like a sort of nettlerash—especially noticeable on arms and throat. I went through the courtyard in a sort of doped condition, not really experiencing it but accepting it. Then when I got onto the throne, things began to happen. I don't know but it was then, I think, that the priest opposite left me: I forgot all about him. I started a chant under my breath to Khonsu.[2] It was queer, I couldn't quite get the words down to this plane. It was a mating call. And He came right across the Lodge, and he kissed me and it was kind of fusion of both of us and I thought it would be more than I could bear. My head began to ache with the nervous pressure and I was flooded with power. Then the priest (I mean the one I call Nefer-su)[3] told me to come and we got down from my throne and went up about nine steps to a dark chapel shaped like an apse... the front was broad and unbarred. And I said "It's all dark and empty" and he said "It is the chapel of the God behind the Gods," and it filled with an unearthly light and He—Thoth who taught Isis—was there. The power was tremendous and the pressure on my forehead again hurt. It's difficult to explain but there was a presenting of me to the God as his priestess and pupil by Nefer-su and the God blessed me. And then we walked down the steps into the grey light of the Isis chapel and I went back to the throne and was very tired. So we came down through the courts, hazily and as soon as I had got into the litter, I came back and relaxed. So far as I was concerned the talisman in my lap was entirely lifeless all evening. I would like one day to do this kind of magic without people who might be disturbed because I always get a strong desire to get up and dance and it is so difficult to hold on to my personality enough to remember I must not move.

CCT

Report on Work done September 8th, 1937

First time I had seen the opening of the Temple and the closing of the doors. Tried to follow but not very successful. When we came to the East and invoked Pan he turned up promptly and I held out my arms to him, he was so very really there.

Very nervous when it came to taking the journey because I knew could not do it smoothly and descriptively as in the Instruction Classes. I think doing it out loud and also with someone to work with helped the strength of the reactions for my part. I was so much aware of the inner sensations: the expectancy, the hush of the hills and the inner knowledge that They had that we would come.

There was a moment when I got stuck not seeing how to switch on to the Pan circuit but I relaxed and left it to Cheiron: if he wanted us to make the contact that way he would open the door. He did, for the hills rolled back and we were on the plain and the world was so young and laughing and *simple*. I've never been there before and the power of the earth life filled me till I thought I would snap and I came back unable to do anything further.

Afterwards when we did the banishing at the altar I remember being so happy and so aware of him that I looked up as he went away and said *"Darling Pan"* (may have been out loud).

Noticeable that since then I have felt pretty well able to throw the world over, terrific vitality, even for me, and a superb serenity and untouchableness.[4]

CCT

Charles Seymour:
Wednesday September 8th, 1937

Time: 8:10 to 9 p.m.
New Moon 4 days old. Weather fine.
Feeling weary and depressed when we started

I worked with CCT alone. We tried for the contacts of the Great Mother in the West and Pan in the South invoking each in turn. I think it is a mistake to try and work a double contact thus.

CCT did the description and did it well. We went to the hills and climbed high and went over the bare slopes to a great cleft in the hillside. After some delay we went through this cleft into an amphitheatre. The sun was vertically overhead there were no shadows. On the opposite side of this amphitheatre was a cave. I saw Cheiron at its mouth and I knew, I heard, the way CCT called him some time before she actually did this invoking.

We could not cross the amphitheatre, which began to fill with shadows that were without any substantiality.

Then Pan seemed to take over and Cheiron disappeared. We seemed to go back into the very dawn of Time, into something very primitive. It was το Παν The All, and not Pan of Arcady the Great God that we touched at that moment.

There was a tremendous head of Power and as I felt that CCT was getting beyond her depth I took charge and closed down. The show lasted only 20 minutes. I felt much better for this rite. Then I taught CCT control of the Aura and the Lesser Ritual of the Pentagram. I closed down finally very carefully. CCT looked splendid at the end, like a girl of 22 or 23. Such a change!

Note: September 9th 4.40 p.m. after a short meditation on last night's work I slept for a few seconds and on recovering consciousness I saw a hypnagogic of the Amphitheatre and Cheiron at the entrance of his Cave.

FPD

Tuesday September 28th, 1937

8-9 p.m.
Temple at 3 QT
Self and CCT
Very fit, fine weather, Dark of the Moon.

Put up the Temple at 6:15 p.m. and banished.

1. Invoked the Great God Pan, and did 20 minutes meditation 7:20 to 7:45 p.m. Left the place ready for CCT. Gave a little talk on technique before we went up.

2. This time we sat side by side facing the altar and the East. We stept side by side on to a great plain with short grass and flowers, I saw them blue and purple. It was as if we had passed through a curtain. Very blue sky, there was a clump of myrtle and pine on my right. I felt two persons, as it were a man and a woman come from that grove. They came very slowly so we ran to meet them. As we got there I knew them for Pan and the Earth Mother. CCT was dressed in a very short white kirtle, with green myrtle and berries in her short hair. I was clad in a Fawn skin and carried a thick club. I was young and felt it. We knelt before them and Pan poured a blessing upon us and as he did so he seemed to change into Dionysus the God of Light. The Goddess opened her arms and formed a ring round us Three with Them. Then the God took of my form and subtle body and materialized himself through it. It left me like an empty shell. And he initiated CC into the Bacchic mystery.

Then They both blessed us and withdrew. When They were gone we returned through the curtain with CC a little shaken.

It was a very wonderful experience for me, and I wonder if eithter of us has grasped its full import?

Note: At 12:30 a.m. I woke up dreaming that we were both with Cheiron at the cave, but we were in the form of the Lapithae.[5] The dream did not stop until I was fully awake and fully conscious. It was a glorious gallop through space with a keen sense of struggle and of conquest.

Griff

Christine Hartley:
> *Report on Rite of September 28th 1937*

Time 8:15 p.m.   Moon Dark.
Weather: Warm   Personal: Normal.

When I went into the room it was full of people I did not recognize but who were very pleased to see me. Then we invoked Pan and the power centralized. When I sat down, I wished we had planned another working because I have been to the plane several times and I did not think anything new could happen unless I invented it. But it was all right. The plane opened in front of us and we stepped out: it is like Alice through the Looking Glass, or like the mirror in "Lilith." You come out of a tunnel into the big space. The grass was full of small flowers and there was a queer, clear light and no breeze but plenty of air: it was if everything was held static in time. We ran across the grass: I had a white full skirt and a wreath of berries in my hair. You had a fawn skin and sandals. We were both ageless, young and as we were then in looks, not as we are now. On the horizon was the pair of people. They developed slowly. She seemed to have arms outstretched and to hold the earth. He came to us, laughing. We were all laughing because it was so very lovely to be alive. We knelt down before him and he was very wise and smiling and he turned to me And I was seized with a passionate love for him and started to get up out of my chair and was pulled down again. And he came and kissed me on the mouth in a way that I did not know anyone could do off this plane and I experienced a complete sense of relaxation and contentment. It was only unsatifying in so far as there was no actual contact, and therefore the top part of my consciousness registered that I could not feel his arms round me. After that I had had about enough and came back. It all grew dark and we withdrew into the tunnel and it closed together in front of us and I woke up very limp for the moment but all right in a few minutes.

CCT

September 29th, 1937

Here it is... as fully as I can remember it. I went back, had a bath, did nearly an hour's work and then slept for seven hours with a curious dream, on the basis of undressing, which would no doubt have intrigued Freud but amused me even while it was happening because the persons concerned were so entirely outside that part of my life... an eminent publisher, a business girl friend and myself. I mention this because I take it that the dream following work like ours may be important. I did the banishment to the best of my recollection, remembering bits of it much too late, but all was quite well. I have, I think, cut the cord all right because when I got home there was a card from O.[6] for the child and the sight of his writing did not move in the least... this is the third time I have seen it on the door mat without any emotion and have also seen him in the distance, without his knowledge, and been untouched.

CCT

Charles Seymour:
Friday October 8th, 1937

8 to 9 p.m.
New Moon about 4 days old.
Weather Fine.
Self fairly fit but weary from a very tiring show on Wednesday with an American Doctor and D.N.F.

We worked in Parker's room downstairs with altar lamp and incense. I banished carefully about 6:30 p.m. Used the 5gm [pentagram] ritual of invocation, and then using the grade signs we both went through the portal on to the 32nd Path. I stopped for the guardian—gave the grade signs and asked permission to take CCT with me. A queer thing happened: a sort of Egg of faint light built round us and enclosed us so that we became two halves of one whole. Then we went along a black road in darkness, then up a mountain path with rocks and cliffs, and onto a snow clad height in silver moon light. An immense star was above the mountain, to the right, and brighter than the crescent moon below it. An immense figure, all radiant, appeared. It was Ishtar.

I told CCT to put her problem to Her which she did and apparently got her answer (I do not know what this was). Here I lost CCT who stretched out her arms, cried and invoked Ishtar and disappeared. I got hold of her again in a grove with a broken altar and broken pillars, the garden all wild and trampled by beasts. Then I saw the temple as it was before it was destroyed. It was the Temple at Babylon. I knew it well. Again I saw it all wrecked and then Ishtar said "look at my earthly temple." A wave of emotion for the Great-Mother seized me and I worshipped. CC broke into a strange sort of lament. Then the Goddess—stopped us—and pointed to the altar. A fire burnt on it. The pillars were rebuilt. The garden was full of scarlet flowers and sweet smelling bushes, and the Goddess said—a dedicated worshipping priestess and priest will always light my altar fires. Will you serve me and bring my joy and life and love to the hearts of men and women? Then the vision faded, we returned through the Moon and closed the Gates.

CCT was very shaken. I was very charged up. So we X hands upon the altar. CCT was soon O.K.[7]

Griff

Christine Hartley:
Report on Rite worked October 8th, 1937

Moon.: Medium. *Personal: Bit tired being*
Weather: Dry   *Friday otherwise well.*

For about three days I had been conscious of someone trying to tell me whom I was to contact. Knew I did not want to do either the Pan rite or the Isis rite in the Temple but could not get clear who was calling me. No hesitation in the Air contact when picking it out of the elements. I did not know if I would get through the Gate but was aware that I must not show any eagerness to go through: it was not a matter for anything but perfect neutrality and obedience. The path was very clear: it was really a path along the top of a ridge above the world. The peak ahead of us was shining like frozen snow. There was a big star overhead and when the crescent moon was shown me it was at the side of it, like the old Turkish flag. At the base of the topmost part of the peak stood the A.A. of the West.[8] I told him what I was trying to get and he stood aside and I seemed to go through a long way. And I knew I wanted Astarte (which is a name I never use myself) "who is Ishtar." And then she came and I asked her a question of my own and she gave me an answer. And then she gave us the message about teaching her people. And I saw the Grove with the broken pillars, the dark trees and the overturned altar, and my heart was very sore. And then it got better and there was a fire on the altar which we had kindled and people dancing round it and the Golden Age was coming in.

The interesting thing about this rite was that I was feeling my way: I was never completely absorbed in it and I did not get the ecstasy and abandonment that I get in both the others. I was rather like a child brought in to help the grownups, understanding some but not fully appreciating. I think this is because I was out of my Grade. It was not frightening or particularly awe inspiring, but tiring and rather more of an effort.

CCT

Charles Seymour:
Friday October 15th, 1937

Time: 8:15-8:45 p.m.
Lovely still warm night with a bright moon.

CCT came with a heavy cold, feeling seedy nearly did not come. Sore throat and could hardly speak. She insisted on going through with the Isis Rite. Banished as usual and then invoked in the name of Isis. Up came the power at once. Built Malkuth in the Aura. Then Yesod in the form of the horned moon. Up came a great silver star which filled the whole room. CCT took charge—journey in the silver litter, past the Lotus Pool. Into the Hall of the Sphinxes. And then into the Sanctuary. CCT sat on the knees of the Goddess, with her head between the breasts of the image.

Then there came a tremendous head of power. I could see CCT (bathed in a sort of silver mist) with the physical eyes. She got up and held out her hands as if in blessing and a stream of pale silver light came off them and on to me. It was so clear that I could see it and feel it physically. We bathed in this for some time, and then CCT told me to get on with giving the blessing of the Goddess to the World. Suddenly it all vanished, and we closed very carefully. Both feeling much better for the tremendous inflow of power. Then we blessed Her and worshipped Her.

CCT looked much better when she left.

FPD

Christine Hartley:
Report of Rite Worked on October 15th, 1937

Moon: Almost Full.
Weather: Dry.

Personal Health: Tired; heavy cold.
Mental Health: Keen to Work.

I was anxious about my voice, wondering if it would hold out and feeling that if I stopped to cough, and I was very hoarse, it would break the thread of both of us. But it held out. I saw the details of the House of Priestesses more clearly than ever before, together with the details of my own dress. Then I got into the litter and rather hurried the journey. (This time, knowing that we had not got to build for the others I could concentrate more on my private feelings and reactions as the high-priestess and get them noted down.) I remember walking up the steps and along the Hall of the Sphinxes and meeting Nefer-su at the curtains. I saw the curtains also more plainly. Then I climbed into my seat and the power began to work through me. I remember insisting most energetically on the way it was transmitted...it seemed to matter. Then at one time the Goddess came right down and I was her mouthpiece and spoke as she dictated, and then I was the priestess giving the responses. It was most strange and very wonderful. I seemed to be carried on without any deliberate volition on my part and all I had to do was to keep myself well held in so that the power should flow freely. After that I remember getting back into my seat and asking to be taken back to the house because I was so tired...but I came active again and described the moon on the lotus pool and the ceremony of disrobing me when I got back. There was not the ecstasy of the other rite but it was extraordinarily peaceful and fulfilling.

CCT

Charles Seymour:
Thursday October 21st, 1937

8-9 p.m.
Full moon on 19th.
Fine clear night, brilliant moon.

Self dead-beat headache probably due to eye-strain. CCT said she was fit but looked white and tired.

Usual sealing and invocation in the name of Isis. CCT got the contact at once. I could not get it till she threw the power to me. Then we went to the Temple. I went to the Sanctuary as the Priest. The priestess then took charge, and joined me at its curtained door. She sat on the knees of the Goddess with her head between the breasts of the image like a Throne. Then with a burst of power that shook me the Goddess took possession of her priestess. There was not much said—a sort of chant of the names of the Goddess which brought a rush of power, and then she gave her blessing. It was like sitting in a blast of hot air. The power filled one almost to bursting point. She gave her final blessing and then she was gone leaving a wonderful feeling of peace and fulfillment.

The whole scene was so vivid, and there was so much emotion and such a feeling of the presence of the holy that the idea that we were watching a bit from my past came to me very strongly.

I worshipped—for the first time for a very long time with a real intensity of purpose.

FPD

Christine Hartley:

Rite of October 21st, 1937

Moon: Just past full. Self: Rapidly recovering
Weather: Dry. normal cheerfulness after
 bad cold and worry.

In the whole of this rite I was less conscious of the power than the priest: I was more anxious to catch what was coming through and interpret it. We rowed across the Nile and the old woman dressed me. She hurried me and I do not like to be hurried when I am going to function: it discomposes my mind. I knew that we ought not to have been so long on the other bank...but we had business. When I came back to the river I was wearing the Double Crown of Egypt. I don't quite know when I discarded it but of course I had the silver and moonstone tiara as the high priestess. We went the usual route and along the gallery of the sphinxes to the door where the curtains are. Then we went inside and I climbed up. I settled myself on the seat and turned my head, as I always do, to look up at her and feel that she is really there. Then the answer began to come through and I got carried up because the Goddess came down and used me as her vehicle. I cannot remember what I said but she spoke through me and I kept trying to get the right words as if I were translating. I saw myself kneeling in front of her with the priest kneeling behind me and she blessing us both. There wasn't the ecstacy as when she comes to me: there was very little conscious feeling: I was being used all the time. Then she went away and we went back and I learnt a little bit more of the ritual ... we come back from the Sanctuary holding hands but our arms held out, till we get to the top of the steps, and then I go forward to bless the people and he stands behind having presented me. The lotus pool was lovely. Then I went back to the house of the priestesses and they disrobed me and put me to sleep in the one shaft of moonlight through the slit window.

CCT

Charles Seymour:
Thursday October 28th, 1937

11 to 11:30 a.m.
Very fit.

Tried the Tejas Tatwa fairly successful. Got into a most desolate mountain place into a big temple very crude: saw a thing like a lion, strangely alive, a great fire, and things that were hardly human. Came back rather tired. Working with Volens in Museum Chambers.

Evening working with CCT and DNF in lecture room 3 QT. Placed the 3 chairs in S. altar N. DNF as High Priestess, self middle, CCT left. I put up and cleared Temple at 6:15 p.m. Then did a meditation and got the Cave. At 7 p.m. I went to my room and changed, came back and invoked Isis as the Primordial Mother. Then I deliberately built the Cave and got the P. of A., and the idea in very general outlines of the evening working. Got the Black Isis and the Cave very clearly and also a fair head of power. CCT came, I went up to get DNF, CCT went into the Temple and bolted out saying it was full of presences and Things and it scared her. So meditation was effective! We used linked hands.

We 3 went in at 8:10. Invoked Isis. Using the Tatwa method we started from the House of the Virgins, CCT in Black, black litter, black bearers, went to empty Temple where DNF took charge, and to Hall of Sphinxes. Then into an underground passage and suddenly I shot out and found myself standing at the entrance of Cave where I waited for the other two. Then all Three went into cave, and past Anubis the guardian at the curtain. Within was the P. of A. waiting for us. He took over—and spoke to CCT. He set her certain conditions which she refused at first, and then agreed to them. She then walked to the stone of sacrifice, through the fire burning on the steps and seated herself between the thighs of the Black Isis. I am not clear as to what happened then for the image of the P. of A. and CCT vanished in a sort of red fog. Later I saw clearly and CCT was leaving her seat, she laid herself on the stone of sacrifice and I saw the P. of A. bend over her as if sacrificing her (!) Then he vanished and I took CCT back to the Temple of the White Isis. We returned through it to the House of the V. where DNF gave the address. Then back to normal. The power was very great, and my eyes were streaming from it. CCT very done at the end, and I think a bit scared. Ended 9:15 p.m. Then while DNF and I were downstairs talking she slept and felt much better.[10]

10 p.m. I found Proctor waiting for me in my rooms and I set to work to get the Osiris contact. Working on my sanctuary I took him through the veil and we found ourselves standing in front of the Ptolemy Gateway and the Temple of Khonsu. We walked through this—and he described what he saw, and then we went to the shrine of Osiris which is to the left (West) of the Temple of Khonsu. We went round this tiny temple and then down into the underground crypt.

Here the whole temple came to life in a blaze of cold soft blue white light. It was so bright that for a moment I thought someone had switched on the light. Then I saw the White Osiris alive—and he turned a ray of power on to us. Next moment Proctor and I were kneeling before him (Proctor right). Isis and Nephythys stood behind him. Thoth was on my left Anubis behind me. Horus was behind Proctor and a little to his right. I was looking into the past and at an initiation. A blaze of light and power came. Suddenly this went and we were back in my room. I was very tired and next moment the people next door began a row.[11]

Proctor was very puzzled because his shoulder was seized by a heavy hand, just before we knelt down, he thought I had done it but opening his eyes he saw my hands on my knees. Anyway I have got that contact, also the curious impression that then l was a woman!

P. said he saw the place—not as he knew it now—but as it must have been in the old days. (Very tired but very pleased—both of us.)

FPD

Christine Hartley:
    Report on Rite Worked October 28th, 1937

Weather: Wet.	Personal reactions: Tired but
Moon: Dark.	well. A bit worried.

This was the new type of rite with the three of us. When I first went into the Lodge I was hit by the Power so much that I stood by the door afraid to go further. It was concentrated at the North side... and I found afterwards that that was where the P. of A. stood for me. The power began to come through with the first invocation and the sealing of the Temple. Then came the journey. I knew the color and difference of the litter before I was told. We went a different way because when I am doing the usual work we don't go through the pylon gate... that is for the people: I go from the House of the Virgins straight up into the Lotus Court. I saw the High Priestess clearly... she wore brownish yellow linen robes with a straight line pattern of dull red bordering and a linen veil. She had a big jewel on her breast.[12] I followed her, not being very sure of myself and got very alarmed in the Hall of Sphinxes because it was all dark and I am used to it with the bright light and the people following me. I was lonely and small and afraid. We went down the passage and out by the desert way and then came to the Cave. I saw the statue of the Goddess and described it fairly accurately, I think. Then I saw the P. of A. in his bluish-gray robes and the high head-dress and the great jewels rather like Urim and Thummin on his breast. And especially I saw his big ring in which he sees the world as it is, past and present and future. And I saw the fire on the altar and got the message to walk through it, though I was not quite sure at first if I was to walk through or pick it up in my hands and scatter it. I went up the steps to the throne and sat down. Then he looked at me and his eyes grew greater and greyer and filled all my world and he came forward and put a crown on my head and I thought it was a crown of thorns, and I could not refuse it but I knew it meant sacrifice. But one does not shirk one's destiny and I have done this before. I could not quite get his message but that will come later. Then I got down and walked past him and everything went dark and we walked back again and I was very tired.

CCT

Charles Seymour:
Friday November 5th, 1937

Weather dull with a very smelly fog.
Self: very fit and full of life.

Did a very thorough preparation with CCT before the rite, and we got the contact very strongly. I had expected and wanted the Bright Isis but the Dark came up.

We went to the Cave and invoked—and got a rush of power. The P. of A. formed the apex of a triangle, we at the base, he beyond the altar light.

There came an awful row from the guild people[13] in the hall— CCT stopped—took a step forward in a shaky way and knocked over the altar and light. This left us both very shaken, and I was very muddled afterwards. Tea put CCT right—after a time.

We must avoid working on Fridays.

FPD

Christine Hartley:
Report on Rite on November 5th, 1937

Weather: Dark and foggy   *Self: Very well.*

Brought a tremendous rush of power down with the Invocation. Could not stop because I got so much that I had to bring Her right through. Then settled down to go to the Cave. Could have started right there myself but we found it better to go by the desert and down the passage. The Cave was lit by the lamp over the head of the statue—or else more centred in the Cave: it must be there because of the shine of the light reflected on her knees and bits of her face. The altar stone had the fire lit on it. The P. of A. was standing there. I went to him and he greeted me. I talked to him as I was desired to do but it was very hard to pick up his message as the wave length was so fine and there was a good lot of noise outside. Then he told me to come nearer and I was just going to him when I overturned the altar and came back with a bump, feeling pretty tired. It was a pity because it was going so well and I had got a strong contact and could have got more.

CCT

Charles Seymour:
Thursday November 11th, 1937

Time 8:10 to 8:45 p.m.
Moon 1st Qtr
Cold and Fine.
Very fit.

Working in Parker's room. I did 1/2 hour's meditation on Isis and Osiris before CCT came. She brought my Ushabti[14] of Osiris, which was definitely alive.

1. We sat building Tree in the Aura, and making the inner bodies glow before work began. This raised a tremendous head of power.

2. Decided to see if we could get Osiris in the temple of OPET[15] at Karnak. This tiny shrine marks the place where he was born and the underground shrine was the place where his mysteries were celebrated.

3. Found ourselves standing in the crypt without any preliminary work. Saw (as with Proctor) the White Osiris, Isis-Nepthys, Anubis and Horus.

4. Got a blaze of light and power that nearly knocked us out. Then came a tiny golden haired child—Horus, which stood between us.

5. We worshipped and knelt before the gods and we meant it.

6. Came back very happy.
7. Closed with great care.
Result a curious sense of peace and security.
Note: invoked in the names of ASAR and AST.[16]

FPD

Christine Hartley:
Rite of November 11th, 1937

Moon: Young. Self: Excellent spirits.
Weather: Fine.

The invocation was extremely powerful and while I was standing behind the priest with my arms outspread like his, someone took both of my wrists and very gently but determinedly pushed them inwards so that I was left more nearly in the Egyptian manner of worship. To test it, I put my arms out and the same thing happened again. The room was so crowded and there was so much power that I practically staggered to my seat after invoking Aast. Then we were in the underground temple and the God came. The Child was at my side all golden and lovely and laughing. When the priest and I held hands as the god and goddess it seemed to me that the child was lifted up on the seat made by our joined hands like a symbol to the world. The power got me pretty badly by the throat and I thought that my body would give out under the strain of containing it all.

The difference in the type of power between O. and I. was very interesting... this was a much more vitalizing, killing, power, like strong sunlight, vitalizing rather than revivifying. I think I mean actively positive against actively negative.

There was a very strong sense of complementary work this time, more than usual, as if I were playing the female to the male and not taking the initial steps as the priestess. There was much more sense of union for the work and I had a curious sensation when being used by the goddess as of the eternal "backing up" wife angle, the supporting woman.

CCT

Charles Seymour:
Thursday November 18th, 1937

Time: 9 to 9:15 p.m.
Full Moon.
Weather cold and wet.
Very fit. CCT in good form.

Talked on the technique of the rites.
Worked the Pan contact and got him, but it was all over in a few minutes. Very strong head of power while it lasted. Then a sudden cut.
I was forced to banish quickly as there came a curious rush of power that was not pleasant in its feel.

FPD

Christine Hartley:
Rite Worked November 18th, 1937

Moon: Almost Full.   Self: Very fit.
Weather: Wet.

The power came almost at once at the invocation in Greek. For the first time I got it by the sense of smell ... there was a strong scent of cedarwood in my inside nose ... not a physical plane smell. I saw the grove and the top of the white temple and then the God came. It was a great rush of power and he came as it were from the side of the priest to me so that we made a triangle. I was very much aware of him. It did not last long ... it could not because it was strong enough to be too much to carry. He went away by the eastern wall and there was a pause and then a lot of nasty little black things like very large insects about the size of mice, came to right and left of me out of the south and were growing bigger and I knew that they would be a nuisance as they were getting up to my knees so I asked to have the banishing done quickly and they all went away.

CCT

Charles Seymour:
Tuesday November 23rd, 1937

8:30 to 9 p.m.
Moon: Dark.
Cold damp evening.
CCT and G.
Lecture Room 3 QT.

Sat for a while discussing methods then worked the Osiris contact, though this had not been planned because the symbol that came up over the altar was a blazing sun.

With the invocation the figure of the White Osiris formed behind the altar. We invoked and worshipped and through CCT I asked about the Red Set and the Red Cave. I was told to get on with it myself but not to attempt to take CCT.

I was given the symbol of the crook to carry, and told not to fear. There was a great deal of power about.

We then closed.

FPD

Christine Hartley:
Report on Rite Worked November 23rd, 1937

Moon: Dark.   Self: Depressed but
Weather: Fine.   enthusiastic.

Did not know what we were going to do but told to see what symbol I saw in the East. Could only see sunlight and then the Temple of Osiris. The power came almost at once with great certainty. I saw a gold cubical altar with a fire of sweetsmelling wood on it that gave out clouds of white smoke obscuring the god. I never saw him really clearly because of this. I was wearing the green robe and it turned me into a man...a young priest with curled wig, sexless so that I could function as the priestess to the priest, but still a man. After a bit the awareness of that wore off but I never quite recovered the assurance of the womanside.

The god came with such force that I went down on one knee and stayed worshipping. I have never held my hands in the Egyptian manner for so long a period: yet I was not tired, though very stiff after it.

The priest asked certain questions and the god spoke through me but I was always in full consciousness which means I have to hold on pretty tight to the contact to get the answers. Then he held out the crook and told the priest to take it, which he did, and then after a bit it faded out.

CCT

Charles Seymour:
Thursday November 25th, 1937

Time: 9:15 to 10:15 p.m.
Moon entering last Quarter
Dense fog and bitterly cold.

CCT had to wait 40 minutes for her bus, arrived stiff with cold, and was then kept waiting.

I felt very little inclination to work a rite, and could not pick up the Gods so we sat in front of the stove and waited and thawed. Then I found myself in a small sort of dug-out rolling on a blue-green swell in flat calm off a small white town built up the side of a steep green mountain. With me was a girl of about 15, I was about 16 and we were brother and sister. I was naked except for a small rag round my middle, my sister had apparently a few beads more as her clothing. She had long fuzzy hair down nearly to her middle. I had a fuzzy mop like a south-sea islander. We were both brown, though not black, features European or rather Aryan, not negroid.

We paddled ashore on to a white coral beach with a small surf edging it in white foam. To the left a tiny fort and a sort of sea wall. In it were large canoes like those of the south sea islands today.

We walked up a wide steep street with paved gutters for rain water. There were quantities of bright red flowers like the hibiscus and a tree that looked like a fig tree. The houses were white, many had two stories, and some had a sort of cupola in the centre. Then we found ourselves in a large house the centre of which was a covered-in courtyard with the rooms opening out of it. This courtyard was full of shrubs, flowers, and a sort of gigantic tree form such as you see in Kew Gardens. The climate was sticky and hot.

Then an elderly man, our Father came in, he had a small javelin in his hand and was wearing a very pale blue robe. He was not pleased with us and sent my sister off to her room. I stayed sulking behind some bushes.

Then a crowd of people came and a very tall handsome man about thirty or thirty-five dressed in a sort of white kilt, buskins and sandals, scarlet cloak and a short sword at his waist. Rather like the picture of a Greek mountaineer. My sister peacocked down to him in long and beautiful robes. He put his arms round her, an old man in white with a paper stood by my father, the three men seemed to sign something, and then all went away to the chief's home where a marriage feast took place. I stayed in the empty room sulky and angry.

Suddenly I found myself looking at the marriage feast. A young woman about twenty-five came and brought me in and made me put on a robe. She made a fuss of me as if I were a spoilt child.

Then came news that an enemy's fleet was on the way to attack us. The Bride and Bridegroom were at the head of a long table loaded with fruits, sweets, and flowers red and blue. The Bridegroom stood up and said to me "You can ask me for a gift," so I said "Take me as a warrior with you tomorrow." My sister wanted me to stay, as did the others.

Then the scene vanished and I was in a canoe standing by my brother-in-law who was apparently the commander of the fleet. There was a great scrap. I was jolly frightened especially when my brother-in-law was knocked over with an arrow through the left shoulder. I remember laying about me with a sword while standing over the chief, for our canoe had been boarded. Then more of our canoes came up and the enemy fled. I felt deadly tired and done in.

We returned to the house of the chief. My sister clung to me while a man in white examined the chief. I knew from the first that he was dead. Here the emotion for both of us got so unpleasant that we closed down.

(I think this was a bit of the past, for the emotions were so stirred and the scenes were so real, effortless. It was probably a scene from an Atlantean colony in South America. It felt very old yet very civilized.)

FPD

Tuesday January 4th, 1938

Time: 8.15—8.45 p.m.
New Moon on January 1st.
Weather very cold and wet.
CCT and Self I was seedy
Working in my room at 2 QT.

Had no feeling for any particular contact so used 5gram and waited. A sudden burst of power came that shook CCT badly. So I took both hands and drew it into myself deliberately. She was then OK and I got a fine head of power. Then we both saw Egypt and the Temples. But we did not know what the contact was. I asked—"Is it Egypt?" and got the answer—"I was with you before Egypt." Then I saw the upper Terrace of the Golden Sun Temple at Atlantis, the pool of Fire, and standing behind CCT a golden clad Priest. I did not know him.

I was asked if I recognized him. I did not. Then I saw Glastonbury, Nibs and DNF. Still I did not recognize him, but CCT did and it was "Himself."[17]

Told us to keep this act to ourselves as it might not be understood.

We closed immediately.

FPD

January 13th, 1938

Time: 7:30 to 9 p.m.
Self very fit but CCT had been ill all day with food poisoning and very nearly did not come.

Started by explaining the centres and their + and − aspects in relation to the chakras and the Sephiroth, and I was going to relate them to the man and woman working as a pair when I felt a presence behind me. I got CCT to take his message and we were told not to proceed with what we were doing. We were not told what to do. Rather at a loss we sat opposite each other hands held. I found myself in the South of France but CCT was in Bristol and could not get away from Somerset and the period of James I. So I blanked and waited and presently she found herself in a small town in the S. of

France at a time somewhere between 1250 and 1350 AD for there was a Pope in Avignon. She was a young girl waiting in the upper room of a well-to-do house in some small town apparently near the Gulf of Lyons. Out of the dormer window she watched me ride in on a white horse. Then I found myself in the room beside her, a man of about fifty, clad in a sort of plum coloured trunks, heavy shoes, a short black cape, red waistcoat or shirt, a flatish hat and wearing a long sword. I got the name Esclairmonde and the fact that she was my daughter and that I was one of the local gentry. She described me as hard, cold, silent, very proud and she feared me. Also that I was an ardent Catholic while she was a heretic and in love with a heretic who had just been killed. I could have saved him and I let him die. Then there was a noise in the house a number of men with clubs and one with a crossbow surged up the stairs. They were led by a big fine looking man in rough clothes covered with flour. I stood at the top of the stairs with my sword and my cloak wrapped round my left wrist. The men waited, and the man with the crossbow aimed at me when Esclairmonde flung her scarf round my arms piniomed me until they rushed the stairs and seized me. Then she told me that she had brought these men to kill me and to avenge her lover who was the miller's son. Then came a blank and once more we were alone, my sword was on the floor she was leaning against a black box, it was dark, and a candle thick and long and very yellow had been lighted. The men were gone but the miller and a curious individual who looked like a saint, was clean shaven with a thin ascetic face a wonderful pair of brown bright eyes, and the voice of a highly educated man was speaking to me, He exercised a very strong influence over me, and in some curious way I knew that I was destined to become a heretic and die for it. Then he faded and the scene blanked. Then the girl and I were riding in the dark over mud and slush into a wretched inn by the road-side opposite was a tree from which two men were hanging.

A miserable looking man took the horse and I saw to his feeding, the girl had gone up to the only room and I sent her food and settled down in a room that stank of onions and garlic, a huge fat woman brought me my meal. Another blank and we were riding south and met a man in light armour of some sort with six men-at-arms. He recognized me and told me the country was up and without an escort I should be killed and the girl raped. Eventually I returned with him, he chaffing me for being unable to control a mere wench. Another long blank, and I was hiding in a cellar with drawn sword and the wench was with me and we were listening to fighting in the street outside. Then the miller's face appeared at a grating and he offered to save us both. I accepted and found myself in his mill and peasants clothing and with the miller was the strange heretic. At this moment the Knight with a big party came and said that he could take us to safety. I would not go but the girl went with him and I remained with the stranger for I had to learn from him. Another long blank, and then I was being led down a long stone corridor in the Palace of the Pope at Avignon. Suddenly Esclairmonde and her husband the Knight met us. We were both much older and I was in the hands of the inquisition. Another long blank, and Esclairmonde and I were standing in front of two stakes in the middle of an immense crowd. She was wondering what the pain would be like when I saw in the crowd the face of the man who turned me into a heretic. I knew what he was doing, he was giving the [there is a blank in the MS here][18] and I knew neither of us would feel any pain. I saw both of us in the flames. It was quite painless, though the emotion was awful.

CCT suddenly gave a shriek and nearly had a fit. She saw her then husband standing with the soldiers, he was mocking and laughing at her suffering which he seemed to enjoy thoroughly. Then everything went blank she recognized in the features of her then husband the face of Oscar.[19]

Note: We were both pretty badly shaken at the end of this, CCT especially. It was the emotion that shook one to pieces. Food and tea very hot and strong however put me right but CCT was very shaken, frightened, and with an awful foreboding of coming evil and sorrow.

FPD

Tuesday January 25th, 1938

Time: 8:40 to 9:30 p.m.
Dark of Moon.
Fine and cold.
Self very well. CCT tired, yet feeling happy and fit mentally.

I cleared the room and lit the lamp beforehand. Was about to invoke but stopped. We sat some time and as I was going to invoke

CCT felt, as it were, the invasion of unpleasant things as once before happened. It vanished without my having to do anything. We waited to see what contact was on. I got a very definite blaze of sunshine and CCT a white glare off a desert. Then we discovered we were on a grey camel and a very tired one. I had a bow, arrows, and a long handled spear. Clothes—an Arab dress of a simple garment. I had heavy black tangled hair and a short beard. CCT had a short skirt, bare uppers, and carried a baby. We stopped near a well got very dirty water, sat in the shade of date palms, while the camel rested. I got the idea of Mesopotamia and CCT said Arabia. Then we discovered that our encampment had been wiped out in a tribal foray and we had escaped. I was taking CCT and her baby to her husband, a man in the nearest big town on the Euphrates—I think Eridu. (CCT panicked badly here.)

She did not want to go. We went on and I was leading the camel and using the haft of my spear as a walking stick. I was tired and bored. Then six soldiers from the city stopped us, they understood us with difficulty and eventually took us to the river, into highly cultivated country, and through the massive city gates into the bazaars. It was hot, very smelly and dirty. Most of the houses were built of mud with date palm roofs and wooden balconies. Here and there bigger houses built round a courtyard. There was a huge inclined temple with a lot of yellow paintings in a white plastered wall. We left the soldiers and turned left down a street and into a small square where we asked the way to a particular house.

We knocked and servants let us in, knew us and laughed at our plight. In the courtyard was a big fat man sitting at a desk under a verandah writing. He was annoyed at my bringing CCT and finally turned us out and disowned CCT and baby. Apparently it was only a passing affair with a country girl. CCT very relieved and happy.

We went out of the city about a couple of miles, plugging through deep dust, and then sat down by the road side near a high canal bank a mud wall, and a date palm grove.

The baby played in the dust. CC was happy at escaping from an unwanted husband and I was wondering where to get food and sell the camel.

Nothing further happened and the picture just faded out.

The experience was an interesting one. CCT was a healthy young female animal about seventeen. The little boy was a topper and so fat. She had no brains or education, and I was heavy dull, a typical desert man very strong and healthy—a fighting man, but slow and thick witted.

It was CCT's emotion and hate for her husband—or seducer—that apparently brought this picture up.

CCT was not in the least tired so we had tea and we settled down for a chat when I became aware of someone standing behind me. CCT took some time to pick him up, and after some questioning I found it was my Irish grandfather, who often turns up.[20] I tested him in various ways and he said he had learned a lot from me that was not in the 39 Articles! He talked about the horses we had when I was small and the place and the black mare Catty. CCT got a regular brogue and used expressions purely local. He wanted us to pay Killagally a visit in the Spring and said H. was in a very bad way, very unhappy, and at cross-purposes with life.

[Pentagram]

I saw the fairy folk, and the big owl on the lawn in the moonlight, and I wanted him to give CCT the sight of the Shee[21] but he refused. He said I had the right, but she had not yet, to see the Elemental people. I was to get on with developing my own sense of inner sight.

Then he said the girl is getting very tired. I must go. CCT finished dead to the world. She picked up after an exchange of magnetism.

FPD

Christine Hartley:
  Report of Work on January 25th, 1938

Dark of Moon.   *Physically well.*

Went back to a very curious life. In the desert. Self, a young girl with a baby. Coloured striped skirt only thing I could remember. White camel with us—brother and sister? Trying to get to the town. Horsemen came down, with cloaks and grey horses. They gave us some sort of escort and I think took the camel... anyway, it was out of the picture. Saw the town and knew it was in Sumer... thought it was Ur. Very strong emotional response to this suggestion. Then we went into the town and wandered down hilly streets to a big house and were admitted into a courtyard, rather like a Moorish one. In the far corner in the angle of the shadows was a big man writing. A nasty big fat man. We expected him to protect me... I think I had given him the child... but he shouted us out and we went into the street and along the canal to the date grove where we sat in the dust and eat dates. I don't think I minded one way or the other... I remember noticing how awfully dusty the baby was and thinking it didn't really matter... but he was in a mess. He was about nine months old and crawling. All the time I was almost devoid of intelligence or emotion... I just did things and went to places. This was troublesome because my top consciousness wanted to be active and positive and see a story—and there wasn't a life to take hold of. Maybe it was a restful one—but dull.

CCT

Charles Seymour:
February 3rd, 1938

New Moon 4 days old.
Self and CCT.
2 QT.
Both fit, fine weather.

CCT came full of the idea that she was a witch. It struck her as she came into my room. After I lit the Three lamps she had difficulty in not going out before I was ready. Immediately we found ourselves in Tintagel. I knew the place she did not. We were back a very long time I should say many thousands of years B.C. We arrived in a small sailing ship, I got the idea Atlantean. I was in armour, leather with some silver like metal sewn on in ⊂•⊃ disks. I carried her up the cliff path. She was wet, cold, tired and was wearing a thin green dress. She complained of the cold of my wet armour and lamented the warm sunny south. She was very young, very slight, rather unformed, called herself Morgana le Fey, or the Sea Priestess from Atlantis. I was about thirty, thick set, very strong and a soldier of the sacred clan. It was cold and wet and beastly on that hill top. We did not know what to do and invoked Merlin then he came but not clearly. Suddenly the sun came out, the wind and rain and mist vanished and we got quite hot. I think Merlin used hypnotic suggestion. He gave us a clear picture of Lyonesse, before it was drowned, and said we had been brought from Atlantis to teach, and that life after life for Thousands of years we should work together as priest and priestess, trained to work as a functioning pair before Atlantis was destroyed. We should rebel and fight and hate each other at times but in the end fulfil our destiny as priest and priestess—a functioning pair.

He gave us a shadowy glimpse of many lives as servers of the ancient Wisdom which then lay before us.[22] Then he told us to look back. And we saw an immense line of ancient Adepts—high priests and priestesses stretching back into the dim ages, and we now work for them as they worked in the past. The vision was strangely clear and I saw L.E. among them. Merlin placed his right hand on my nape of the neck and on CCT's and drove an immense current of force through me and through her. It shook me like a leaf in the wind. And he told me that CCT was far in advance of me as a trained and initiated priestess, but I as a soldier was to look after her. L.E. then took his place and told me that I was free of the world in a way that she was not. She was bound to the world by her karma in way that I was not. That in the future she would break away often from me, but her initiation at Atlantis would drive her back to serve with me. I have to be patient.

They left after a little time and we both felt splendid.

Time 8:30 to 9:45 p.m. CCT out much further than usual but remained fully conscious.

At 10:30 p.m. after tea I gave CCT a block of stone from the cave under Arthur's castle at Tintagel to hold.

She described the castle accurately, position of the path, towers, the gate. The well and the rooms as they are now.

Then a band of raiding Saxons or Norsemen from ships with a blue banner and a horse. Gave a minute description of the methods used to defend the castle.

She had not been there and did not know the place at all.

FPD

Christine Hartley:
Report on Sitting on February 3rd, 1938

Left to see what "came" in an empty room, I kept getting "Morgan le Fay"[23] hammering at me, so we started on that. A headland with coarse grass, a strong wind, grey skies, the surf beating below but out of sight and rain at intervals. Myself, long black hair and a green dress blowing around me. A cromlech...a little footbridge joining the headland to the mainland and a cliff path up the mainland to the bridge past the Cave where Merlin sat. I was cross and bored...hating the place and wanting to do magic but unable to begin till Merlin came. The sun came out for a few moments, a very watery sun and a very few moments and I thought of the Cornish Riviera posters and jeered.[24] Then we talked and remembered how we had come in the little ship from Atlantis, carried forward on one enormous green roller after another, and you reminded me how you had had to carry me up the last of the cliff path—and how cross I was. And then Merlin[25] came and I went into a queer state and there were questions and answers of which I remember very little now except that "they" must not have to work with much yet because they might recognize me for who I am. I have a pretty strong idea myself of who I am, but they don't know it yet. Then I came back and was very tired for a little while. I remember L.E. and Merlin behind me and the feeling of being at the end of a long line of very important people and of somehow "mattering" but not knowing quite how.

CCT

Charles Seymour:
February 10th, 1938

Time 10:15 to 11 p.m.
2 QT. Fine, cold, 1st Qtr.

We had just finished a sitting of Completed 3rds[26] with DNF. Lighted the 3 Lamps, and L.E. came through bringing my paternal Grandfather who is very Irish. CCT got quite a brogue after a bit. Then we were at Killagally in the moonlight, with the people of the Shee. Two came and stood beside me and held my right hand then they danced—a pair of silver misty semi-human figures, and the great owl came, and then the little people in green and brown formed two rings and danced too, I wanted to seize CCT and dance with them.

Then I saw the river in brown flood—early spring.

Then G began to talk about going over. He did not seem to be happy about H. and B. He kept saying the place wanted me and Rowena. I knew the fairy folk, they did not.

I pointed out that my work must go on here. He agreed and I said I must go there in the Astral and CCT could bring it in these meetings to me. That would keep me in the heart of the place.

Then CCT went to Scotland (so G. said) with L.E. and we finished suddenly and much too abruptly—a distinct shock for CCT.

CCT seemed quite O.K.

FPD

Christine Hartley:
Report of Rite worked February 2nd, 1938 (Isis)

Moon Full.   Self: Perfectly fit.
Weather: Cold and dry.

Came in and sat down not quite knowing at what point I had been fetched. Picked up nothing at all at first. Found I was trembling violently all over and teeth chattering but not cold. Felt the hands of the priestess[28] gripping me till I thought I should never be able to stand the pressure. She was burning hot.

I never saw the Temple at all but spent all the time out of doors on a wind-swept plain: grey sky...might have been dusk but seemed more like a suspension of time: no wind, no movement, just a period held. Ground covered with heather stubble—or something like that—brownish. Small, rather stunted grove of trees on a line with my left eye and grass at their roots and in front, between myself and them, running water that did not seem to flower but was not stagnant—again, as if the motion were in suspended animation. One time during the chanting I saw the full moon clearly reflected in the sea, at the appropriate moment, and at another there was a second stream of swiftly running water between my feet and the altar whereas the main picture was the other side of the non-existent altar.

I remember being filled with expectancy and then with a great happiness and came back a bit shaken but otherwise all right.

CCT

Charles Seymour:

Thursday March 3rd, 1938

New Moon Yesterday
Time: 8:30 to 9:30 p.m.
Weather cold and dry.
Contact sought—Joan of Arc. CCT and Self. Both fit except for my sore throat.

Waited after usual preparation for about 10 minutes. L.E. came up then a figure in silver armour with a very bright aura. After a while scenes of an old walled town, and an attack. Then crossing a river, more fighting and a confused scene in an old castle with a lot of women. J. of A. in the thick of it.

Then a long blank.

Next came a prison cell, a woman in man's clothes, two warders in black. Then a procession, with the woman being suspended by two men. She was drugged and I am sure not Joan.

Then the burning which was very clear and tragic.

Next a blank.

Then saw a small country manor, Joan in purple dress, looking very happy with a thick-set man. This picture with its small well-kept garden and farm yard was very clear.

There were a lot of people about and everyone seemed very cheerful.

Conclusion Joan was not burnt, but a drugged substitute was.

At the end L.E. came again. CCT asked if the pictures were historically correct. He said you must judge that for yourself.

Then he laughed and said that our conclusions were substantially accurate.

FPD

Christine Hartley:
   Report of Work on March 3rd, 1938

Tried to pick up Joan of Arc. Saw a Maid on a horse, she was wearing armour. There were men around her...I picked out Dunois, the Marechal. The most striking thing about it was the radiance that came from her as though she were wrapped in her golden aura. This was the vitalizing identification mark, so to speak, which was the key note afterwards. Then I remember a castle with pepper pot turrets and a river or moat. The Maid forded it with her troops. They shouted "Vive la Pucelle." The English were on the other side. I was afraid because it seemed to me that they were going through without properly covering the ranks in front but it worked out all right. They got into the Castle and seemed to relieve the siege. There was fighting because I remember the sort of horror that got me at the sight of the killing.

And then we swung right away to the cell at Rouen and a woman in man's clothes lying there.

Then the great square with the soldiers round it and the stake in the middle and a procession of priests and soldiers and in the middle a woman muffled in white. She moved heavily, slowly, as if she were drugged and the most salient thing about her was her lack of life: there was no aura at all, no radiance...just deadness. And they burnt her.

I saw a pannelled room next and a man in a very dark or black suit at a heavy oak table...a tired, worried man with aquiline features. And a woman came to him and consoled him and I knew that it was John, Duke of Bedford, Regent of France for Henry VI, and that he was worried over the burning of the Maid and that the woman was his wife, Anne of Burgundy and Luxembourg.

There there was a country manor house with farm buildings and stiff ornamental sort of little garden...rather like those in sampler stitching, and people came out of it, cheerful people And one was a women in a mulberry dress with gold tassels and embroidery and I knew that she had been the Maid, and there was her husband with her and I got the name Armoise or Amboise.[29]

CCT

Charles Seymour:
Thursday March 10th, 1938

Time 10:30 to 11:15 p.m.
CCT and Self

    CCT very drawn on at the 3° sitting. After tea we went to the temple of Atlantis and saw it by moonlight. There was a line of priests on the upper Terrace and a line of soldiers. They came from opposite sides. CCT came from below and was met on top step by L.E. in full high priestly dress, and she was shown to the Ss and the Ps. He was wearing a golden lamen with a great emerald or cat's eye* in the centre and on the chain supporting it were links with the signs of the Zodiac On the Emerald was a ✡. This he showed her again and again. He had a great gold head dress and he was in a long golden green robe. Then he took her into the great Temple, and to the altar. They faced each other across the altar, and he projected power upon her until she grew to twice her size. Then he took her to the (her) left to that end of the temple and through a narrow door. I was waiting behind the door and he told me to teach her for the next grade. We turned down a passage towards a dark room and the scene ended. I was one of the priests.
    Then we closed down. Later I showed her how to expand the aura and we stood giant figures above an altar.
    But when I explained the *modus operandi* she panicked and looked at me as if I were the Devil.

                                                                                       FPD

Christine Hartley:
Work done on October 3rd, 1938

    Told I could choose my period: Egypt suggested but did not feel any pull that way. L.E. turned up and told me to go to Atlantis but not by way of Cornwall, which I had thought of doing. We were to take the short-cut and go straight back.
    Settled down and closed my eyes. Saw the great Temple in the

---
* Probably the Emerald Tablet of Hermes.

moonlight instead of in the sun... very clear-cut and with a sort of bluish radiance over everything. From the left door facing us came a file of priests: from the right a file of warriors. They all came down to the top of the big white marble steps that lead down the hill to the lower levels and they stopped there on that sort of "landing" which is below the three steps and waited. And then between them L.E. appeared wearing his robes. And he, too, waited.

And then I came up the great white staircase, wearing a white robe and feeling very nervous and rather"'young." (I was about eighteen?) I came up to L.E. and he made me look at his insignia and I tried to describe them: he wore a sort of crown of which the only thing I can recollect was a gold serpent. Round his neck he wore a long chain of chased designs which were the Signs of the Zodiac: it reminded me of the heavy Mayoral chains worn by worthy citizens. And from that hung his lamen. It was set in a circular gold setting, unbacked, and was green. I got the impression of an enormous cat's eye or emerald—but inclined to the former. On it was engraved the double triangle which we call Solomon's Seal. It was not a flat stone but "humped" like many rings, and was very large.

Then he drew me to him, turned me about and put me before him on the step with his hands on my shoulder and presented me to the priests and warriors as if I were a Queen. And I felt enormous vitality flow into me from his hands. Then he turned and I followed him into the Temple by the great folding doors of the main entrance The doors were open and they closed behind us. The Temple was quite empty and the sun-slit in the roof was closed. The black altar was at the far end and I followed him there. There was a perpetual fire on it. He went to the far side—that is the east—and I opposite and he threw the power across to me with upraised hands and I took it. All this was without a word being spoken that I could recollect.

In the North-east corner of the Temple there was a narrow door to which we went, he first and I following. This door was opened for us on the far side and you were there. L.E. told you that he had brought me to you for safekeeping and instruction and I gathered that later on he would be expecting me again. We went into a bare sort of room and I came back.

CCT

Charles Seymour:
Tuesday March 15th, 1938

Time 10 to 11 p.m. Full Moon.
Fine weather, both fit.

In accordance with L.E.'s instructions we started work as follows:
1. Built the Moon Symbol [?] the aura of each of us. (Sat facing each other).
Built the Tree in colours within each aura.
Built the Middle Pillar and the Sephiroth belonging to it a second time.
Called down the Cosmic light and power upon me, I *drove* it across to CC and she *drew* it from me.
Then we opened up the Sephiroth of the M.P.[30] as lotus flowers beginning at:
1. Kether which was pure white flame.
2. Daath which was a white colourless transparency.
3. Anahata which was a Blue lotus with scarlet centre.
4. Tiphareth which was Golden sunshine.
5. Yesod which was Purple with silver edges.
6. Malkuth which was a yellow lotus with russet centre, olive green stalk coming out of black mud.[31]

This took a long time. CCT's came to life as flowers at once.
She missed the Ajna centre.
Later we opened the Ajna centre as a butterfly with two wings of flame. Then we put the auras together and sought for the Ego using (instead of self-analysis) a mantra:
"My Physical body is not the I. It is a part of me. I use it as my instrument.
My etheric body is not the I. It is a part of me. I use it as my instrument.
My Astral body is not the I. It is a part of me. I use it as my instrument.
The Mental body is not the I. It is a part of me. I use it as my instrument.
I am the God and Goddess dwelling in the secret Moon Cave that uses these instruments."

Then we imagined the Ego in the Ajna Centre as the two winged flaming butterfly and from there contacting and using all its instruments.

This produced a feeling of tightness between the eyes. Pictured a flame passing through these two centres, by entering the back of my head and passing out at the back of CCT's. She complained of a bursting feeling until the power was visualized as passing out at the back of her head then she became comfortable and a tremendous flow of vitalizing force passed between us until we could hold no more. It was a glorious sensation.[32]

2. Talked with L.E. who said that we had begun on the right lines and to go on with this work as given above. He warned me not to bind myself too tightly to my present work as he would move me on to new work when he wanted me to do it. (I had asked about a feeling of no longer being wanted at 3 QT.) My job is to look after and train CCT, his child.

3. Then he came and magnetized his photo for us to work with.[33]

We finished at 11.30 p.m. I feeling splendid.

Griff

Christine Hartley:
Report of Work March 15th, 1938

Moon: Full. *Personal: Very tired, but*
Weather: Dry. *otherwise well.*

Called on L.E. and he came at once in the Old Robes. I asked him a question but before that, I went up the steps to him and he held out the lamen and I put it to my forehead. Then he talked to us. I don't remember a great deal except that he was very pleased that I have taken my Initiation earlier in the evening and called me "my good child" as though he had thought that I might jib at it. I know that he laid a great burden on me and that all the way it seems as if it were to be sorrow—not my sorrow but the sorrows of the world that I must carry. And then he gave me very much into your charge and I remember his saying more than once that you were to take care of me and teach me.

CCT

Charles Seymour:
Thursday March 17th, 1938

Time 8:30 to 9 p.m. Then 9:15 to 10 p.m.
CCT and self 2 QT
Both fit, weather fine.

1. Each built the Magical Personality standing opposite to each other. Then built the Tree in colours. Then built the centres and opened up the lotuses with their colours, and placed the Egyptian gods on them. This produced a tremendous head of power and nearly knocked CCT out.

2. Talked for a moment with L.E. who said we had done enough.

3. CCT, had a longing for the Norse contacts for some days so we sat together to see what would come. Got a fjord with a tiny wooden village on the side of the hill, mud bank, with the long-ships lying on them ready to sail. Myself tall, golden beard, winged helmet, spear in left hand, sword on hip, laughing heartily at a tall golden haired girl, my sister, who wanted to sail with me on the expedition to Northumbria. Next picture at Flamborough Head as we with four or five long-ships passed slowly. Then a great muddy river probably the Humber. We rowed a long way up it, and then seized a small village, very poor, which had been left empty, the inhabitants hiding in the surrounding thickets and wastes.

Next scene the British trap and kill one of our men and cut his head off. A very tall fair Saxon is their leader and he challenges me to single combat with the sword between two forces. We went for each other with heavy double-handed swords and he wounded me slightly. I noticed a little ditch to his left rear and managed to edge him to it so that he fell into it. I pulled him out and gave him his life.

Next scene we and the Saxons were building more ships, the village was much larger, and we had some of our women folk and had settled there, and combined forces with the Saxon chief. CCT had fallen in love with him.

Then the ships finished he and most of my men and the long ships go off on an expedition to the South leaving only the smaller fishing boats. As they start our priest blesses them, and Odin appears with his one eye covered and his ravens on his shoulders, very black and terrible. CCT prophecies death and disaster as they sail away on seeing him.

The village has a strong palisade round it on the land side only and though we are few men and many women and children we did not expect attack. One night the whole village was blazing. I carried CCT who had an arrow in her thigh, to the bank and put her in a boat. Then I collected the others and with some difficulty got them all out of the blazing village into the smacks. There was no further attack and then I examined CCT who was unconscious. I saw she had not long to live and cut the shaft of the arrow off. She became conscious called for the Saxon chief. Then, declaring she saw Odin calling her, died—as a warrior should die and I watched a Valkyrie on a great white astral horse bear her soul away as if she had been a warrior.

The scene loosed a great deal of emotion and for a time it knocked us both out badly. I should say that the date was 700 to 800 A.D.

FPD

Christine Hartley:

Work on March 17th, 1938

Weather Dry.   *Self: Very Well.*
Moon; Full.

After being taught how to build the M.I.[34] L.E. came and said we might do pretty much what we liked, so we went back.

Had had a strong Norse contact for several days calling me. Suddenly found we were in a country close to a very green and rather cold sea with a grey sky and knew that we were North. Then I saw a Viking long-ship and then you in a golden winged helmet and a sort of tunic studded with metal knobs and spikes and sandals and puttees. You wore a broadsword on the left hip and a small circular shield on your back and carried a spear, on which you leant. You had a long golden moustache and plaited golden hair and you were very tall and large and laughed from deep down in your chest. And I was in a blue woollen dress caught up under the breasts and had long plaits of yellow hair and blue eyes and I, too, was tall. And below us in the fjord were a fleet of ships ready to sail and I wanted to go with them and you were laughing at the idea and saying it was not yet for women. I was your sister, and I tried to persuade you to let me come as a boy.

I must have succeeded in the end because the next thing I saw was the coast line, somewhere about Flamborough and we sailed up a river that must have been the Humber, and found a township. It was empty, the Britons (Saxons) had run away: we burnt it, or it was set on fire by them: I remember the horror of the burning houses and the smell of the fire. Then it came out that we were there to settle. We did, but before that you had a fight with the leader of the Saxon crowd: a big man. You and he fought in single combat and you pushed him back till he fell into a ditch. I came up to see what was happening, because I was terribly interested and you were angry with me. Then the man got out of the ditch and you made friends.

We lived in that town for a while and more people came back from Norway and we settled there peacefully. And we built or re-built boats and got a fleet together and the enemy, whose name was Ragnold the Terrible, was in command of the fleet and his boat was called Wave Cleaver. And he went off one day but before he went we saw the priest and then Odin himself looking so grey and "distant" with two ravens on his shoulder and his great twi-bill in his hand and the black cloak misting out behind him. Arid I felt a great sorrow on the ship, where I was standing.

The fleet went away and while it was going down South the town was attacked. I don't remember much about this because I was wounded early on by an arrow in the side. You carried me to a dugout canoe and then to a bigger boat and lots of our townsfolk got away into other boats and we made a sort of encampment in the middle of the river out of range and round a bend.

I remember wondering what was going to happen next and then you told me I was dying. And that seemed a great pity, and such a silly feminine thing to do. You got the arrow head out ... and it hurt no end ... but you couldn't stop the bleeding. And you reminded me as I'd been killed in battle, woman or no woman, I was eligible for the Valhalla of the Heroes and even that didn't really comfort me because I was filled with the most awful disappointment that I shouldn't be able to wait for Wave Cleaver to come back. I wouldn't have minded so much if Ragnold had been there once more. You told me you could see the Norn coming for me but I saw none of that: I kept trying to say "Tell him I'm sorry I couldn't wait" but I was crying so much that I had no voice. And then I died and woke up.

After that we talked and much later L.E. came in and said good-night and looked at me in a sideways kind of manner and said "Well you asked for it, and you got it!" to which I couldn't say much.[35]

CCT

Charles Seymour:
Friday March 25th, 1938

Time: 8:30 to 11 p.m. Moon on last Qtr.
Self fit but very fed up with the Belfry Isis Rite.

1. Built up the Magical Personality, then built the Tree in colours. Then woke the 7 centres and built them as coloured lotuses. Finally placed the Egyptian gods on their lotuses. (Note this time Har-Par-Krat came up first on Tiphareth next Herakhti.) Then we stood visualizing the White and Black pillars and cross linking the centres, and calling down both the powers of the Pillars ran them through the Magical Personality.

2. Placing hands on each other's shoulders, we used the M.P. and grew to an immense size and floated high above the Earth. Suddenly I saw an immense rainbow which became Bifröst, and over which we floated looking down into unfathomable depths, between two cliffs of black rock, which was Nifl-heim and the abode of the giant in flames.

And as we crossed we saw Odin the All-Father waiting for us. He was smiling and not terrible as he was the last time we saw him. He was, one felt the God of Universal Wisdom. His image was dark clad, a dark cloud about his head, and one eye was bandaged, his two ravens Hugin (Thought) and Munin (Memory) were perched on his shoulders.

Below his feet were the two wolves Geri and Freki, and behind him was Valhalla. He offered CCT three gifts which she might ask for. First she asked for Courage and he said you have it already. Then she asked for Judgement and he said you have it already if only you will stop to think. CCT delayed over the Third boon, and he said wait, you can ask again when in real need.

Then we saw the Gods Balder, Freya and others. But we were pushed back across Bifröst, and looking down I saw the Tree Yggdrasil and below it in the roots the dark forms of Evil and destruction.

Suddenly we were back.

It was vivid and powerful, and this symbolism was intensely real, and CCT was rather shaken. She slept a few moments while I got tea.

After tea we decided to sit and see what came for the last vision had come as we were standing working the Tree.

I gave CCT my plaque with the ibis which had come from Karnak.

First came bright sunshine and then CCT got the name Karnak and the Desert. I had in the meantime seen a great Temple and a small Pyramid and a lake near it. I knew it to be the city of Hermopolis or Khemenu. After a little while CCT found herself in a court with colonades she was sitting by a pillar and I was leaning against it. She was about twenty-four or twenty-five, I was about thirty. We were in the scanty dress of the Egyptians. She wore a wig, some beads round her neck and a sort of thin wrapping like a sheet, all very conventional. I was clean shaven not a hair anywhere. We were waiting for sunset. Then an older priest rather fat, and his wife also middle-aged came, and they smiled at us for we were rather nervous and they took us into a small temple at the foot of the pyramid which was also quite small. Then I knew that we were in for an initiation of some sort for I saw the symbol of a great veil or net, and I knew it to be that of the "House of the Net."[36]

The Priest led us through the little temple to the left hand corner of the Pyramid and with a long staff he pressed a stone and a block of stone swung aside showing a narrow passage. CCT and I went in, and the door swung back and we were blocked in and without lights. She hung onto my girdle and with hands and feet I felt my way down the passage which seemed to slope downwards fairly steeply. My sandal struck a stone and it fell into a deep hole which blocked the passage. I searched for a way over or round and could find nothing.

Then, as I knew it had to be crossed, I decided to jump it, and in pitch darkness I had to jump standing; it proved to be quite narrow and we crossed with ease. Then we got into a chamber, and I trod on a beastly great snake and we both panicked a bit. I offered to pick-a-back CCT but she said snakes were a part of the job, so she would feel her way round the wall with me. We found some steps and went up. There were eight of them and at the top we ran into a great statue and feeling our way round it we found ourselves in a small vault, and in it were two Sarcophagi. So we lay in them went into trance and then stepped out into the light of the Astral plane.

We were in a small temple chamber with Ptah, Sekhmet and Thoth forming the three points of a triangle of light. CCT went to Sekhmet and backed into her arms. I did the same for Ptah. And power poured through me until I thought my forehead would burst. It was agony. CCT and I walked to meet each other, took hands and keeping within the white △ went to Thoth and went down on our knees and hunkus. Thoth put a hand on each of us and blessed us as married in the Mysteries. Then he signed us both on the forehead CCT with the ♀ and I with the sceptre.

We went back to our bodies following a △ of light the points of which rested on the breast bones. CCT got on with little difficulty and came to at once. I had a great deal of trouble to get round and CCT had to help me in and she sealed the point of entry at the breast bone. She was much better at this than I was.

Then we sat up in the dark, very cold and shivery until the priests came in the morning with cloaks and took us into a big temple just at sun rise. Here were a crowd of neophytes, a veil between them and the initiated priests and priestesses. The priests who came for us in the vault had examined our auras for the Marks of Thoth. And having found them, as initiated priest and priestess we were passed through the Veil, out of the Hall of the Neophytes, into the temple of the initiates of the priesthood of Thoth and joined those in the House of the Veil (Net) who formed the 3rd Order that lay behind the Greater and Lesser Mysteries of Ancient Egypt.

CCT had been a priestess of Sekhmet, I of Ptah before we were both sent to the Temple of Thoth to take our initiation into the teaching order that ruled the inner priesthoods of the other magical cults.[37]

Then we came back very tired and very pleased. Something new seems to have come to me—a sense of confidence, and a reality in the work that now lies before me.

FPD

Christine Hartley:
Work done on March 25th, 1938

First we built the magical images and then went out into the air. I saw London at Westminster below me in the dark with the lights shining and then Paris and the Champs Elysees and something inside me said Barcelona next and I was bracing myself for the destruction when you told me we have gone on to the Rainbow Bridge and asked me if I knew of one. I said Bifröst, and we were there. I saw Father Odin all smiling and pleased at the edge of the cliff, and near him was Baldur, shining green and gold, and Kiordis, who was Sigurd's Queen, smiling and welcoming me as a sister. And Thor was behind me and in front of you. And then we went back across the Bridge and looked down at Yggdrasil in the chasm and I got worried about the height for a moment—it is all right floating in the air but not so nice standing on a bridge, even in the astral. And then we came back.

Secondly we went to Egypt. I picked up a sort of cloister with pillars and stone seats and a pyramid in the middle distance, framed between the pillars, and you and I together. You told me it was a Priests' College. I was sitting on one of the stone seats and you were standing beside me, leaning against a pillar, and we were watching the sun set behind the pyramid. There were figs and grapes in a basket at my side and I had been eating fruit. When the dark came the elder priest and priestess came to us and we made a little procession to the pyramid. The priest raised his arm and said something and a door in the solid stone slid to one side and showed us a dark narrow passageway, and we had to go in. It was very dark and frightening and you made me hold on to your belt while we went along. We came to a gap and jumped it, finding actually it was only a foot wide though a stone dropped down it went rattling for hundreds of feet. Then we went to a round room where there were snakes, and I hated them. You offered to carry me but I would not agree because that would not have been fair. Then we came to a door at the top of eight steps, and someone guarding it, but we pushed our way through and came to the centre of the Pyramid with two stone sarcophagi in front of the gods... Thoth, and Anubis, and Ptah and Sekhmet. We got into the sarcophagi and then went out of our bodies and in our astral forms we were initiated. Sekhmet poured the power into me when Anubis led me to her. Then we were the two basic points of a triangle with Thoth at the head, long fine light lines like tapes guarding us within. And we progressed up the sides of the triangle till we came together before him and knelt down and he signed us on the foreheads...me with the circle and the line and you with the sceptres. And then we retreated down the lines which led each to our own sarcophagus and terminated between the breasts of our bodies. And I slid down the line and into myself again, stretching myself rather as if I were fitting my fingers into a glove. And you had a little difficulty so I sat up and helped guide you into the little opening.

It grew cold and I was getting tired so I came and sat in your big sarcophagus with you till the dawn. And at dawn the priest and priestess came and looked at us and knew that all was well. So we went out by a much quicker path and back to the College and then we stood in the axis of the great halls and looked at the dawn coming through the eastern pillars. Then we went into the big hall and were taken to the initiated ones on the far side of the veil.

CCT

Charles Seymour:
Tuesday March 29th, 1938

1. Built the Magical Personality which came up very clearly.
2. Built the Tree in colours.
3. Built the 7 lotuses on the Central Pillar.
4. Built the 7 lotuses in their colours.
5. Built the Egyptian Gods but only got as far as Yesod when Isis changed into Ishtar, and we were away in Babylon. As we were standing up this was very short and confused, everything out of gear.

Then we had tea.

Later CCT picked up L.E. who gave the following curious message: "When the corn is ripening the wise man does not hurry to use the sickle." She went out much further than usual and came back tired.

But we used the system for warming up and soon she seemed OK.

FPD

Christine Hartley:
Report of Work of March 29th, 1938

First we built the magical images and then began on the lotuses. When we got to Daath I went right out and remember nothing more until I heard the name of Isis and then Ishtar. And I seemed to struggle back to consciousness and to focus on the Goddess. I got the contact, but broken and difficult and a much greater effort than when I do it alone. This was explained later as being due to the method of working.

Then I contacted L.E. and talked to him. This was very hard because I had to go to him instead of his coming to meet me. I got the conversations all right but I came back to report them and then went back to him, and then back here again ... and when it came to an end I was awfully tired.

Much later in the evening He looked in to say good-night and then he came down to the astral and came over to me.

CCT

Charles Seymour:
Thursday, March 31st, 1938

Time: 8:15 to 9:10 p.m.
New Moon

(a) 1. Built the M.P.
   2. Built the Tree in colours.
   3. Built the 7 lotus centres in colours.
   4. Placed the Gods on them.
   5. Linked up the two auras by lines of light.
   6. Amalgamated the two Trees and the 7 Centres into one.
   7. United the magical auras into a composite hermaphrodite form.

(b) Then we sat facing the picture of L.E. and went back to the "House by the Wall" in Babylon where we met the Master of the Magicians[38] who showed us Aaron's rod in blossom. And asked us to interpret it. I did it as (i) The cauduceus (ii) The letters ש א מ .[39] Thereon (iii) the Tree of Life with the Ten coloured blossoms (iv) The human spine with the seven coloured lotuses. Then he smiled nodded to us that this was correct and left us. We came in broad sunlight and returned to the temple of Nabu the great God of Wisdom,[40] the scribe messenger of the Gods. His temple was empty and together we went to the altar and cast into the fire upon it frankincense and myrrh. Then we went for the first time to the inner shrine which was on our right through a curtain. This shrine was empty with a black altar and an astral light above it. We knelt at it with foreheads on the altar for a long time as priest and priestess of Nabu. CCT suddenly went limp and seemed to fade away and come back tired. So we had tea after she had slept heavily for about fifteen minutes.

Then we started building and using the "Sphere of Sensation" and after a bit we were bathing off Greece. I saw two centaurs and changed myself into one. CCT jumped on the back of the other and away we galloped until we arrived at a glade. Then I went blank and presently CCT said she wanted to return so we came back very carefully. She was not a bit tired this time.

FPD

Christine Hartley:
Report of Work done March 31st, 1938

First we began to build the magical images and then I got the name of Cheiron and began to see the hills of Macedonia. You turned me around at once and we sat down to work; we went to the House by the Wall. It was very hot, with the heat of the mid-day sun. We were a priest and priestess of Babylon with stiffly curled wigs and a good deal of paint on our faces and I got the impression of gilded finger and toenails. We went down the street between the booths to the House, which was cool and dark. We went into a room that had a sort of divan on one side and cushions on the floor and there the G.M.[41] came to us. He was wearing his scarlet robes with the gold chain: his complexion was olive and his features aquiline. He sat down on the divan and talked to us: I cannot remember what he said but it was to do with Aaron's Rod that blossomed. Then he gave us the Blessing of B... and we left him and went back to the Temple. The Temple entrance was a triangle, with the priests' apartments on the left, the priestesses' on the right and the temple proper in the middle. We went into the temple and knelt for a long time on either side of the altar, which was rather to the eastern end of the big bare hall, with a low smelling fire burning on it. And then it all went black.

Secondly we found ourselves off the coast of Greece, bathing. We were quite young and when two Centaurs came down to the beach you suggested we should take their shapes. I funked it—not quite sure why but an instinctive apathy. So you became a Centaur and I rode on the back of one and we raced up the valley and into the low hills, you chasing us until we came to a glade. There I slipped to my feet and the Centaur disappeared. You came up. It was sunny and warm and the grass was very soft. You lay down as a horse does and rather reluctantly and shyly and I did the same. And I knew what was going to happen and asked to come back because I did not feel up to seeing it all. When we got back I felt entirely different; my voice was warm and vibrating and I have a sense of complete fulfillment.

CCT

Charles Seymour:
Tuesday, April 5th, 1938

Time: 8 to 8:30 p.m.
CCT and Self.

Built the centres and linked them sat down to see what would come.

Got a blue sky, blue sea or wide river with little boats and white sales. Then a falling back into darkness. Then huge green waves breaking over palm trees and gardens. Then CCT, L.E. and a few others were standing with me on the topmost plateau of the sacred mountain in the courtyard of the great temple of the Sun. The mountain was slowly sinking into the waves, L.E. called an old priest, CCT who was a young girl, and self, he puts us in a boat behind the temple and the waves floated us off and we drove N. before a furious gale, and later saw the golden temple of L.E. vanish beneath the waves. After days of misery, cold, thirst and hunger, we sailed up a little river and landed on an island where the Priests were expecting us and they bowed low to the old priest and put a blue cloak about him and there was Merlin.

They fed us on a lovely hot stew and then rubbed our salt water sores with oil and put us to sleep in beehive huts. I just slept and when I woke CCT was sitting near me clad in a white woollen robe, and Merlin outside in his blue cloak. We were on the edge of a rounded green hill such as one sees in Dartmoor. The villages of hut circles.

Later after we had rested and were well Merlin took us to a cave on the headland. The people treated us as if we were gods. I hated leaving the warm beehive huts for Merlin's cold cave—then the vision ended. We were both very tired, and a lot of emotion came when L.E. went back to the drowning temple. We were both crying when we came to finally.

After tea both were quite OK. CCT left at 9:10 p.m.

Griff

Christine Hartley:
Report on work of April 5th, 1938

We built the magical images and then opened the centres. I did not have any desire to "go out" and it was quite easy to keep full consciousness.

Then I swung back and back to Atlantis and was sick with terror as I saw great green waves over the island and the big Sun Temple sticking up on top and the four of us there... you and me and Merlin and L.E. And there was a little boat, rather like a fishing smack, that was tied to the balustrading of the Temple—the water was so high. And we had to go away in it. Merlin got in and you got in and I didn't want to go but L.E. said I was to, but he wouldn't come. It was dreadful to leave him there alone and I cried and cried. I remember his more or less lifting me over the gunwale and putting me in your arms and saying "Take care of my child," and then we were adrift and a great wave came over the top of the temple.

We came to ourselves later off the the coast of Lyonesse. We went up a sort of gorge and there were beehive huts and people with a priest dressed like the pictures of the Druids. They welcomed us and gave us food and clothes and a hut and looked after our cuts and bruises. Then they told us of a holy place at the end of the island where we could have a cave to live in and could work our magic.

CCT

Charles Seymour:
Thursday April 6th, 1938

Time: 8:30 to 9:15 p.m..
Moon 1st Qtr.
Very Fit.
CCT at 2 QT.

I. 1. Working on the centres.
    2. As we finished I saw the ☽ above CCT. We then sat for what came.
    II. Got the Pylon Gate and the path of ה [42] went out swiftly across a dark plain past the guardians and up an immense mountain with a narrow steep path overhanging or overhung by great precipices. At a bend a shadowy figure met us and took us up on to the mountain peak. Here was a throne or stone chair on top of steps on a tiny plateau behind this chair were three grey veiled figures. CCT sat in a chair and a fourth veiled figure came down and stood before her. I was standing at the foot of the steps and rather to the left.
    I could not see what the figure was doing, but presently CCT and I went up the path of ב [43] in the sign of ♐ [44] and reached an altar at the crossing of the paths of ב and ה [45] Here there was a great veil and we saw the ☉ [46] dimly through it.
    Then we returned with care for CCT was knocked about. The 4th veiled figure had given her a double edged sword which she had to plunge in her breast before she could go on.
    Ill. After tea CCT tried Psychometry. I gave her a photo of Kha-m-uast but she got my grandfather, his old brown dog, the armchair and dining room at Killagally, then the walk by the little garden, the crab trees and stables. She gave an accurate description of the yard, the mare Catty and Rat the pony. She described my grandmother and I found that K-m-u-t had been lying on top of this photo.

FPD

Christine Hartley:
> *Work done on April 7th, 1938*

We built the magical images while I got ready in the big chair so that I did not have to move again. I was shot out suddenly on to the Path with the star shining above me and much nearer to the peak than I have ever been before. You said you were guiding me up the knife edge of the cliff but I was not aware of you, oniy of going on and on with a purpose behind that I could not define. Ahead of us went Some One for I saw the flutter of a robe going round the corner of the mountain. And then I was at the top and there was a sort of chair or throne cut out of the stone and on either side and behind it was a veiled figure, shadowy and grey. I sat in the chair and the light of the big star poured down on me. While I sat there a Shining One came down from above, all veiled, and in his hand was two-edged sword. He held it out to me and I tried not to take it but I could not refuse and I took it in in my hands and deliberately set the point between my breasts and something or someone said "Yea, a sword shall pierce thine own heart also." But after the pain there came a great sensation of light and sunshine seen veiled and not too bright to bear, and I came back.[47]

CCT

Charles Seymour:
> *Tuesday April 26th, 1938*

Moon last Qtr: 22nd. New, due on 30th.
Weather fine with cold East wind. Setf very fit, CCT fit but tired and a little cold. Worked in 2 QT began at 8:30 p.m. ended 10:45 p.m.

CCT and self did the Aura exercise very carefully and got a great head of power. CCT's work very steady no upsets, used the Egyptian god names for the Sephiroth.

Went out on to the astral through a dark grey sphere. A guardian as a dark veiled shadow put one arm on each of us, my right, her left, shoulder and took us into a lovely green sun lit land of trees and marsh marigolds. Then on to a hill with a thick cloud over the top, this lifted and showed a tiny white temple which appeared to be built of a single moon stone and it was shaped like the Ajna lotus thus: ▷◁

In the centre were—a crystal globe and a crystal bowl filled with water. The Globe was masculine this CCT took, the bowl fem. I took it. (Note the change of polarity on the Inner Planes.)

Then shadows began to form in each of them and we both saw: as it were from above the Astral Temple of Lonsdale's initiation into the 1° next door at 3 QT. We followed the ceremony from the time L stood between the pillars. The Temple was full of Elementals and angels.

M.C.K. of S. was there. I rather missed being out of the ceremony and he said: I want you two to serve—not L.E., not even me, but the Logos of all. Your job is to teach and go on teaching others: they will build later on. You just teach them now. Teach and teach. Then he blessed us in fire with the three symbols: wheat, honey and asbestos. Then we were brought backwards through the globe and out again.

After tea and just before going my friend the Gnome turned up. I turned out the lights: lmmediately the Owl turned up on the lawn at Killagally. And from out the trees came the tree spirits—beech, oak, poplar and may. They were glorious. They said they wanted to tell me how to work the lecture on Tir nan' oge on Monday next.

1st To say what the ancients thought about the elementals drawing on the Greek mythology.
2nd Bring it to the Celtic ideas.
3rd Try to make the audience see the pictures.
CCT finished not in the least tired.

FPD

Christine Hartley:
Report on Work on April 26th 1938

First we built the Tree and the Images. The Yesod Sephira was very strong and seemed to pull itself out of me. When the God names were used I got a strong sensation with Kether and Daath and then with the S.P. it seemed as if the lotus grew out of me on a golden stalk and cupped in it the little golden baby. The Isis centre was even stronger, for it sent me chanting and invoking and then the shadowy Osiris came to my side and embraced me and held me as at the initiation. After that when I stood up I could have floated out with the merest touch of assistance.

When we turned round and sat down I went out on the 32nd Path by a new way, a long black tunnel that curved to the right with a circle of light at the end when we were round the curve. There was a white temple at the top of the hill, circular with wings from it. We went in and there was a plinth with a crystal on one side and a plinth with a bowl of water beside it. I went to the crystal and you to the bowl... I facing East and you West. And then One came in the East in white with a golden aura of sword like flames behind him and I knew it to be M. and told you. And you told me that there was an initiation going on next door. And I saw the candidate between the Pillars and M. behind the Magus blessing him. And he came forward to do it and took out of the breast of his robe a wheat ear and a piece of honeycomb and held them out while he was in the flaming aura. And the whole of the walls of the Temple were filled with angels and archangels and their coloured rainbow wings, mingling one with another, and all singing triumphantly the Benedicite. And then it went dark and I couldn't see any more.

Later on we got the earth contact with the Little People and I could see the tree spirits quite clearly and they gave me the synopsis of the lecture you want to give on Monday: it was a very interesting experience for me because while they gave me the steps and I brought them through I still retained my critical brain and could check the logic and connection of what I was saying and could see that it would make a proper precis from which you could work.

CCT

Charles Seymour:
Thursday April 28th, 1938

New Moon on Saturday
Weather fine with cold east wind. Self very fit. CCT and happy Worked at 2 QT began at 8:30 ended at 10: 25 pm. when we had tea.

Built the Auras and woke the centres. Just as we began there came a rush of power—very cold which chilled CCT. So I placed my right hand on her and willed a warm current which came. Did not use the God names—only visualized in the colours but C went out. I knew this because she was so limp—so I brought her back. Both ended the exercise filled with power.

Sat for a little while and got fields, flowers, blue mountains and bright warm sunshine. Nothing happened until it blanked out. Then someone came and stood behind me and placed his hands on my shoulders—and I felt a great current of power running down my spine. Then I saw the Cave of the Black Isis which CCT had not as yet got. I saw the P. of A. and another whom I did not recognize then. CCT was at first rather out of the picture and could not pick up the replies. She was asked if she would take the "Linking" initiation of the Black Isis. She said yes. Then she went and stood between the legs of the great stone image with her head resting in the fork made by the legs of the image.

The P. of A. stood behind me and in some way absorbed me into himself, and I was left with an empty shell of a body. My life had gone into him and I was conscious through him. The P. of A. linked the centres of CCT with the cosmic centres in the body of the image (Note her Kether [Sahasrara] and the Malkuth [Muladara] of the image formed on glowing centre.) Then C's Ajna between the eyebrows linked with the Yesod of the image (Svadisthana) and a great clarity of seeing came to her. Then C's Daath and the Solar Plexus of the image linked.

Next the Heart Centres (Anahata, junctions of the 13th and 19th path) united in a blaze of blue light and in some way C. seemed to be the image and to grow to its size for a while.

Then the solar plexus of CCT and the Daath of the image linked up.

Then her Yesod centre and the Ajna of the image linked. But I could see no Muladara centre in CCT.

Then the P. of A. left me and stood at my left, and another figure came it was Kha-'m-uast.

The P. of A. put CCT in a sarcophagus and said use the Ajna clairvoyance you have been given. I went away with Kha-'m-uast and CCT described what she saw. (I *felt* it before she said it as a rule.) We went out of the cave turned to the right went down a ravine and then into a rock tomb which opened as K. touched it. We went down a long sloping passage into a small chamber. K. raised the slab in the floor and we both floated down a deep well. At the bottom was a small chamber half full of running water with two chambers, opposite each other, cut in the rock and just big enough to take our bodies. We stood in these, K. to the East and I in the West. K's Ajna centre lit up and so did mine. A steam came up from the water and my body below the heart centre seemed to have died. Above that I was intensely and vividly alive. K. stretched out his two poles and touched my hands with them. And he seemed to flow along the poles and to vanish into my body. He said I never forget those who served me and I will now work through you and you shall have my magical power for your work. I felt as if extremely well and powerful and I left the chamber closed the slab with the sign ⟁ and then sealed the tomb. Then I went back to the Cave of the Black Isis. Raised CCT who was dead tired took her on my shoulders over the desert to the Temple of the White lsis. There we went through the narrow door at the back of the sanctuary into the sanctuary which was dark and we stood together on the steps of the priestess throne facing S.E. instead of the usual position opposite each other.

The Moon Isis came and lit the whole sanctuary from herself and blessed us as her heirophants no longer just priest and priestess. The moon fire entered into us and we walked out into the Hall of the Sphinxes where the temple priest and priestess greeted us. Then into the lotus court where we blessed the people and we walked out into the garden but CCT did not go to the priestess's house. Instead we both went to the House of the Heirophants.

We stood together in a small hall with a wonderful pavement of birds, flowers and fishes. It was brown and yellow and green very vivid. We faced each other as if doing the Aura exercises. I said—this is our home—and then we were back in my room.

I was dead to the world, and so stiff below the chest that I could hardly move. CCT very done.

We had tea and biscuits and then were both as fit as could be.
FPD

Christine Hartley:
Work done April 29th 1938

Conscious of amazing cold in the back and shoulders when we started. It went after a while. I think there must have been a good deal of power because I could not hold consciousness all the time though I was fighting to do so. I very nearly went out again when we stood up.... I could have gone but I would not.

Then we seemed to be falling through blackness and I came to a circular field covered with wild flowers and with blue sky but we were only on the edge of it, rather as though we were seeing it through a large port-hole. It went and we dropped again till we came to the cave of the B.I. The P. of A. was there. He put his hands on your shoulders and held you facing me. I went up to the image, which was standing, and took my place between the legs with my head touching her. At first I could not see how the centres could be joined but you showed me. I felt the power pouring in to me and then for one moment I had a frightful temptation because I stood there completely charged with the power of the gods and a chance to take the Left Path if I wished. I refused to accept the idea of what this unlimited unlawful power could give me and the moment passed. Then I came down from the statue after the P. of A. had given me a box of brownish wood which seemed to contain the Book of Thoth, by which I take it that I was made free of the wisdom of the Gods. He led me to a sarcophagus and made me get inside while you went out with an old Egyptian man with two staffs in his hands... one red and one brown. You went along the ravine to where the cliff blocks the end and he struck the cliff with one staff and it opened. You went into a long narrow passage and proceeded till you came to the centre chamber. There was a moveable flag in the floor: He lifted it and you followed him down a narrow ring ladder into a well. At the bottom there were two niches like the ones at the Glastonbury Well, and you each took one Then the water began to rise and he passed the sticks across to you so that they were a link between you. Power was passing from him to you all the time. There was a white mist rising off the well that enveloped you to the waist and then cleared off... when it had gone, He had gone. You came back to the cave and took me to the Hall of the White Isis. I was deadly tired and only wanted to get home. Somehow we got through the crowd of priests and priestesses, who were cheering and congratulating us as Great Ones and then we went down to the House of the Heirophants where we stood for a moment in the hall and then came back. I was too tired in my astral self to notice any special details.

CCT

Work done May 2nd, 1938

Sat in the seat of Hod for a lecture on Tirnanog.

Unfortunately, I went out at the beginning of the lecture just as soon as the mooncloud formulated. I came back at the moment when we were meeting the beech tree. It was curious because there was no shock, no surprise, I slipped from the unconscious to the conscious medium without any effort or break in the subconscious continuity. I saw the wood with the aura and the great oak tree. I contacted the spirit of the pine and stood among the hills. Then I was lifted to the peak of the hills and saw the great spirit behind them and the spirits of the country called me and said, "You've come back at last," and they gave me the freedom of Fairyland.[48] I stood in the meadow among the small flowers and felt the life around me and the pulsing of the earth. It was an amazing sensation of at-oneness—a sort of home-going—and a great reluctance to come back again.

CCT

Charles Seymour:

Thursday May 5th, 1938

Moon within 24 hours of 2nd Qtr
Very fit, fine weather.

Nothing doing. A horrible atmosphere in Paula's room where we wanted to work as Honey was in my quarters. Forced CCT out with me and then me the Symbol of Saturn. So we did nothing for the rest of the evening.

FPD

Tuesday May 10th, 1938

Weather fine and much warmer. Self fit. CCT worried over private affairs. Began at 8:30 ended 10:15 p.m. Moon 4 days after First Qtr.

Banished with Pentagram beforehand, room felt very peaceful. Odin came up very strongly and gave CCT a message. His image was very clear. Then as usual as we began to open the centres, but I suddenly found myself standing on a wet cold afternoon at the tower by the eastern end of Hadrian's wall. There was a wild red cloudy early sunset behind me, and I was looking at a headland. I was a Roman officer but I think of Germanic birth or at any rate born on the Rhine and Germanic in ideas though an initiate of Mithra. Beside me stood my subaltern a fair boy about nineteen and I recognized him for N.N. and I was very fond of him. As I watched I saw the long galleys come round the headland—about twenty of them. And I knew the Roman fleets that used to protect the Wall by sea had gone. Our flank was being turned. Then our commander joined me—I recognized him for General Orton whom in this life I had known in India. A very fine soldier.[49] (CCT I did not see.)

The trumpets went and in the afternoon drizzle and mist the men fell in and we hid "en echelon" in the heather and mounds just above high water mark, with the light troops and slingers, and a few bowmen in front on the beach and out covering our right flank. We had about 400 men in all. The tide was far out over the mud flats.

The ships came in rather carelessly one after the other and beached in a long line they had perhaps 300 men, and they were led by a huge man with the design of an eagle on the sails of his ship. Their crews jumped into the mud and boldly attacked with their right leading. Our slings and arrows took a heavy toll of the men floundering in the mud and directly they landed we charged and in five minutes the raiders' right wing was smashed.

Then the raiders centre and left wing got on land formed at right angles to the sea and charged our right. When they were well into the attack our reserves echeloned behind right charged, took them in flank and that was soon over and the remainder of the raiders ran for the ships, leaving their leader dead. We then set to work to kill the wounded and strip the dead of weapons. N.N. discovered beside the dead chief a girl of sixteen dressed as a man. (CCT had now come into the picture.) She was senseless from a blow on the head. (I had a hell of a headache after this,) and at N.N.'s suggestion she was carted up to the tower. The dead leader we found was a celebrated pirate and raider. His name I think was Wolfmar. The actual fight was very short and quick and was over long before dark. N.N. wanted CCT for ransom.

We tried to get information out of CCT and learned that the other half of Wolfmar's fleet was near at hand and they were under the impression that the Roman legion had gone and had expected to find only a few native British troops. I promised CCT swearing by Odin, that if they came back I would give her her liberty if she would be quiet. N.N. tried to take CCT's dagger from her and I watched with considerable amusement a scrap between the two in which the big boned Norse girl scratched and smacked my tall slight good looking subaltern thoroughly. I laughed but N.N. wanted to cut her throat, and for some reason seemed jealous of the interest I took in the girl. Then he and I went to the Mithraic chapel under the wall where I took the silent meditation as the senior Initiate.[50] The night went quickly and at dawn the alarm was given that the complete fleet was coming back. I made CCT put on Roman armour and a helmet and we formed up again in the same place. But before their attack began reinforcements came into view and we were more than stronger than the raiders who drew off out into the bay.

Then a small single ship came in. They asked for the chieftain's body and his daughter. I was on the tower with CCT and N.N. and fed up with the fighting between them told CCT who reminded me of my oath by Odin that she could go.

She went about half way to the shore with N.N. when he suddenly brought her back and said she was too valuable a hostage. I agreed and kept her in spite of my oath, and her reproaches.

Finally I went down to the beach with CCT and the interpreter and met a rather crafty looking raider who had come off to parly.

FPD

Christine Hartley:
Report of Work done on May 10th 1938

We were just sitting down to work the centres when I got a strong pull from the Norse contacts and turning round I saw Odin at my side He took me in hand—I had been very nervy and stupid—and pulled me together and told me off for letting myself go like that.

Then you saw the Bay and the Wall and we plunged right into things. At first I could merely see things objectively with you since I was not in the story. We saw the Wall and the soldiers of the Legion. You were a captain of fifty and there was a boy, tall, young and good looking, who was under you: he had a tremendous admiration and affection for you: he was a bit spoilt. You were afraid of a raid from the sea by which the ships could get behind and attack from both sides while the Picts and Scots would attack from the front.

We could see the Viking fleet coming in round the headland. Then I began to take part and was in the foremost ship with the chief. I was a girl of about sixteen, with a helmet and a short dagger. We landed out in the low water and waded to shore and up the mud flats, going rather slowly. The trumpets had sounded on the Wall and your men were on the grass dunes above us and the slingers came nearer and attacked. A lot of our men went down. I was behind the chief all the time and he attacked on the right. Our left wing wheeled round (this is vague because I was naturally occupied with what I could see at the end of our line) and after pushing you back a bit you executed a flanking movement and turned us on ourselves. We were pushed back on to the flats and the Chief was killed in a sword fight. A stone must have hit me on the head for I don't remember much till I came to on my face in the heather with the boy bending over me. The wounded had been killed off but he thought I was valuable having been near the Chief. My helmet was off and he saw I was a girl, so he called you and you had me carried into the officers' quarters in one of the Wall towers.

The centurion came in and ordered wine and you gave me some and I came back to life, and remember getting my back into the angle of the wall and sitting on the bedstead and the heap of skins more or less spitting and snarling. The boy saw that I still had my dagger and he bent forward to get it. I wrestled with him for it and then scratched his face hard. He was furious and turned to you and asked you to have me beaten but you and the centurion were laughing at him.

Then the centurion went away and you sent for a soldier who could speak some of my tongue. First you gave me your short sword, hilt first, and I looked at it doubtfully, took it and gave it back to you, again hilt first. Then the interpreter came and someone brought me food. You and the others were Germanic by origin, not Latins. You swore by Odin that you would not harm me, and that I could go free if I wanted to. I swore not to try and escape by myself. The trumpets sounded and someone said that the Vikings wanted to collect the dead. You took me up on the Wall and on to the dunes and sent me with the boy to my own people. But suddenly you saw the boy dragging me back, and he told you that I had betrayed the fact that I was of the Chief's house and therefore you must not let me go as I was a valuable hostage. You agreed and took me down to the room again. I was furious and blackguarded you all I knew for breaking your oath but you said you must do it for the sake of your men's safety. The boy lost his temper with me for my fury with you and took me by the shoulder and shook me violently. I swung round and smacked his face pretty hard. You ordered him to let me go, told me to stay on the couch in the corner of the room and took the boy to the Chapel of Mithras, of which I could see very little.

When you came up again it was dark: the boy went to do the rounds and you came to lie down. As you passed the boy's bed you laughed and picked up his softest dressed skin and threw it over to me for the night was bitterly damp and there was a howling gale... the walls of the tower seemed to be wet.

Early in the morning the trumpets sounded again and you made me put on some Legion armour and then go up to the Wall with you. The second chief was there and asking for me. You bargained with him for the safety of the rear attack and he promised. Suddenly we were both aware of Odin standing at your left hand as a warning and you felt you could not trust the Viking. Suddenly he stooped and picked me up and ran for the boat, holding me as shield between you and himself. Someone ran round on the angle and slung a stone that dropped him at the edge of the water. I fell to the ground in the mud, scrambled up and ran back to you dropping more or less on my knees as I slipped about. The boy caught my hair and dragged my head back and begged you to cut my throat then and there to avoid further trouble. You knocked him down and told me to follow you and we went back again to the Tower. I remember crouching again on the bed with my back in that angle of the wall and then it faded out.

CCT

Report of Work done 12.5.38

Moon: Half full.   Self: tired
Weather: Breaking.

We sat in the circle and I acted as one of the priestesses for the reinforced power in the invocation; the power was very noticeable and almost as soon as we sat down again I saw the unnamed one to the south of the mirror. After that I began to see the Temple and then I went out for a little but came back fairly soon. The current flowed very evenly and strongly and I could feel that the power was going out of me to the altar though I could not see the power shape that was described. The temple came clearly with the unnamed one,[51] the P. of A. and Another, whom I could not place, on the dais. When we were told we might ask questions I felt my astral body being drawn out and into the mirror. I walked into the Temple quite easily. He had come down to the front of it to meet me: he took me by the hand, led me back to the dais and stood me at the foot while he mounted again and put a crown on my head. Then he put his arms round my shoulders and "showed me" saying, "This is our beloved child with whom we are pleased." Then I asked him certain things and got the replies, partly in words and partly in very clear picture making... the persons in question appearing as it were astrally in the Temple. I had hardly ended when we were brought back and I felt the power altering and so it ended.

I was very tired afterwards but soon recovered.

CCT

Report of Work done on May 19th, 1938

Circle of eight formed... self as one priestess. Clairvoyance completely dulled owing to having taken 5gr. of aspro ten hours earlier. Therefore unable to see anything though aware of what was going on in the Inner Planes.

The power ran smoothly and strongly round the circle I found myself in the Inner Temple and saw the Three. I fixed my attention on the third, whose name I learnt since the last sitting. He unveiled his face and the beauty was such that it caught me in the breast and I could not stand the pain. His eyes were marvellous. I saw the U.M. but could not visualize him as clearly as usual. I did not see the clouds or the formations over and round the altar.

Later I asked the U.M. the question I had wanted to have answered. He gave me an oracular answer and I pressed for something a bit more clear so I got it. Again I pressed, wanting confirmation, and got that again. I suppose he really was very patient with me, but I do like to be sure of what I want to know![52]

Not at all tired afterwards... much less strenuous than the time before.

CCT

Report of Work done on May 26th, 1938

Sat in the Circle Preliminary building pretty clear. More conscious than usual of the four Archangels when helping the Magus[53] with the invocations. They all appeared enormous and clear and their outstretched wing tips touched each other at the corners, shutting out all ingress from the outer world.

The current ran pretty smoothly and then the building of the lower Temple was completed. Saw the three Masters sitting there. Greeting L.E. I was, as it were, passed on to K.[54] and told that he wanted me that evening. K. unveiled his face to me and the beauty was more than I could bear. It caught me in the breast and made me try to elude it. Presently he shifted and I was only conscious of his eyes. All at once I was aware of my son kneeling by me in front of K. and K. telling me that in some way I was the mother of a greater than I and one who would work on different lines and that I must be prepared for this. I was still the child of L.E. but my child comes of different stock.

Then I came back again and the regular work of the pyramid and the fingers of light, etc. went on and were pretty clear.

CCT

Charles Seymour:

May 31st, 1938

Time 8.30 to 9.45 p.m.
New Moon on 29th.
Weather Wet.
CCT, self at 2 QT. CCT arrived tired mentally and not feeling too well.

1. Drove power into CCT.
2. Built the Aura, the Tree in colours and the Centres.
3. Sat down in the temple and awaited what might come. After

a fairly long pause someone came. I did not recognize him it was Cleomenes III and with him was L.E. and after greetings he told us he would show himself unveiled as he had work for us to do. He also told us that L.E. and he were working together and that each spoke for the other. Then we were suddenly in a small horseshoe shaped Temple built of immense blocks of stone. Then Cleomenes took each of us by the hand into a very narrow dark passage which sloped downwards. He went in front while we followed behind him. After a little time we came out into a small courtyard in which were some women and a number of officers. He took his place in a chair to give his decrees. I was the middle-aged commander of a company of some three or four hundred men, CCT was a woman. I was given my orders to hold a certain hill and a disk which I was to send to the king only in dire need. I was looking over my command with much pleasure and starting to march when the scene blanked.

Next I was on a small hill near a small town and to my right rear was a small river. The hill was a shambles, dead and wounded everywhere, and a filthy stink of blood and refuse. There was no food and the thirst was awful. I had only a handful of men left. The hill had been taken and then retaken. I was waiting for reinforcements to make it secure again, when I saw them going off to the left away from us. Then the enemy counter-attacked and we were cut to pieces. Myself and a dozen men one of them a great black-bearded Giant, a freed helot captain, cut our way to the river. There was a long fight and flight over the countryside and then only half a dozen of us were left. Then I saw a boat waiting for us; in it were a lot of women and CCT. We charged our pursuers and the helot captain got a spear in his throat. I just got into the boat in time and dropped off and when I came to myself we were at sea in a fresh wind, heading for Egypt to which the King and his family and most of his nobles had already gone.

Next I was in a small Mystery Temple under the King's house in Egypt. I think it must have been in Alexandria. It was oblong with stone benches on three sides and a low dais on the fourth side. In the centre was a black cubical altar with a light upon it. At the four points of the compass were four immense winged and coloured beings, and their wings made a roof over the temple Their colours were golden yellow in the E, red in the S, blue in the W, and dark green in the N. Before each burnt a lamp coloured to match their robes. I thought of the Sons of Horus. On the dais were three dim forms, apparently those of the demi-gods. I did not know Them.

Before the altar facing them stood Cleomenes with his hands on the altar. CCT and I stood just behind him. He appeared to grow immensely big and bright and then as it were floated in a blaze of golden glory up through the temple roof. We stood there beside the dark empty shell that was his body.

After a time he came slowly back and entered his body which became transfigured and glowed with an exceeding brightness. We knelt before him and he laid a hand on each of our heads and drove an immense force into and between us, a living triangle of which he was the apex.

He told us that he must be killed and the free state of Sparta must die in order that this life and his ideas might take a new form. This new freedom of the individual which he had tried to give to Sparta must be born out of the teaching given in the Mystery Temples in England today: it is Man's complete freedom in religion, in thought, and also in life—so far as the interests of all the State permits. England is to be the home of that personal religious freedom which he had striven to give to Sparta. He would teach it, and CCT and I (later another) would be his present instruments in the Temple at 3 QT.

He would remain veiled and unknown to the rest, and the teaching would have to be given gradually for not all could bear it. Later he would give us more.

He then blessed us both. I blanked while he gave a private message to CCT. Then we both came back suddenly with a bad bump, and shot out without a chance of closing properly. CCT was a bit discoordinated and swaying as if about to faint. A few passes down the body and up the head put her right and she slept until tea was ready.

A wonderful experience and after tea I was very fit.

FPD

Christine Hartley:
Report of Work done on May 31st, 1938

Weather:Fine.
Self Fit

Opened the centres and felt a strong head of power. Then sat down to wait. Dropped back and back to old Sparta and picked up K. and a battle, which I did not know. It was vague to me because I know nothing of tactics but it was the holding of a hillside against overwhelming forces in the plain. Gradually the defenders were beaten back and forced to withdraw down the hill. They fought a rearguard action losing men all the time. At last a few got through to a ship which was waiting in a tiny cove, between very high cliffs. The sea was very blue and the trees on the slopes were pines and olives or something of that kind. The shipload had women and children on board as well and the boat picked up the few warriors who survived the struggle and went off to Egypt—a journey of several days. It was a little ship and it was rather doubtful if it would get through.

Then there was a black out for a bit and we found ourselves in an underground temple with K. This was Egypt. There was a cubical altar and we were both acting as assistants to him in a rite which we hardly understood. He was a captive in Egypt and as such had advanced in the priesthood unknown to the world. There was a tremendous cone of light over the altar which came from him and I could see his astral self as it were ascending to heaven while the black shell of his body stood before the altar with outstretched upflung arms. It was like the Transfiguration. And I knew that we were witnessing a touching of the Sixth Level of a Master. Then he came back into himself and there was a sort of stillness over everything and a complete black out.

CCT

Report of Work done on June 16th, 1938

The room was full of power when we went in and sat down. I was a little anxious as to my perceptions, having had to take aspro in the morning for a headache but although the edge may have been blunted, I got as much as usual and more than on many times.

The circle of power ran very smoothly and it was difficult to hold back till the Temple was built. Then I saw it clearly with the Three Masters in their usual places. L.E. spoke to me and then I went on to see K. who asked me more about the child again. There was a great deal of her about and more than once it seemed to me that L.E. was going to materialize.

The cloud formed above the altar again and I saw the hands on the long arms of smoke, especially touching an individual most clearly and I shall be very interested to see if that person eventually turns up.

The Archangels were clear, though not so distinct as the time before. Someone came in after the banishing and stood behind the priest staying there to the best of my knowledge all the time, but I could not tell who it was, other than it was someone of great power and friendliness, someone more of a teacher than a warrior.

CCT

Charles Seymour:

Tuesday June 21st, 1938

Time: Evening 8.15 to 9.15 p.m.
CCT, Paula, and Self

Went straight to Chiron's cave, via the pass and the lawn and found Paula was as one of us.

Paula and CCT went off with the centaurs riding and I stayed to commune with the Master. I got the idea of linking the old symbolism of indigenous women's mysteries with the pagan mysteries of England right down to the present day, and through the witchcraft period.

I could not get the title but CCT got it for me later. It was "The Wisdom of the Cave in the Mountains."[55]

He promised to help me with it, but I was to keep his name out of it.

Paula as we returned tried to bolt back to the centaurs, and I found a little bay filly that I was very fond of, and I wanted her badly. Cheiron promised us that at death if we served him we might come to him and be with his children. Had great difficulty in getting Paula to return, but she came like a good un.

FPD

Christine Hartley:
Report of Work done June 21st, 1938

Weather Midsummer.
Self Very well.

Worked with the three of us. First aware of green-leaves and branches. Then we seemed to be climbing out of a beech wood and up the hills. We were moving swiftly and were soon above the great rhododendron beds and on to the grey rock and the peaks above. We took the turning through the cleft and Paula found she could come easily. We came to the arena and at the far side of it was the cave. Then we called Him by name and he came out of the darkness to the sunlight. But whereas we had seen the shadows of the Others, he, present, cast no shadow. Then we went into the cave and he sat down on a kind of raised divan with skins on it, and we squatted on the floor of the cave at his feet. He took up his lyre and played to us and the music was marvellously sweet.

He told us that we were welcome for we were all of the Blood. That he had trained the Heroes and that we were of the Heroes Seed today. Then they came back, neighing and stamping in the doorway of the cave. We suggested riding with him and he said we might, if we could find the way back. Then I lost everyone else and went off on mine. I saw the Danube like a glittering silver snake and then the Black Sea, miles below. And then it seemed amusing to try and ride straight into a low star but when we got near it, I thought it was beyond a joke and insisted on hurrying back to the cave.

There, after a little more talk, we left Him, escorted over the arena by themselves, nickering and rubbing against it. As we started down the cliff I saw that Paula was lingering behind trying to stay with them and I was a little afraid so we had to get her back between the two of us and so we went down the hill.

CCT

Report of Work done on June 24th, 1938

Formed the circle. Felt very cheerful and definitely not psychic. The banishing was potent and I was conscious of the archangels though not so definitely as the time before. When the Magus called me to see what I could find in the mirror, I was rather taken aback and troubled for at first I could not see anything. Then it came clearly and was L.E., lamen, the square green one with signs on it.

We sat down and the power ran clearly and strongly in the circle and I was aware that there was a hooded figure behind each one of us, taking part as from an Inner Lodge.

K. very nearly materialized on the S. window and L.E. was clear behind and beside the Magus at different times though not materialized.

The streamers of fire were as clear as I have ever known them and the power was running strongly all through.

CCT

Report of Work done June 28th, 1938

Started when I walked over the threshold of the house and felt witchcraft all round me. Went upstairs extremely desirous of being a witch. When we had settled down I kept getting little pictures of Ishtar worship through the ages, the most constant being one of silhouetted witches in pointed hats and ragged skirts dancing round a fire. Then it seemed to focus a little more steadily and I was aware of the goddess standing before us mistily veiled.

She spoke through me. I do not remember everything she said but she stressed again the necessity for Joy in worship and that she was the goddess of Love of Life as well as of Love in the more conventional sense. She said that people had forgotten her and that her altars were broken down and that she had been transformed into the Virgin Mary which was not the fulness of her worship but only one side of it.

Then she gave you roses and violets from her hands, she gave Paula a silver star and she set the diadem with the star and moon on my forehead. Then she drew me to her and enveloped me with her veils and we were closely wrapped together and in this way began to rise up to Yesod. I could see the earth planet below me, strangely small, but I could not leave consciousness and this held me back from getting really away with her.

I could see Yesod misty and cloudlike and at last I got the beginning of the vision as I stood with her just inside a tunnel and saw the Fields of Ishtar through the circular opening but because of my inability to let go I could not pass right into them.

CCT

Charles Seymour:
Tuesday September 6th, 1938

Time: 8:30 to 9:50 p.m.
Weather: thundery
CCT and Self

CCT started without any preparation in the green woods of Ireland and got the oak and beech people at once. She said they were in the room when she came in. I had done an hours Green Ray meditation before she came. She was met by a tall figure in an ancient Irish dress with spear and round shield who led her to a ford over a deep stream in a little clearing. It was called the "Ford of the Moon" i.e. AnnaRea. He crossed and told her to follow after she had looked into the river. In the river she saw a great green city all transparent under the river and the wooded hillside. She hesitated to cross and wanted to go down to this City but the moon mist came up and she and I floated on it to the other bank, and then we went to a circle of very ancient birches on a small rath. The fairy people were there and in front of us was a tall single frond of bracken. This began to wave violently and I told her of its significance and how it should be greeted, when if we were accepted the bracken would suddenly grow quite motionless.

We then went up the lane onto the wide open heather and stood by the two stones of the "whispered truths" on the "High place of the Moon"—Aurd naRea. One stood before us in a white robe holding a small shield and spear which he gave to CCT, and then placed a gold crown on her head and led her to the Throne of the Great Mother—Dana.

CCT knelt before her and the cloak of the Goddess was thrown over her shoulder, and she was blessed.

We came back by the same way. CCT was very tired. After tea we saw the "Hosts of the Shee" riding. But deliberately refrained from joining them. Later again Pan came but something broke the contact and Pan came back upon me with a rush which upset both of us for a while

FPD

Time: 8:30 to 9:30 p.m. [undated]
Moon: Nearly full.
Cold fine windy.
My rooms.

Vision

After falling and falling down through Time, CCT and I walk up out of a dark wood of olives or evergreen oaks on a ridge of short grass and then down a little meadow in which is a small ring of rough standing stones about 4 feet high, in the centre a stone altar about breast high. We were short dark with black hair and very sunburnt and clad in a short white smock and a kilt in my case, a simple Greek dress in CCT's. She carried flowers and fruit. I a small lamb over my shoulders. We went to the altar and I tried to keep the lamb on it, but it jumped off. CCT then put the fruit and flowers on the altar. A white dove came and sat on her shoulder and I in the E. she in the W. face each other across the circle with the altar between us and our backs against the stones. We began to chant and invoke.

We waited and a golden mist came off the flowers and formed into the Earth Goddess with a sheaf of corn in her left arm and a sickle in her right hand. She showed very clearly and an oval band of spinning light sprang up between the Three of us. We slowly moved in until our hands were on the altar and the oval band had become an orange shaped vertical circle of pale golden light embracing the three of us.

Then a very old woman with thin grey locks and walking with sticks appeared in the N. As we saw her an horizontal triangle of light formed between the three humans and the old hag came slowly to the altar. When she placed her hands upon it she began to grow young and very beautiful, a duplicate of CCT, and when this process had ceased the goddess had flowed into her and into this bright golden symbol △ (We got very cold and empty).

The new arrival said I am life from my womb, came live at birth, and life goes back at death. I was the priestess at this altar, you are the priest and priestess, and I will be again, when you are gone. Then CCT grew very old and vanished but the goddess and the young priestess were there in our places.

We finished very cold and dead tired.

FPD

December 6th, 1938

Time 8:30 to 9 p.m.
CCT and G

Started with no idea of what was coming. Then saw Odin in his cloak patch over one eye, two ravens and two wolves and spear.

Then up came the Wall with CCT as the Norse girl myself as the middle aged Roman commander (a German by birth), and the "Boy." The Norse were landing south of the Wall and attacking the rear, the Picts were attacking the Wall from the North. An attack had been beaten off but as no help could come we knew we were doomed, besides the girl could see Odin waiting for us, and above were the choosers of the slain. The three of us were in our living tower. I sent the Boy to his post as the attack began again, the girl I had offered to send to her people but she refused saying Odin was waiting for both of us. At her request I cut her throat (now she understands this gesture of hers) and a few moments later was killed on the Wall.

Then Odin showed us the Boy with a sword through his back laying on his face; self my chest smashed in lying on my back, but with a smile of relief on my face; the garrison exterminated. Dead lying in heaps and the ships behind us.

Next came the ride to Valhalla—but not as the dead. We were the joyous warriors returning to real life and well we felt.

Then came a blank. And we were back in this room rather shaken and very tired. But Odin was still with us—He blessed us and said "You are still my children. I still live, and I lay a command upon you two: In my service work. And let not your interest in ancient Egypt make you forget that there is a great Norse trad···

your own islands. Seek for the mysteries of the Norse men that were in the islands."

(Twice in October and November 1938 we picked up again this incarnation but nothing much seemed to happen, just cold and wet and worry round the Wall, the "Boy," the Norse girl hating each other like poison.)

FPD

Christine Hartley:
Work done January 9th, 1939

L.E. came almost at once between the curtains, very clearly and strongly. Then I found it impossible to settle to any one thing. G.[56] got a whirling figure which I could not see: then a great horror came over me and I cried out that it was the figure of a Hanged Man. He said no and reduced it to the figure of a dancing girl: he wanted to go East but I could not get away from the West of England.

Slowly the thing clarified till we were standing on Brean Down looking out to sea. There was a mist over the water and a clear patch of moonlight. In that there was a little ship, and I knew it contained a Great One, though I could not place the person. It did not seem like Ishtar and I got a feeling of Atlantis connected with it, although it was the wrong part of the coast.

Gradually the ship came to land and the mists cleared and I could see the dark men getting out of her, and then I saw Who had come. There was a Golden Boy with them, and I knew that we were watching the Phoenicians coming to the lead mines and bringing the Child Jesus with them. And He ran ahead down the village street, and buxom women leant on their fences and loved Him, and the rabbits and the moorhens came out to play with Him. They mounted ponies and rode across the fenland and up Cheddar Gorge till they came to the mines on top of the Mendips before you dip down to the Bath Valley. There were sheds and works at the top and the Phoenicians had come back to their former concessions. There was a sort of windlass at the top, with a bucket that dropped down a circular shaft. Some of the men went down in it and the Child insisted on going too. I got a clear view of Him, sitting in the bucket, the golden aura all round Him from head to heels, holding on to the sides of the bucket and laughing.

After that it grew faint and I could not see the return to the ship ... it just blurred out and I came back.

The most notable technical thing was the extremely cold air round my ankles before I began to see anything. I had my coat over a rug, which I have never needed before I was not cold during the "seeing," as I have been before: it was an objective seeing and therefore much less emotional than sometimes, but the cold came at the beginning. I was pretty tired when I had finished.

CCT

Work done January 16th, 1939

The room filled up very quickly and I was conscious of the presence of four of the Great Ones ... L.E., Merlin, Odin and Cleomenes. They all said things in turn, which I cannot actually remember but the gist of it was that they were the bearers of the Torch and that it was being handed on to us. I remember C. saying ... "And I went down into Egypt."

After that there came a sort of blank and then a great light and M. of S. came in the middle of it, all shining and wonderful. He gave us bread and wine symbolically and then actually gave you a crown and frankincense. And then he turned to me and I was very disappointed because he did not give me anything, but he smiled and said "Daughter of the Morning Star" and pointed to a golden chariot at my feet.

And then we were out on the plains with the hills dimly outlined on the horizon through the golden light that was round him ... and gradually it withdrew and he faded away.

Later on, we worked again and I picked up Merlin and a cove on the West Coast. And as usual it was beastly cold and wet and I was cross, and the fire wouldn't burn. And then M. came out of the cave and walked over to us where we were by the fire and said various things I can't quite remember but chiefly, "Take care of my Morgan ... take care of Morgan le Fay ..."

CCT

Charles Seymour:

February 13th, 1939

Time: 8:30 to 9 p.m.
CCT and Self

Room was very quiet and had been carefully sealed before hand. CCT and Self both fit. Dark of Moon near, weather fine and spring like.

Waited for about five minutes and picked up a place that looked like Avebury as it may have been 3000 to 4000 years ago, except there was a long altar stone in the middle and over it had been built a sort of roof of leaves that looked like beech. It was very early in the morning just after dawn and I think it was about May Day or Beltaine. I noticed the dew on the grass. Then came two priests one carrying a gold hilted bronze (?) sword about $2^1/_2$ feet long. This was a big man heavily built with a wide face, a big mouth, large teeth with very prominent and pointed eye teeth. The other was a smaller man thin and fanatical looking who carried a large gold cup. Following them were men carrying a rough litter on which lay a young woman about twenty or thirty. Fair hair blue eyes. She was naked with finger nails, toe nails, and nipples painted red. She was not bound.

(Note: I was feeling awful, my back all creepy and I was unable to move in my chair.) Then the woman was placed on the altar stone with her head (face) facing N.E. looking into a notch in the hills where the sun would appear. This woman was paralysed below the neck—or hypnotized or drugged. But she could move her head a little and her eyes rolled and she was fully conscious. The big priest stood behind her head waiting for the sun to rise to plunge the sword between the painted nipples. The smaller priest with the bowl squatted at her feet to catch the blood from a runnel in the gently sloping stone of sacrifice. The whole temple space was filled with figures. The sun came up after a long wait the priest raised the sword to stab and I recognized him as DNF, the other was Chris, and I was the girl sacrificed on the stone. The big priest had the face of a devil. I ended dead beat both physically and emotionally.

FPD

Christine Hartley:
February 13th, 1939

I kept getting a very strong impression of Salisbury Plain and at first I picked up Stonehenge. Then I knew that was not the right place and suddenly I found myself looking at Avebury—which I have never seen.

I found the long avenues between pillars leading like spokes of a wheel to a small circle surrounded with pylons. It seemed to me as if sometimes this was roofed in by boughs.

It was late Spring so far as I could judge by the grass and the general air of the place.

Along one of the avenues came a procession of priests and near their head was a girl lying on a litter. She was very fair with a milk and roses complexion and very white pale skin all down. She was drugged, evidently, because she seemed to be paralysed below the throat though her eyes, very blue, were alive. She was not bound because she could not move—this had something to do with the "Willing Sacrifice."

The procession came to the centre of the ring and all the priests stood round inside the pillars. The sacrifice was laid on the altar and two priests took up their positions, one at the head and the other at the foot. The one at the head had a horrible face—square with long canine teeth and something of a great cat about him. It was almost sadistic in expression—a kind of beastly gloating over the girl who was lying there, completely naked. The priest at the foot was darker and somehow less positive but none the less terrible by reason of a certain secretiveness. They waited for what seemed a tremendously long time for the sun to rise over the centre pylon and strike on the blade of the knife held by the fair priest. The dark one had a cup to catch the blood as it dripped down the stone.

Then the sun came over the pylon and it was all finished.

I seldom if ever remember such a tremendous discomfort and vibration in my spine as if rills of water were pouring in and out of it: it was impersonal to me and I did not really suffer but I was acutely aware of the objective vibrations all round.

CCT

Notes

1. The Priest of Anubis, who can be identified as Ne Nefer Ka Ptah, which means "The spirit of Ptah is good (or beautiful)." Anubis is the "Opener of the Way" or "The Guardian," the god of magic.
2. Khonsu, the Moon-god, usually represented as a man with a falcon's head surmounted by a lunar disk. With Amun and Mut as father and mother he completes the Theban Triad. In *A Case for Reincarnation* Hartley describes themselves as having been followers of the moon gods, from Thebes, who had been persecuted by the Hyksos kings.
3. Nefer-su was the name of Seymour from his Egyptian incarnation, meaning "He is good (or beautiful)."
4. The Pan workings were prompted, in part, by CCT having confessed to a phobia concerning woods. She could never enter even the smallest copse without feelings of panic. After the Pan contacts the phobia disappeared.
5. The Lapithae were a mythical race who had defeated the centaurs, in Thessaly.
6. Oscar Cook, her first husband.
7. It is interesting that while the pair have frequent contact with the Gods as opposed to high-grade discarnate entities, the divinities in question rarely have much to say. No sententious philosophies, no prophecies. In magical parlance this was because the two were functioning at the level of the Greater Mysteries. These are essentially non-verbal experiences above conscious mentation, suggestible through symbol and metaphor only. What passed between the Gods and the two coworkers can be described as follows:

    The relationship between a magician and his goddess is like that between a baby and the mother giving him suck.

There is a profound and loving bond, nourishing and giving—but a very quiet one. Whatever the mother may croon or whisper to the child is lost to its conscious mind, but sinks into the web of the subconscious to be brought out in years to come as an original discovery.

8. Archangel of the West, being Gabriel, associated with the Cup.

9. In *A Case for Reincarnation* Hartley comments "... it was borne in on me that where I really worked was at Philae, the temple which is now submerged except for a few weeks in the late spring when the Nile is at its lowest. This was a Temple of Isis and I have strong affiliations with the moon."

10. In the magical system Isis is invariably described as White or Black, neither having any moral implications but relating to the positive and negative aspects of the psyche. See Dion Fortune's *Moon Magic* for fuller accounts of the Black Isis rites.

11. Possibly a reference to the violent domestic quabbles between Dion and Merl.

12. These are the robes that Dion wore on astral levels.

13. The Guild of the Master Jesus. Seymour and Hartley were presumably working in 1 QT on this occasion.

14. An ushabti is a statuette in the shape of a divine mummy, usually carved of stone, wood, or frequently blue faience.

15. The OPET festival was the annual feast when Amon-Re visited his consort Mut in the Temple of Luxor.

16. These are early names and forms of Osiris and Isis.

17. Nibs was C. T. Loveday, so called because he handled the accounts and records; "Himself" was of course Lord Eldon.

18. The blank occurs within the line and is of a decided length as if Seymour knew the Word in question—a long word—but was reluctant to commit it. It was probably the "Blessing of Release," an autohypnotic key word that had been built into the subsconscious of each priest during his training against the day when his heresy might provoke just such punishment.

19. Seymour explained to CCT that this was why she and her hus-

band had had to get together in this life: Oscar had to atone for his earlier betrayal.

20. This was the Reverend Donelan Bolingbroke Seymour, the Dean of Clonmacnois.

21. More usually spelled sidhe. Seymour was spelling it phonetically.

22. An interesting comment in that the great adepts are said to be able to see future as well as past incarnations. Which makes it necessary to revise, somewhat, the traditional speculations regarding karma.

23. Morgan was Arthur's half-sister, comparable to the Irish Morrigane, both triple-goddess figures. The name means "borne of the sea." In the system of Qabalah suggested by Christine Hartley in the Western Mystery Tradition Morgan equates with the sphere of Binah, the "bitter sea."

24. A deep-trance medium would not have been able to do this. The conscious mediumship taught within the Inner Light would allow CCT both to explore the past by vision and yet retain her critical faculties.

25. The records are not very clear here, but a distinction must be made between the discarnate semi-divinity/archetype known as Merlin, and the earthly priest bearing his name as an initiatic title. In the latter case the references are to Thomas Penry Evans, in a previous incarnation.

26. 3° initiations.

27. His daughter

28. Dion Fortune.

29. To an extent there is a similar controversy about all such popular figures from Arthur up to Che Guevara, in that they did not die but somehow survived. Nevertheless a recent and controversial book about the Maid by Pierre de Sermoise entitled *Jeanne d'Arc et la Mandragore* tends to support this vision of the two magicians. It is known that a woman called Claude des Armoises pretended to be Joan after her death.

30. Magical Personality.

31. The spheres on the middle pillar of the Tree of Life were equated with the yogic chakras:
    Kether – Sahasrara
    Daath – Visuddi and Ajna
    Tiphareth – Anahata and Manipura
    Yesod – Svadisthana
    Malkuth – Muladhara

32. The writer William Thompson states that "prana enters the physical body from the back of the head at a point in the medulla oblongata; while the other point ... is directed at the third eye..."

33. See Figure 3. There are several other depictions of Eldon, but none have quite the same quality as this painting by Thomas Lawrence.

34. Magical Images.

35. In *A Case for Reincarnation* she describes another Norse impulse which came to her some ten years before she began proper magical training. It came to her that she had been Hiordis, the girl whom Sigmund the Volsung had married at the end of his life and who was herself the mother of Sigurd. Years later when Dag Hammarskjold died in a plane crash she was drawn into contact with him and thereby learned that he had been Sigmund Volsung. One suspects, however, that this was the sort of impulse that the Colonel might well have suppressed, as Hiordis later appears on the other side of the Bifrost bridge as a separate entity. It might be that the explanation is to be found once again the idea of overshadowing. Although I am not at all moved by the various Norse contacts I have no doubt as to the authenticity of CCT's contact with Hammarskjold.

36. No reference to this was found in any source. It has been suggested to me that the veil, or net, was a symbol of the hymen.

37. It is noteworthy that Ptah the artificer god is the dominant one behind the far memories of Elizabeth Halch and Joan Grant.

38. Melchisadek of Salem.

39. The 31st, 11th and 23rd Paths.

40. Nabu was the moon divinity of the Assyrians.
41. Grand Master.
42. Tau, and the 32nd path.
43. Samekh, and the 25th path.
44. Sagittarius.
45. Samekh and Peh, the 27th path.
46. Sun.
47. This seems to have been a veiled version of the Vision of the Chiefs, described in *Psychic Self Defence*.
48. There is a curious passage in the *Western Mystery Tradition* referring to Tir n'an Oige: "It is the resting place of our mother race; sometimes, looking down through clear water, it can be glimpsed faintly where a little stream runs silently beneath a bridge with a birch tree and an elder at either end." She elsewhere described the dangers of approaching Glastonbury Tor when the Sidhe were hosting. This was the Green Ray mysticism described in many of Dion's writings usually with attendant warnings.
49. General Orton was born in 1874. His regiment was the Royal Dublin Fusiliers and he took part in operations in China and Persia. Along with Seymour and many other military occultists he was also involved with Intelligence work.
50. Possibly the Romano-Celtic temple as Benwell dedicated to the god Antenociticus, destroyed in a barbarian raid at the end of the second century. Mars Lenumius was also invoked there as well as three lamiae, a local trinity of war-fertility goddesses associated with ravens.
51. Was this Eldon or Erskine? After fifty full years CCT could not recall the reference.
52. This would have been typical of Eldon during his lifetime too, never being renowned for rapid pronouncements on any problem.
53. Dr. Evans.

54. This was Kleomenes. It seems from the record that these Three Masters were Eldon (the U.M.), Kleomenes, and either the Priest of Anubis or Kha'm-uast. However, in the light of recently received inforniation it is obvious that the topic is far more complex than I have suggested, and that I have certainly erred on the side of simplicity. Hopefully, this will be amplified in due course.
55. See his essay, *The Old Religion,* which contains a section of that name.
56. Griff.

The Old Religion

by Charles Seymour

A Study of the Symbolism used in "Woman's Mysteries"

PART 1
INTRODUCTION

*Fate that is given to all men partly shaped,
Is ours to alter daily till we die.*
—John Masefield

These articles are a study in imagery. They have been written round the results of experiments (carried out by some of the senior members of this Fraternity in group meditation) upon the use of ancient Pagan symbols. These experiments had for their objective the linking up of memories dormant in the subconscious minds of the members of those meditation cups with ancient cult memories that still live in the subconscious mind of the Great Mother of all-that-exists on this planet.

Most of the members of these groups have, in the past, served at the altars of Pagan Religions and have met, face to face, the Shining Ones of the forests and the mountains, of the lakes and the seas. Such memories never died, either *Here* or *Yonder*, and they live because of their power or, shall it be said, their vital energy. They are *Within* man's memory, as well as *Without* him in the memory of our Great Mother, who is called the Lady of Nature, the Bona Dea, the Magna Mater, Isis.

In the course of these experiments it was discovered that if any one of the members of a group had in the past a strong contact with a particular cult at a certain period that individual, by means of a special technique, could communicate these memories to others, and could link them with the cult memories that still lie within the Earth memories of Isis as the Lady of Nature, that term being used in the sense that Fechner used it.

At first difficulties, contradictions and disappointments were many. It was almost impossible to distinguish between fancy and the results obtained by the imagination trained magically. Then, as the result of years of work carefully recorded, a system of cross-checking grew up and in the experimental work of those groups a reasonable degree of probability was obtained. One discovery was made that cleared up many contradictions. Religions change their status. Bergson's philosophical concept of life as an ever-becoming applies to religions, to the Gods, both great and small, as well as to an individual man. Also every man's concept of a God is an ever-becoming, even when that man proclaims that his God is Being or the very Essence of Being. Man creates his own Gods.

From this conception of religions as changing without cessation (Bergson's dictum—*Je change sans cesse*) gradually (for us) grew up the idea of the Religions of the High-roads, and the Religions of the By-roads, an interesting theme that will be developed in more detail later. It will be sufficient to point out here that most great religions start in their youth as religions of the by-road. In maturity they become one of the great religions of the high-road, and in old age they return to the obscurity of the by-road. Yet strange as this statement may sound it is in the cults of the by-ways that power (not material power however) is greatest.

The members taking part in these experiments have in the past served at the altars of these cults of the by-ways. And, again and again, life after life, to most of us, there comes the necessity for making the choice between the popular religion of the high-road and the religion of the by-road, despised and rejected of men.

A study of the history of religion shows that the way of heresy usually is the way of the by-road, and since the Prince of Peace came the by-road has only too often been the high-road to the stake or to the gallows. Before the Prince of Peace came history tells us that cults and religions often changed their status. For example at one time the cults of Isis and Osiris were religions of the high-road. Times changed, and the cult of Isis became the cult of the simpler folk living in the village and the country. To use a modern term the religion of Isis became pagan, that is the religion of the paganus or country folk. Still later Isis-worship once again became fashionable and she developed into the divine ruler of most of the Mediterranean civilization. Isis today lives on in the modern cult of the Virgin Mother of God, rightly beloved by certain sections of Christianity.

The feminine cults or Woman's Mysteries when working with the ancient moon symbolism are, even today in so-called Christian England, exceedingly potent as a means for obtaining and using the "energies" of the Inner Worlds on what the Qabalists call the level of Yesod. But this aspect of life is, and usually remains, a *terra incognita* so far as the rich, the prosperous, and the happy are concerned. Isis was, and still is, the Divine Consolatrix. The powers of Isis are often to be found manifesting through the old hag in the hut—they are not very often given to the fashionable woman in her town house.

It is easier to get in touch with the Isis power by tapping the memories that pertain to a period when the Isis cult belonged to the religions of the by-way, when it was neglected by the wealthy, the educated and the hierarchical classes who lived in or near the great Egyptian towns. This too is a theme that will be developed later when dealing with the old conflict between Patriarchy and Matriarchy. For it is *the* Woman that holds the keys of the inner planes for *a* man. If you want to pass the Cumean Gates you must become as a little child and a woman must lead you. You must find your Deiphobe, you must turn up the by-way that leads over the wild heather-clad heaths, you must pass through the forests, you must sacrifice to the "Goddess Three-wayed," if you would reach the "Cave in the Mountains."

"*Cherchez la femme!*" has a hidden meaning which is known only to the initiate who understands the significance of Omar Khayyam's lament:

There was a door to which I had no key,
There was a veil past which I could not see.

It was Deiphobe, daughter of Glaucus, priestess of Phoebus, and of the Goddess Three-wayed who, for King Aeneas, opened the keyless door and drew the veil that hides life from death, and death from Life.

Chapter I
The Cave In the Mountain

In lives that now belong to the distant past most of those who today seek to leave the broad highways of the orthodox World Religions and to adventure along the various by-paths that lead to the Cave in the Mountain have served at altars belonging to Woman's Mysteries. The key to these mysteries is only to be found in the dark cave that lies in a wooded ravine just beneath a tree-crowned summit,

Today after some fifteen hundred years of exclusion woman is once again beginning to take her rightful part in Religion. Here Religion must not be confused with the idea of Sectarianism: for when this word is used in these articles it denotes something that is wider than any single sect such as Buddhism, Hinduism, Christianity or Mohammedanism.

In the past of long ago Woman held the Keys of the Kingdom of Life. *De jure* she holds them today. Her womb admits man to physical life; woman's greater aptitude for psychism admits man to a religious life that is a conscious communion with inner, subtler realms that are supraphysical. Before the darkness that enveloped Europe at the fall of the Roman Empire came, woman was recognized as the holder of the Key of Life and the Key of Death. As a priestess her position was then equal to that of any male priest. In much earlier times it may well have been superior for matriarchy was prior to patriarchy. *De facto* woman still holds these Keys, for man has not as yet sought to take upon himself the pangs of physical childbirth, though he has successfully managed to claim any worldly profits that may accrue from spiritual rebirth.

During the period of Matriarchy the woman was the head of the family and the children knew who was their mother, but the mother selected her mates, she owned the property and so was not economically a dependent. Often she was the nominal if not the actual ruler of the State, the tribe or the village. The men hunted and fought, the woman kept the home fires burning. They were essentially the priestesses of the sacred fire. And from what is guessed at by anthropologists and by those who make a comparative study of religion it would seem that woman's real power then lay in the fact that she was not only the *de facto* but also the *de jure* ruler in religion.

Today in Christian lands there is a curious superstition or a tabu that woman as the weaker sex or vessel cannot be competent to act as a full member of a priesthood. But, in the various religions of the by-roads such as New Thought, Spiritualism, and the many other -isms that have sprung up in America and Europe during the last hundred years or so, woman is slowly yet surely being trained to take once again in religion the position that rightfully belongs to her: for woman spiritually is the stronger sex. She is not as some of the Christian sects have so often taught either a "vessel of wrath" or "a snare for a pious man." By turning aside into the by-paths of religion, woman is gradually learning to use spiritual power. The power, or shall we say the energy of the inner planes, is now being placed at her disposal. She is now, through practice, beginning to realize that her power as the prophetess, the healer, the seeress, the sibyl and above all as the pythoness is, very often, stronger than the power of the male priest.

(It must here be added that the ideal is the harmonious teamwork of a male and a female of equal or nearly equal training and development.)

The Christian ministers complain of the weakness of organized religion in England. Is this not due to the fact that in England most of the organized sects are unpolarized and without rhythm? Many churches and chapel have an atmosphere that can hardly be distinguished from that of a lecture hall. Are not most of the clergy well-informed scholars who strive to become good organizers? Do they not wish to pose as the defenders and administrators of the social tabus that pertain to the Law of the Herd rather than aspire to the mantle of the prophet and the seer? Even the feminine garments in which the priestly castes robe themselves when officiating have failed to give to their teachers and pastors that spiritual intuition, sympathy and understanding which is in its highest form so typically feminine.

Nevertheless it is freely admitted that the great religions of the high-roads have their part to play in civilization, and a very important one it is. For not only do they shepherd the very ignorant sheep along a broad and safe track, but they also act as a heavy (and a very necessary) brake upon the wheels of human progress. Being rich organizations they are naturally conservative and so are a guard against anarchy. The modern ship of state is often a very crazy vessel, and organized religions make excellent ballast.

The word Druid comes from the old Irish *drui*, a magician. Druidism, among the ancient Gauls and Britons, was not an unpolarized system. There were Druidesses who were prophetesses, and also magicians in their own right. That great authority Professor Rhys seems to think that Druidism in England and Gaul was derived from pre-Celtic and non-Aryan races (*Chambers' Encyclopedia*, Volume IV, page 96). If this surmise be correct then in Druidism we have a continuation of that ancient practice of the OLD RELIGION in which the man and the woman worked harmoniously as a psychic unit. This is the marriage which is made in heaven, the marriage in the mysteries, which man cannot put asunder.

In ancient Egypt the priestess held a highly honored place until religious degeneration set in about 1200 B.C., when the priesthood of the sect that was then dominant seized temporal power and became politicians rather than prophets. The priestesses became the singing women of the Temple at a time when a gorgeous ritual took the place of conscious magical working. The Egyptian religions had entered upon that stage of ever-becoming which is usually marked by an attempt to compensate for failing spiritual *force* by increase of ritualistic *forms*. They were suffering from spiritual arthritis, and there are some today who are afraid that Christianity as an organization is suffering from this disease of the aged.

As regards the Christian sects this fear may or may not be well founded. But as regards Religion, as distinguished from Sectarianism, there seems to have come about in England a sort of spiritual rejuvenation which is the reverse of the process described in the last paragraph.

Throughout the British Isles there has dawned slowly but surely during the last fifty years a Celtic revival. To a great extent, certainly in Ireland, woman, as a sex, has been responsible for the headway that has been made. Her contribution may not have been as public and spectacular as that of some of the male supporters of the Celtic movement, but it has been more effective, because as the mother in the home, as the teacher in the school, as the psychically stronger sex, woman has, as it were, provided the energy, while man has provided her energy with suitable religious and political forms.

In the group soul of the English peoples the subconscious content is very largely Celtic and this statement will be enlarged upon later and reasons will be adduced to support it. From the psychological point of view as taught in the mystery schools the conscious mind of man is considered to be predominantly male while the subconscious mind is considered to be largely female. The subconscious mind is, as is well known, a storehouse of emotional power. It is the source of that energy which drives a man into action. It might almost be called the human power house. In the same way the generating station for the power that animates the group soul of any nation lies in its subconscious. If the argument that has been put forward is historically and actually sound then the driving power of the English race lies in the Keltic potentialities of its group soul.

The immediate task of the womanhood of the British Isles is to make manifest these Keltic potentialities. If this is to be done then the best and the wisest of the womanhood of England, Scotland and Wales will have to turn away from the highway of an Ultra-respectable Orthodoxy. When the Emperor Julian died on the field of battle that Cause that (from the religious aspect) enslaved woman triumphed. For the early fathers, who were often but half-crazed sex-maniacs, woman was the chosen vessel of Satan. In their ignorance of psychology and fanaticism they strove to kill out of life joy and to destroy beauty. For them it was wrong to be happy. To be beautiful was to be evil; even artistic perfection was but a snare of the Evil One.

Today, if woman is to regain in religion the honored place she once so worthily held, she must turn up the by-way that leads through the woods, over the wild heaths, to "The Cave in the Mountain." There and there only will she gain the freedom that once was hers. There, through learning the wisdom that is taught in the Cave in the Mountain, will she regain her ancient power, her religious freedom, and the spiritual prestige which is hers because she is spiritually the stronger and intuitively the wiser sex.

Man creates theologies; Woman is Religion. This is true only if you feel religion to be man's link between the physical state of consciousness and those inner states of consciousness which pertain to realms that are more subtle than this material one. Of course if religion for you means the man-made dogmatics of comforting sects then woman is but man's helpmeet, i,e. one who is fit to help *him!*

"A wife to help your ends, in her no end..." as E. B. Browning so aptly describes the situation in "Aurora Leigh."

In the realms of religion man, if left to himself, is only too often content to remain in a bog that is named Psychic Research.

Deiphobe, daughter of Glaucus, put the matter very neatly to King Aeneas when she said impatiently: "Non hoc ista sibi tempus spectacula poscit." ("Now is no time that commands staring at sights, as you stare.")

If a man wishes to pass the Cumaean Gates he must first leave the highways of religion and seek the by-ways that run steeply upwards through the woods of the Good Three-wayed. But let him not forget as he enters Her woods that a woman must lead him if he wishes to pass through the Cumaean Gates; for Cumae is, for us, a western land of death and of rebirth, The Druids taught this in the story of Connla and the Lady of the Sidhe. Jung explains it in his preface to the *Secret of the Golden Flower*. Practical experience in group meditation confirms its truth. It takes two, a positive and a negative, to make an efficiently functioning psychic unit.

PART II
THE HIGH-ROAD

If one makes a comparative study of religions, if one can sympathize with the good that is undoubtedly in each and in all of them, if one can understand that the weaknesses so apparent in all religions and in all sects are due to human frailties, one can learn much that is outside the comprehension of a man who sees all religions as vestigal. The great religions, dwindling and degenerate as they may appear from the points of view of modern psychology and of modern science, are something more than the vestiges of an earlier civilization, even if their outward forms and pompous pretensions are but monuments of a dead and gone ever-becoming.

These great religions are almost invariably governed by old men living in a scholastic past that has been deserted by the living and vigorous manhood of today. They have forgotten Bergson's dictum—*Je change sans cease*. They may sing "Change and decay in all around I see," but they forget that change and decay are but the outward symbols of an inner ever-becoming; and ever-becoming is the essential principle that governs all life and all progress in manifestation. Existence is but an ever-becoming.

Religion is greater than any or all religions for it is the essential principle that stands behind then all. Religion has no need of any god. It is man who needs a god in order to get in touch with his religion. In other words God is a figment of a man's imagination which enables him to link up in his own microcosmic mind the Seen and the Unseen, the Here and the Yonder of the Macrocosm. "No man hath seen God at any time" said a Great one; "No God exists" is one of the great teachings of all the ancient mystery schools; but neither of these sayings can be taken literally for they are incomplete. It is only the Bona Dea that is seen of man. It is She who has said: "I am all that was, is, and shall be, I am Isis of the many names; I am She that exists." The multicolored tapestry of life is woven between two pillars, the silver and the black; and so far as man is concerned it is he, himself, who is Tao, the ever-becoming, the way between Boaz and Jachin.

Again, an unbiased study of religions will reveal the fact that at all times and in all places known historically the religions of the high road have been among the most profitable commercial enterprises known to man. To its astute devotees such a religion offers golden rewards in cash in this earthly life, and it also issues post-dated checks to be cashed in the heavenly life. The ancient temples were the schools and universities at which the professional classes were educated for the civil services. They were also, in many cases, the great national banking centers. Their revenues ware immense and they were often too strong for the monarch to humble. The religions of the high road have in the past offered to the religious Napoleon the quickest and often the easiest way to temporal power. Some of the ancient religious inscriptions of Syria have now been deciphered. Their language is strangely like that of the Jewish Bible. And from them it is not very difficult to discover that the common phrase: "And the Lord said" really might be translated "And the priests wanted." This state of affairs held good even in England until the sixteenth century, as the story of Cardinal Wolsey shows.

The religions of the high roads cater also for those religious soldiers of fortune who are able and willing to hire themselves out for rewards given both here and hereafter. These men police this broad and gently sloping highway, and they have power to protect and to punish those who march along it. The rank and file are those who are unable or unwilling to think for themselves, as well as those who obey the herd instinct and who fear to face the unknown or the unusual. There is a tremendous sense of security and of fellowship to be found in the pomp and ceremony of a great religious caravan on the march. Psychologically speaking, it is an undoubted truth that when after due preparation all shout together, the Halls of Jericho must fall down.

Again, the religions of the high road in return for compliance offer security. Weary man longs for security, and cares little whether it be the security of Nirvana or a Paradise thronged with eager houris, or just a heaven with the appropriate music.

The high road religions of today are guarded, guided and governed by males dressed in female clothing—a subconscious tribute to a long forgotten she when in religion woman was the guardian, the guide and the governor. So strong are these long buried subconscious memories that today God has been given a mother—the Virgin Mary, she who once was Isis, Astarte, Astor-eth, Diana the ever-virgin, but not ever-chaste, queen of Heaven and Star of the Sea. The Great Mother of All has been ousted by the male rulers of most of the official religions of modern Europe. She no longer EXISTS for them. But in religion the common people are wiser than their leaders, and Diana of Yesod, whether entitled the "Ever Virgin Mother" or "The Compassionate Harlot" is the actual source of the energy that animates the only branch of the Christian Vine that today shows much real vigor.

Woman is a man's inspiration, Woman is the *energia* (actual being as a potency or activity) of the Magna Mater. Woman is man's link with the Goddess that EXISTS. For, as the Ancient Mysteries rightly taught:
$\quad\quad\quad\quad$ NO GOD EXISTS

The By-Road

As Dr. Harding has so clearly pointed out in "Woman's Mysteries" the worship of the Moon Goddess was an education of the emotional life by means of a series of initiations. An initiation ceremony may be acted upon the physical stage in a dramatized myth, but initiation *per se* is an education of the emotions and its field of experience is in the subconscious mind. Its culmination (which the ancients called the summons of the God or Goddess) take place sometimes before, sometimes not until long after the physical plane ceremonies have ended, For these latter are only intended to stir the *heart* of the man, that is, his subconscious mind. Initiation is not a ceremony, it is the beginning of a new way of using the mind.

But in addition to their educational import these ancient Moon mysteries were meant to be a cure for emotional starvation. It has been said that emotional starvation is the cause of much of the neurotic troubles that are so common today in England. If one makes a habit of watching the expressions of the people one sees in the parks, trains and buses one will soon notice how rare it is to see among the humans who are over thirty a face that is happy when in repose, or when its owner is relaxed and off guard. This tendency is far more noticeable in England than in France, Italy or Germany. Perhaps it is the religion that has produced the English Sunday as the national expression of a joyful thankfulness for God's mercies that is largely responsible for this confirmed melancholy of the middle-aged of the nation.

Now these articles, as a study in moon symbols, are intended to show the reader a way to combat this national tendency of the middle-aged towards a settled habit of joylessness. If they are studied with care they will enable a self-initiation into the symbolism of the moon cult to take place. For by means of a system of the training of the image-making faculty, subconscious memories that have been gradually accumulated over a long series of lives are stirred up or brought into consciousness.

As a study in imagery and in order to practice "composition of place" as described by Ignatius Loyola, build in detail the following word pictures as if you were preparing them in your mind before setting them out on the stage of a theater. Picture clearly each of the characters in the various scenes and then try to live yourself into these scenes. AS IF you were one of the principal characters, taking in the first place the character that most of all appeals to you.

This study is meant as an exercise in practical meditation upon the information that has so far been given you. Invent as you please little turns and twists to make the scenes and the characters live more clearly. But at the same time it must be remembered that as mental and emotional training this type of meditation is potent for good or ill. It embodies much of the practical technique that is used in this mystery school, and if persevered in, it will bring the student out of the highway and on to the byway that rightly is his.

Let it never be forgotten that a man is what *subconsciously* he pictures himself to be, for, as Coue discovered, the subconscious wish is more potent than the conscious intention.

Exercise I

Along the border of a wide, green and fertile plain rises a range of high hills with many steep jungle-covered spurs that are separated by deep ravines which run far up into a mountainous country that lies to the North. Picture range after range rising between you and the perpetual snows that glisten and sparkle upon the far distant northern horizon. Vivid green are the lower slopes that come down into this rich and well-watered plain. Brown and russet are the bare crags. Blue is the sky that overhangs the peaks, their ridges, and the rivers to which they give rise. Bright are the colors of this hidden land that abuts on silver and purple Yesod.

Across this plain and up the widest of these blue-misted valleys runs a broad road built carefully to a very gentle gradient. The eye cannot see whence it comes; whither it goes is also unknown. Its beginning and ending are incomprehensible for they are lost in that illusion which the conscious mind calls time and space. And the reason why you and the rest of humanity have to traverse this road is beyond human understanding while it is still in the flesh. All that anyone can surmise is that having climbed those far-off snow-clad heights, man sheds his humanity and prepares to take upon himself Divinity. Even now potentially man is as the Elohim, and we know not what we shall be then.

Having carefully constructed in the mind's eye this brightly colored picture, continue for several days to build and rebuild it until as soon as you turn your attention upon it as a completed picture it will spring into being within you. Next proceed to elaborate this picture, then analyze your reactions to it and to the pictures that rise from your subconscious mind as you cogitate upon it, noting most particularly the colors in which the latter show themselves. These latter as your own personal contribution to the process are very important, for your mental *tone* will color them brightly or otherwise.

* * *

The road itself is crowded with a long serpent-like column that slowly moves northward towards those distant snows. This column is composed of men, women and children. It is humanity, in the process of evolution, seeking experience usually, as the Buddha taught, through self-inflicted suffering.

The Great Mother has children other than humans. And winding up other valleys that lie to the right and left of that up which climbs humanity are yet other roads. These too are broad and gentle of slope. Up them, in a manner similar to humanity, toil your brethren of the other evolutions. They are hidden from sight by steep jungle-clad ridges and humanity as a whole knows nothing of them.

There are however individuals who have left the main column on the high road and have climbed the mountainside to the white temple of Diana Three-wayed. These individuals on that sacred tree-clad mountaintop have in "The House of Gold" received from the Priestess of Phoebus the gift of clear vision. It is however a vision which is not just mere seeing, for it is a gift which enables the one who has received it worthily to become aware of many non-human aspects of the One Divine Life of the Many-Breasted One. For She too is seeking experience by means of an ever-becoming. Nothing in that Divine Life which ever flows from Her sacred black and white breasts is stable. Everything that has life and can reflect upon itself can ascertain this one thing for itself—*Je change sans cease*. Her life is change and with cessation of change Her life that comes out of the YONDER disappears and its form fades out from our view HERE.

Now picture yourself as moving upon that road, a unit of that column. Imagine clearly what you can see and feel. Next try to catch hold of the thoughts that would fill your mind as suddenly and upon an impulse you step out of the caravan on to the grassy edge and watch it roll slowly past you. *You* are now a spectator but *they* are busy living each their own life in that column. It may come as a shock to you to notice that you are now outside the herd. You are alone, and it is said that the lone wolf away from the pack, as a rule, perishes quickly.

Is that to be your fate?

* * *

That sudden impulse which made you, at a certain spot, step out from the main column is the stirring of old memories. And it is well to pause here and realize this stage with the utmost thoroughness for it is here that the soul takes up once again THE PATH. It is here that it is necessary to learn to be alone yet not lonely. It is here that one surmises that for each one of us life holds a special type of experience, something has to be done but no one else can do it for one. It is here that people begin to look askance at the one who watches the herd from outside the line of its march. Then there are the guardians of the caravan, men dressed in female garments to whom the caravan pays reverence, calling them its priests. These guardians look at you uneasily. The unwise guardian seeks to head you back into the column, the wise guardian watches to see that you do not seduce others who are in his charge.

See yourself watching and waiting expectantly. Then a little later feel yourself wanting to rejoin the column and wondering what all the pother is about—for nothing happens—just yet.

* * *

Loneliness and boredom are always the primary experiences of the path and it is well to be prepared for them. As you gaze about you, wondering why you obeyed that sudden impulse, you see a narrow path leading up the hillside. There is a notice at its entrance—"No Road. Trespassers will be Persecuted." This path is forbidden, and immediately a black-clad guardian warns you that to travel by this road means madness, disgrace, perdition, hell for ever and ever, etc.

Now if you believe in Hell, or in a personal God or in an equally personal Devil, or if you believe that any savior can save your soul for you, then you had better hurry back to the main body. You may not attempt that by-road in safety until you realize clearly and fully that each man is his own savior. You are your own priest or priestess; no one, except yourself, can stand between you and your own divinity. Potentially you are divine, but actually you are as yet only human. This is the age of the age of the free man who carrying his own burdens on his own shoulders strides manfully across the sky. The age of Aquarius is to be the age that will free man from the bogies of an outworn superstition.

If free from these superstitions, then press boldly up the path until a small plateau forming a halting place that overlooks the main road is reached. This plateau, the first stage leading to the Path, is occupied by a wrangling crowd that disputes vigorously, and its members are as dogmatic and fanatical over their particular doctrines as the guardians of the highway. For they have not yet discovered that the disputations are not really on the Path that leads to an inner freedom.

There is a steep track leading up the hill from this plateau and it is closed by a gate. Its Guardian asks you what you know. He does not want your beliefs. He wants to know your knowledge, if you have any—and until you can distinguish between belief and knowledge you may not pass him.

You will also be asked your motive for seeking this particular bypath. And the only answer that will open the gate is:

"I desire to know in order to serve."

Any other motive is considered to be impure for only the pure in subconscious intention (this the ancients called the heart) can, with safety, invoke the powers of the Bona Dea who was and still is the Celtic Goddess Anu or Annis, and Dana: Isis of many names.

Having passed the first gate a long and steep climb leads to another plateau, which appears to be empty, except for a small bench which is just long enough to seat two. Sitting on this bench one can see the column far below; its advance guard is beyond view and its rear guard is not within view.

"All will reach their destination—in time," says a voice. And then a stranger draws attention to a notice board marked with an arrow that points straight up the mountain, and bearing the inscription: "To the Cave on the Mountain."

If you questioned him, the stranger will say that in this cave is to be found Wisdom: the Wisdom of the Cave in the Mountain. He will also explain that this path is called the path of death in life. In any case he will point out that this hill cannot be climbed alone; the wisdom of the Cave in the Mountain is not for any man who is a solitary: "for that which is solitary is barren."

This stranger will tell you to return to the High Road and to get a woman, who if she is the woman of your choice and you are the man of her choice may be an unknowing Eve or a very knowing Lilith. It matters not in actual practice which she is for women are intuitive and adaptable, and usually take to the routine of THE PATH more quickly, though perhaps less thoroughly than a man.*

But back to the high road you must go until you have found what is in truth your better self. Anima and Animus must be MATED, so that the ONE becomes the TWO and the TWO *are* FOUR.

---

* Women readers must simply adapt this as appropriate.

Chapter 2
The Watcher at the Ford of the Moon

At the end of each day when he goes to bed a would-be Magus as a symbolic action should wipe his brow with the back of his hand and say to himself: "Has my brow today been wet with mental sweat?" This little rite has value not only as a reminder of the great work that has been undertaken, but also as a mental and emotional catharsis, for it has been truly said that the chief temptation of any would-be magus is creation without mental toil.

Now these articles, although they are elementary, are not intended to set forth any new teaching yet involve an intensive and somewhat unusual mental effort. Their object is, by the use of symbols and imagery, to enable the reader to educe from the content of his own subconscious mind much that has hitherto lain fallow. A technique is set forth first by giving the principles on which it is based, and then by showing in an actual meditation how such a technique is to be used; the result should be that by visualizing each exercise carefully and accurately a freeing of the subconscious mind takes place, the dark prison in which the frustrated emotions are shut up is opened, the life force flows OUT with greater freedom and mental energy is thus released.

This technique has been used for some years. The records of its successes and its failures cover many thousands of pages, and they represent many hours of both group and solitary meditation, for the students who have taken part in them can be counted by the score. It is advisable, at first, to stick closely to the methods as given here, but later on when more proficient each student should work out for himself the technique that suits him best, for Moon Mysteries have widely varying stories to tell to the many different kinds of souls that seek their initiation in Yesod, the Sphere of the Moon, where the Moon Goddesses are each a triple figure—dark and destructive in waning, bright and constructive in waxing, integrating and perfective at the full. And this is true psychologically as well as cosmically.

One of the first difficulties that an attentive and philosophically minded student will meet when meditating in this sphere is that of the "Observer." And it may console him to know that modern science has also come up against this difficulty, and considers the Observer to be an obstacle in its search for that external reality which is the goal of science. To obviate this difficulty the modern scientist has invented a puppet which it calls a standard observer, who is supposed to be the normal individual. Unfortunately, as the records of past controversy show, the normal observer is nearly always the person or persons who agree with the individual who for the time being holds the platform. Those who disagree are often called abnormal if not something worse.

If Bergson and the great sages of Ancient India are right and if everything as they teach is changing and developing as it evolves, then this normal individual is nothing that is actual: certainly he is nothing that is real: he is not even, so to speak, non-existent; non-evolving human stagnation. For neither in life nor in death is there stagnation. He is merely a modern convenience for use in controversy. A handful of dust to be cast in the eyes of the less highly educated man-in-the-street.

The initiates of old in both the West and the East were well acquainted with this problem of the observer. They called him (or it!) the Watcher at the Threshold, or at the Gate. They also called him the Genius, the Higher Self, the Horus Within, and a number of other titles. And they gave this Watcher a very active role in their systems of meditation, while modern materialistic science strives to drive their "Observer" as far as possible into the background of scientific consciousness, and quite rightly makes of him a nonentity, which is what he is, though not in the sense that the scientists mean.

This reversal of role is simple to understand: science seeks to know an outer reality as it exists independent of any human observer. The Mysteries sought (and still seek) in their first stage—which is all that concerns us at present—to understand an inner reality as it exists within the mind of the human observer, for their motto is "Know thyself." Therefore the student must realize that the technique of modern science and that of meditation have as little effect on each other as two trains would have after each has started from the same station in opposite directions.

For science the watcher is of no great importance except as a possible source of error, and thus he is merely a nuisance. For the Mysteries, however, the Watcher is the primary objective.

Meditation in Moon Mysteries may be defined briefly as the pursuit of inner active objectives. And in some of the quieter moments of deep meditation, which is an inner process that is not externalized, one becomes at times very strongly aware of an observer or watcher. He (or it!) almost seems to be something or someone that is external to oneself. Some authorities consider this watcher to be an entity external to that Unity which is A MAN. Others consider him to be the higher self that forever dwells in the most secret recesses of a man's being. Really it is the conscious finding of this "hidden one" that is important; the labeling is actually of little value, and it does not matter if he be YOU or NOT-YOU.

In this school we think of Man as a unity which consists of a cosmic atom that is unmanifest and has its home in spheres that are uttered beyond all human conception. This cosmic atom or monad, as some name it, has no beginning and no ending as limited human reason conceives of these two things. It sends forth from its own essential being what is called a higher self or genius, an individuality, which is an ever-changing entity that evolves through the immensely long period that a man has to spend in the bosom of the Great Mother in order to gain his full quota of experience as a unit of the human race.

This individuality or genius in its turn sends forth from itself a portion of its own substance which is called the lower self, and this latter is that natural phenomenon which is known during earth life as Mr. Jones or Miss Smith. And let it be said (you can disagree if you like for no proof is possible) that as Mr. Jones and Miss Smith you incarnate. But Miss Smith and Mr. Jones only *incarnate*. THEY NEVER REINCARNATE. It is the higher self of each one of us that seeks reincarnation by incarnating A LITTLE BIT at a time. And the non-incarnating portion of Miss Smith and Mr. Jones is the Watcher, the Observer, the Guardian at the Gate, etc.

The older, wiser and more perfectly human a soul seems to be, the greater is the extent to which the individuality is able to shine through its temporarily incarnated personality.

Really man is of course an integral unity, though there are some that would deny this statement, but for the purpose of empirical instruction it is customary to think of him in this threefold fashion.

Thus it can be said that the personality is the unit of evolution for the period of a single incarnation on the material plane Earth; it is the Miss Smith or Mr. Jones of everyday waking conscious life. The individuality is the unit of evolution for that immensely long period which the Hindus and Theosophists call a Manvantara, or "A Day of the Gods" as it is termed in the Western tradition. It (the individuality) is our Virgin Mother, the immeasurably ancient, very wise, infinitely patient Watcher at the Gates of the Unseen: the Judge who has to be faced at Death.

The cosmic atom or monad is the unit of a period of evolution so immense and of such divine, super-human potentialities that we call it Unmanifest and label it indescribable.

The above is a simple and convenient empirical system for beginners. There is no need for the student to believe in it. It may be, perhaps one percent accurate, and it is almost certainly 99 percent inadequate, but if used intelligently as a convenient working hypothesis, which is all that it pretends to be, it will enable the student to cooperate with his own far wiser "Watcher on the Threshold." To learn how to use this system is the first step that has to be taken when on the path of the Moon Mysteries that leads to An-na-Rea—the Ford of the Lord of the Moon according to the Celtic Mystery teaching.

After meditation—but not during it—when analyzing and comparing and during the process of recording results, let the reasoning spectator of things noticed in meditation watch carefully for "The Observer" and the part that he has played: also watch the inside of your own soul and see WHO has been there.

Now having studied these brief and elementary points with regard to the art of meditation, it is necessary for the student to think very carefully about the relationship between the Watcher and that which is called the Universal Subconsciousness, the Collective Unconscious.

Behind the physical body that each of us inhabits during this our earthly life is a purposive entity that may in some far distant eon transcend the limitations of human intelligence and begin a new stage of evolution as a Divine Intelligence.

In the subconscious depths of the human mind lie hidden all the experiences of Humanity, for there is the subconsciousness of Humanity as well as the subconscious of a human being. Man is an integral part of that greater whole which is called the human race, and the theory that there is a racial subconsciousness common to all humanity is fairly generally accepted because it explains much that is not easy otherwise to understand.

Behind this physical earth that we and other evolutions inhabit during physical existence is a purposive entity that is divine: a non-human entity that is intelligent and evolves through the expression of its own essential nature. As man evolves through an ever-becoming, so also this entity, which we call the Great Mother, Great Isis, Dana, and by many other names, evolves by means of an ever-becoming. The law of ceaseless change is the law of Her being just as it is the law of that much smaller entity—Man.

This does not mean that the Divine functions according to limitations that are set by human reason. The functions are analogous, which is not the same as identical.

"As above, so below" is a very ancient maxim which in effect means that man is a microcosm of the macrocosm. Man's mind is an integral portion of that larger whole which is called the Universal Mind: Man's subconsciousness is an integral portion of a much greater universal subconsciousness; man's memory is an integral part of a much wider universal memory in exactly the same way that man's life is an integral and indivisible part of the Universal Life, and man's material body is an integral and indivisible part of the material body of the Earth Entity.

This as a method of description is, of course, pure anthropomorphism, and quite rightly it should be condemned as such, for anthropomorphism as an unreflecting way of thinking is deplorable. But in meditation, especially in its deeper levels, anthropomorphism works most successfully. And until you have found empirically some other and better method of working, you will have to be content with this anthropomorphic method if you wish to have life and power in your work. Of course, if meditation subjects are purely abstract ideas or just ethical, this question will not arise, because imagination is not being exercised.

Nevertheless, practical experience, which has been carefully recorded immediately, will soon teach that any real depth of communion with the Great Mother with Isis as Nature, is only possible on the condition that one works with Her as if She were like unto man: though of course without mankind's all too obvious mental, emotional, and spiritual limitations.

Many years of experience has taught that if you want to meditate in a manner that will spiritualize and intensify as well as recreate your mental life you have, in actual practical work, to make use of the two following maxims *as if* they were true:

(i) "There is a Principle of Life which is universal; it fills all space and it is immanent in all forms. The substance of this Principle of Life is Mind."

The second maxim is its corollary:

(ii) "Man's mind is an integral portion of this Universal Mind."

If these two maxims are true, and practical experience seems to show that they work as if they were natural laws, then all idea of mental separateness is an illusion. All minds are joined together as integral parts of a complete whole. They are parts of the Universal Mind as waves are parts of the sea.

What the Gods have joined, let not human delusions tear asunder.

* * *

When a man is meditating with power, his mind is in action and affects its surroundings in this sea of Universal Mind-stuff in much the same way that the propellers of a ship churn the ocean through which it is passing. Steam sets the propellers working. Imagination fired by desire drives the human mind into purposive mental action. Imagination driven by desire is almost always stronger than mere reason; as Ignatius taught: "ACT AS IF."

It is well to remember that just as a man's mind is an integral part of the mind of Nature, i.e. of Isis as Mother Earth, so, in turn, Her mind is part of a still greater Mind that is in its own degree Universal, and so on ad infinitum. Be spacious in your outlook on infinity, remembering that speaking comparatively the cosmic outlook of an earthworm is probably but little less narrow than a man's outlook when compared with the Cosmic Consciousness of such a Divine Being as the Great Mother. After all, it is true that all knowledge is purely relative.

When contemplating the gifts of the Great Mother that are to be obtained through meditation it must be kept in mind once and forever that one's meditation is not done for one's own personal benefit. This life force must not be drawn upon selfishly, but only to enable the life of the Great Mother to flow more freely, to manifest more strongly. The object should be for each in his own small way TO ENABLE THE GREAT GODDESS TO LIVE MORE PERFECTLY THE EXPERIENCE SHE NEEDS FOR HER OWN DEVELOPMENT.

There is no need to accept these hypotheses as true, but better results are to be got in one's practical work if they be accepted and used as if they were true.

To obtain "cud" to be gently chewed during meditation it is necessary to accumulate facts and sound theories about such facts.

It would do no harm, if you are sufficiently mature in your religious development, to get that excellent book *Woman's Mysteries*, by Dr. Harding. It is a mine of information with regard to the Old Religion, which essentially was concerned with the "negative" feminine principle in Nature, that which the Qabalists call the Black Pillar of the Tree of Life, and the Hindus in Raja Yoga name AKASA. Note for example that the Jewish and Babylonian Sabbaths were observed at the quarters of the Moon, as were also the Egyptian *taboo* days which were sacred to Osiris considered as the Moon God. The Christian Sabbath is a Moon festival taken via Judaism from the Old Religion and on page 53 Dr. Harding has given some interesting theories that afford food for meditation if you can digest them.

The Celtic, Assyrian and Egyptian rulers at certain festivals wore horns which were emblematical of the horned moon. Cernunnos, the Horned One, is to be found all over western Europe as well as in England and Ireland. In Ireland he is called Buarainech—"Having the face of a cow," and is generally considered to be the All-father, the elemental god of night and death, while it is said that "his horns are the crescent moon, queen of night." (*The Irish Mythological Cycle* by Jubainville, page 218.)

Buar-ainech (father of the Irish triad Bress, Balor and Tethra who are as it were his doubles) is, even today, to be found in at least one of his old sanctuaries by those who know how to invoke him, and are able to worship him. But, as certain worthy and inquisitive dabblers found to their cost, not every one is prepared to stand before him and remain still in silent worship.

Like Cernunnos, Buar-ainech is connected with serpent worship, which is not, as so many ignorantly think, the worship of evil. The serpent stands in the Old Religion for the principle of Wisdom, and is no more evil than is Woman—no matter what in their delusions sex-crazy saints may say.

The modern man and woman owe a deep debt of gratitude to the great psychologists of this century who are freeing mankind from some of the insane terrors of religion. In terms of alchemy these psychologists are performing the first operation of SOLVE—the breaking down process of the Alchemical formula "SOLVE ET COAGULA."

Exercise II
At the Ford of the Moon

The man found his woman. As a modern Adam and Eve going back to THE GARDEN of the Great Mother, they left the second plateau above the High-way by a path that ran through a steep cleft in the hills and up onto a spur covered with rocks and dark juniper and small green thorn trees. There taking breath, they looked about them.

In front, but some little distance away, is open country, a wild broken heath-land, basking in a sunset glow of green and gold. Its shallow valleys are filled with a light mist of turquoise blue. Its heather-covered spurs slope gradually upwards to the crescent-shaped ridge of Drum-na-Rea, the Ridge of the Moon.

Behind them no portion of the broad High-road is to be seen, no sound of the tramping of weary feet upon its hard surface can now break the fairy-like silence of this green, grassy byway. The Alchemical operation of SOLVE has been carried out. A new land has been entered. The frontiers of the country of the High-way have gently closed behind them and strange by-roads lead down into the greater freedom of "The Oldest Land."

Below them is a shallow valley filled with green beech and oak woods that are slightly veiled in a faintly violet mist. The path turns down suddenly and steeply into this valley which it apparently crosses, for the narrow ribbon of the green by-way can be seen winding up the heath towards the center of the ridge of Drum-na-Rea.

After a pause the man, and the woman he has chosen to be his guide, leave the spur and turn down the path that enters the wood. Once within that warm, moist atmosphere it feels as if one had gone into another dimension of soft, green, translucent spaces: spaces that are very still and windless, yet they seem to reflect something that is vividly alive. One gets the impression of looking into the green and pale blue depths of a woodland pond that is reflecting the sky and the aliveness of the green leaves above its surface.

This is the fairy greenwood that surrounds An-na-Rea, the Ford of the Moon. It is lit by an inner light of brilliant fairy gold and green in which phantom-like forms appear only to disappear once attention is consciously directed upon them.

Actually nothing is heard, nothing is seen, but it feels as if many unseen Presences hoping for recognition are waiting just behind this veil of green stillness to greet these wandering from the

Broad High-way of everyday experience.

In spite of the utter absence of any visible form or movement, this wood appears to be pulsating with life. The trees are motionless in the early evening stillness, yet the Tree Folk, children of Dana, the Great Mother, are holding their evening revel. One is never quite sure, until it vanishes when one stares hard, whether a tree is really a so-called inanimate thing of wood and soft green leaves, or a vast, tenuous, brightly colored living elemental with an almost human-like form that seems to slip in and out of the imprisoning bark.

Laughing Dryads, if not watched too intently, seem to peep and peer with the curiosity and shyness of wild things from behind the thick boles of beech and oak; the ferns and bracken are alive with the smaller fairy folk all waiting for their playtime. Fauns with tiny knob-like horns people these green spaces that seem to close in upon one as if a wall of transparent, tenuous, very still water was preparing slowly and gently to pour through this wood which is now a fairy wood that is colored with the greenish starlight of Netzach, the sphere of the Elemental Gods—who are the Shining Ones that wear emerald green robes.

The note of this wood is that of friendliness, for all its dimly seen inhabitants are glad that this man and woman have come away from the hard glare of the great white highway into the softly shining greenness of the Celtic Twilight. All around are the children of other evolutions ready to greet these *accredited* newcomers as their Brethren. For, have they not also for their Divine Parent, the Great Mother, the Green Isis, ruler of the still, transparent, shadowy green woods and all that therein dwell:

> *Give to these children, new from the world,*
> *Silence and love;*
> *And the long dew-dropping hours of the night,*
> *And the stars above ...*

sings W. B. Yeats in "A Faery Song" sung by the people of faery over Diarmid and Grania in their bridal sleep under a cromlech.

On the short sward some little distance away stands Caoilte (pronounced Kilte), a royal figure with hair burning as if touched by a golden ray of sunlight. He is clad in green and gold with a spear in his hand and a rounded shield slung on his left arm. As Lord of the fairy wood he gives greeting, and then turns to the West. He passes down the road, saluted by all, for is he not the Prince of the Sidhe! He halts in a wide, open glade through which a deep stream glides silently and without ripple. In the brown of this clear bog-water is reflected the still sunlit evening sky as well as a great golden harvest moon. For this is the season when the moonlight and the twilight or early Autumn strive for mastery, the fairy time when "The Host is rushing 'twixt night and day."

This glade is called An-na-Rea, the Ford of the Moon. Caoilte points with his spear into the dark, shining depths and bids the pair of humans look therein. The man, his thoughts bent on climbing the distant hill whereon is the temple of the Goddess Three-wayed, sees but a long dark ridge mirrored in the still water, and the shimmering silver-shining rays of the round golden-silvery moon that is Her symbol. But the woman, more open to the fiery fairy magnetism that flows from the golden leader of the Host that is in Knock-na-Rea, has seen in its depths the glitter of the green and gold palaces of the Sidhe.

In a flash without breaking the still surface by even a single ripple, she has dived deep into the fairy pool and down, far down, into that fifth dimensional world which the Irish Celts called Tir-na-mbeo (the Land of the Ever-Youthful).

"Your guide has proved more clear of sight than you," explains Caoilte. "Yet look not behind you, but cross by the moonbridge if you can."

A white moon-mist gathers on the water: it swirls up into an arch and forms the moon bridge over An-na-Rea. Alone the crossing is made and the western bank is reached.

Caoilte has gone, but in his place is a woman of the Sidhe, holding a branch of silver-like blossoms.

Chapter 3
The Watcher: His Symbols and Symbol Systems

The process through which is developed an awareness of the "Watcher Within" is meditation.

The tools that are used in this process are symbols and symbol systems. These are usually borrowed from active existing systems or from the so-called dead religious systems of the childhood of man. These ancient systems however are not dead. They are merely quiescent in so far as the ordinary man is concerned. For those who make a comparative study of the psychology of Religion (not sectarianism) they are dormant like the sleeping princess in a fairy tale: but they can be awakened into an intense spiritual, mental and emotional activity when the right stimulus is given at the right time.

Professor Jung, in the chapters on the "Symbolism of the Mother and of Rebirth" and on "The Song of the Moth" in his valuable and suggestive book, *The Psychology of the Unconscious*, has set forth an almost inexhaustible supply of ideas that will repay careful and open-minded brooding upon in the quiet moments of meditation. But the prude and the bigot had better leave them alone. For as Paul of Tarsus wisely pointed out, strong meat is for the full-grown man. Babes—spiritual ones!—require feeding with carefully prepared pap, lest they feel unwell.

Meditation has been defined as "the pursuit of inner active objectives." From the point of view with which these articles are chiefly concerned these active objectives are symbols or systems of symbols. It may also be said with very fair accuracy that "a symbol is something that is used to represent or suggest that which is not capable of portraiture as an idea, a quality, state of action." (*Century Dict.*)

It is proposed to elaborate somewhat the ideas to which these two definitions give rise, partly because meditation as used in this Fraternity is something that differs in many important respects from ordinary religious or even ethical meditation: also because these articles are written for the beginner who worships in the outer court of the temple and not for those who work the sacred rites in the Sanctuary.

In theory both these definitions are inadequate, but in practice the beginner will find them sufficient for his needs, especially as he will soon discover that they are not nearly so simple as they appear on first reading.

For the moment let us consider that common symbol the Roman Numeral I. For a very large number of people I stands for one o'clock and is the symbol for lunch in most nicely regulated middle-class families. It therefore stands for an idea (food), a quality (appetite), a state (stomach empty) and finally the action of eating.

But, *per se* this Roman numeral which is on the face of most dining-room clocks, bears not the remotest resemblance to or has direct connection with any of these things. Its importance lies in the fact that we have become "conditioned" to this symbol and for this reason it has for us a special meaning.

Now "conditioning" is the first and the most important process in the art of using symbols. Unless you are conditioned to a symbol and can react to it either in an orthodox or unorthodox manner (it matters not which), it is not for you a symbol. For a symbol must bring to mind active qualities. It is not just a portrait.

A symbol may have many meanings and these may vary in different persons. Make the symbol ♀ which is but a circle above a cross. For the zoologist this means a female as opposed to ♂ a male. For the poet ♀ means a pleasant form of restlessness that usually attacks a young man in the early Spring of each year. Astronomers and astrologers use it for the planet Venus, but each gives to it a different content. The astronomer thinks of ♀ as a bright body in the sky. For the astrologer ♀ denotes certain tidal energies in an ever-flowing cosmic life-stream that comes from the Unmanifest source of all life.

It may be just as well to point out here, for it is an important point that is often forgotten, that the educated astrologers know well that the planet ♀ no more causes these cosmic tides than the Roman numeral I on the face of the clock in the dining room causes lunch. The immediate cause of lunch is the cook who remains, or should remain, so far as the dining-room clock is concerned, in a state of unmanifestation in another dimension—the kitchen .

If this idea be extended to other symbols and groups of symbols it soon becomes evident that the importance of a symbol lies in what you can learn about it. You can learn much from reading books, but you can learn a great deal more by turning over in quiet and regular meditation the knowledge you have already acquired from sources external to yourself.

Now meditation (as used in this Fraternity) in its early stages is a training in the art of using symbols. And the details of the examples and exercises which are given at the end of each chapter should be repeatedly studied with care for many days in succession for they are exercises that have been used with good results in both solitary and group meditation. Never forget that if you want thoroughly to become familiar with a symbol you must meditate upon it again and again and again. Follow the example of Napoleon who said "Read and re-read." His method of reading was really, as he himself has told us, a system for training his visualizing imagination, and his re-reading took the form of a visualizing meditation. A symbol is meant to be incubated over a considerable period if it is to be hatched out into action.

In pursuit of these inner active objectives it can be said truly that in most cases (i.e. for the ordinary individual) it is better to work strictly to a daily timetable, as well as to sit in a comfortable chair where the body is forgotten. Ten minutes daily methodical work done thus as a consciously directed exercise is usually worth ten times as many hours done without method when the whim to meditate is felt. Of course there are eccentrics who say they get wonderful results by violating all the above rules, even to meditating when standing on their heads. But such methods are unusual and even if effective for a few, are for the average Westerner abnormal.

These visualizing exercises seek to present the internal activities of the meditative life, and their repercussions upon the psychical makeup of the student, with a reasonable clarity and in such a way that he can understand with ease what is being done. Making a clear representation to another or even to oneself is not an easy thing to do, for the realities of the internal activities of meditation are not to be described by means of a language that is limited to objects in three dimensions. Such realities can only be described by means of analogy. For example the Moon is often used for the group soul of women as a class: then the moon is dynamic. Materially speaking, the moon in the sky is a passive ball of rock which as a cold dead sphere reflects the light of the sun. In the former case, though a three-dimensional language is used, one is not dealing with science nor with facts, but with delicate and all but intangible feelings and moods and yearnings that are peculiar to a group soul and to the individuals, who make up that group entity.

One talks of woods and bracken, of fords and ridges, and of horned moons, but it is the effect (upon the subconscious mind of the reader) that is produced by the inner substance or the essence of these material things *as holy places* that is being referred to here, and not just their three-dimensional externals that are so fully and carefully outlined. The outer symbol is described with what may seem to many an unnecessary wealth of detail, which is often repeated with intention, because it is by these means that subconscious feeling and emotion are stirred up. This deliberate repetition is an important part of the process and it should be studied carefully, for the subconscious always works in terms of picture consciousness and it is the representation of colors and sounds and smells that tug most effectively at the strings of its memory.

The symbol of the physical moon and certain color effects are described again and again. Not however in careless repetition, but deliberately, in order to stir up the energies of the sphere of Yesod that dwells in the soul of man as a microcosm of the macrocosm. The object is to call into activity the immensely dynamic and purposive inner nature of BOTH these spheres of sensation, for one is subjective and the other objective in a meditation. Here is the same idea as that of shattering a glass by the repeated sounding of its note. For the sphere of the moon within the sphere of sensation (subjective) of the soul of a man is directly linked to the moon sphere that is within the soul (objective) of the planetary spirit of this earth, and the physical moon is thus but the symbol of that cosmic tide which then acts upon man's subconscious moon-sphere. The rise of the tide in the North Sea will fill a London Dock that is many miles away from the coast but still in connection with the sea. And so it happens when the soul of a man is linked *consciously* with the soul of our Great Mother—Nature—Her tidal flow becomes our tidal flow—Her life is consciously felt in our life.

Once you have thoroughly mastered this system you can begin to build these images in your own way, and thus put the stamp of your own individuality into all your work. For if this is not done you can never become a true magus and nothing that is real can be achieved by you, for you are working mechanically and without inspiration. Inspiration is the result of repeated efforts and with it you create magically a *something* that will work quite independent of your volition. This something is what the priests of the Old Religion sought deliberately to create for use in their rites, rituals and meditations. It is the link between the magus and the cosmic energy he seeks to use. In the Old Religion the object of the priest or priestess was to work with inspiration which was deliberately visualized and intentionally invoked.

Let the motto of a would-be magus be: *Labor omnia vincit*. Act and react to these inner representations until you have lost all sense of the HOW, the WHEN and the WHERE in the feelings spontaneously created within you by these visions which have been so often built up mechanically by daily mental toil. When this happens a representation is no longer just your subjective mental picture. It has become (for you) an entity which is not only objective but also vibrant with life, and it is real upon its own plane of being, though that is not this material plane of physical sensation.

When this happens you have taken the first long step that leads to self-mastery as a true magus: that is, as a person who has trained his subconscious mind to create by means of the ancient technique of the Western Mystery Tradition: a technique that is, in its own way, as sound for us, as is that of Eastern Yoga for the peoples of Asia.

With the flowering of the powers of the subconscious mind comes inspiration, and then the magus pours into the visions that he is creating ALL the energies of his own soul. Read Ezekiel's vision of the Valley of Dry Bones. Then very carefully visualize it, for you have in it, barely hidden behind a transparent veil of commonplace words, a practical magical technique with each step described in detail and the final result clearly indicated. There is much sound magical lore in the seemingly strange tales of the Hebrew Bible.

Working in this way, the would-be-magus is developing in a perfectly safe manner his own inner life. With steady development character is being rounded off and matured. This development will tend to show itself in his mundane activities.

Thus one gives life to one's visions by living them in meditation and in ritual with a desire that is made as strong as possible, even if in the early stages such desire may have to be stimulated artificially. The vision is lived by experiencing the appropriate feelings, and each time this is done with intention reinforced by desire more and more life is infused with the vision. Ignatius Loyola based his wonderful magical system of training on this fact.

Again, never build your visions if you are bored with them lest you undermine their vitality. Instead visualize another totally different but familiar symbol as a mental drill for a disobedient mind. Drill your mind during periods of "dryness" with the visualization of the Tree of Life and vibrate gently its God-Names. They are a potent cure for what some call "The dark night of the Soul."

It is a great help when building symbols in vision to feel that behind one is the life power of the Unmanifest waiting for any opportunity to find expression through forms that are created by a visualizing imagination. Feel strongly that you have behind you and flowing through you the limitless energy and everlasting harmony of the Great Mother of All. Then by working AS IF this were so, one's natural abilities are transcended.

In working a moon ritual in group meditation, there are certain phenomena that practical work has brought to notice. Among these is the important fact that better results are to be got by working as a trinity. For example, the hierophant, if a man, will find that his powers are immensely enhanced if he will think out the implications of the following facts.

The Roman Church uses three priests for its High Mass. In the Vignettes of the "Per-t em Hru," i.e., "Coming into the day," Osiris as the hierophant is supported by Isis and Nephthys. "Hecate Triformia" is a combination of Aphrodite-Selene-Hecate and represents the Powers of Heaven, Earth and the Inner World. Sinn, the Babylonian Moon God, was also Triune in his inner nature. In Mohammedanism, the Three Daughters of Allah retain the ancient names of the three aspects of the Arabian Moon Goddess. They are Al-Ilat; Al-Uzza; and Manat. Again the three Celtic Bridgets are three aspects of the Moon Goddess Brigantis; in Ireland they are the three aspects of the Great Celtic Moon Mother Anu and so on (see *Woman's Mysteries*, Chapter IX).

There is much to be learned concerning the use that was made by the ancient initiated priesthoods of the fact that the gods and goddesses in the sphere of Yesod are three-aspected by watching with the inner eye what is done in group meditations by those Orders that have recovered something of these ancient methods from their own unpublished manuscripts as well as from the published works of Briffault and Frazer, from Hastings' *Encyclopaedia of Religion and Ethics*, and from the books of many other modern scholars.

This however touches close upon the practical work and so far as is known it is never attempted in public today, except perhaps at High Mass by certain Christian sects. For a meditation ritual does not lend itself to the pursuit of external objectives, such as a public ceremonial demands from those who officiate.

Exercise III
At the Pillars of Aurd-na-Rea:
The High Place of the Moon

In the place of Caoilte in a faint haze of golden light stood a smiling woman of the Sidhe (Shee) very soft and young and graceful, and the man wondered if this were Niamh of the Golden Hair. But seeing his perplexity at this sudden change of guide the woman laughed and said: "I am old, very old as you men count years, and yet I am ever-young, for unlike Eve I made not for myself a coat of skin. Your former partner Eve is now renewing her youth in TIR-FA-THONN, the land beneath the waters. And now that you have passed safely over An-na-Rea by the Bridge of the Moon I will take you by the long green way over the wide spaces to Aurd-na-Rea. There between the pillars of the Whispered Truth you may learn of the Great Mother; for it is She whom we also serve, who are of the Dedannans, the children of Dana. But first look once again in this deep brown pool of An-na-Rea and tell me what you see."

He gazed into the still dark water that now, seen from the West, reflected the trees of the fairy wood and the steep dark mountain beyond it. A faint mist rose and then cleared, and in the pool was a seemingly drowned land. A land of high towers, lofty trees, and bright colors where dwell a people ever young, ever happy, ever advancing in a wisdom that is not the result of human experience and suffering.

This is the land that some call the Summer Land of the Astral plane. Long ago it was called the Garden of Eden and Adam dwelt there with Lilith for his first wife. But because progress is slow in perfect happiness Adam was filled with a divine discontent. And so, when in deep sleep, he dreamed of Eve as the imperfection that should complete his own perfection. And when his dream exteriorized through intense desire he sought with her the golden wisdom that the sacred green all-wise snake would give him through failure. And so the two wandered from that golden land "on the verge of the azure sea." For Adam was divorced from his first inner and subjective love when he sought for the objective as Eve.

Lilith remained in Tir-fa-Thonn, the bright land that is in the Astral Sea, until the Moon Mother who rules the rise and fall of Astral tides called her to her temple that is within Aurd-na-Rea, the High-place of the Moon. There it can still be seen, it is said, as O'Brasil: as long ago it was seen by Maildun—the Irish Seer, who saw it without the sight of his physical eyes by means of the Two-petalled Lotus that is between them.

The vision vanished and the woman of the Aes-Shee moved up the green way through the heather, purple with its summer blossom and smelling like new honey, past golden furze bushes bright with yellow blooms. There was no sun nor were stars visible. Yet all details could be clearly seen in the green and faintly orange lights that cast purple shadows of the sphere of Yesod where rules the Lord of the Moon who is the king of this land of Life, He who is the first-born of the Great Mother Dana, the Ruler of the non-human peoples of the Etheric and Astral planes of consciousness.

They stood before two great pillars. Beyond these pillars only faintly to be seen was a temple and before it a throne—that of the Great Moon Mother who sat thereon.

The man stood alone before the Pillars of the Whispered Truth for his guide the Bean Sidhe (banshee) had vanished, and he sought to pass between them, but could not. Then he saw the sword of Life that flames red as blood between the pillars of Life and Death, the Jachin and Boaz of the Temple of Solomon. He heard the right hand pillar whisper, "Moy Mell is barred to you without Eve." The left pillar whispered also, "Moy Mell is barred to you without Lilith."

And then the blood-red sword whispered, "If you would pass while living, here is the Key of the Door that is barred by me, for I am the sword of Azrael. Come again as Adam bringing your Eve and your Lilith."

* * *

The functional nature of the unit for leaving the Astral Garden is dual, for returning however it is Triune.

Chapter 4
The Watcher and the Triune Divinities

In the Old Religion a snake symbolizes the Inner Wisdom that is intuition. Also in vision it is a symbol for the Lord of the Moon Sphere. Cernunnos is often shown with serpents as is Hermes, and so are other wisdom gods.

Eve is the Moon. She is woman as the man of the earth-sphere knows her. Lilith is woman as the Lords of the Moon-sphere know her. The moon-sphere is positive and the earth-sphere is negative and both are contained within the etheric of that purposive Entity which is called the Great Earth Mother, or the Great World Mother. She is a macrocosm and the human entity is a microcosm. The latter is also bi-polar. And the four poles of these two entities—the World Mother and the human being—can be linked so that the more potent will charge with life energy the less potent. The process by which the microcosm consciously charges itself from its immediate macrocosmic superior is the so-called "Yoga of the West." It is the wisdom of the serpent according to the non-Semitic religions of pre-Christian times.

This Yogic process can be carried out by a single person working alone in meditation. It can also be carried out by two (or three) persons of opposite sexes in what may conveniently be called a ritual meditation. The most powerful trained unit is either a man and two women, or a woman and two men. That is, Osiris supported by Isis and Nephthys, Adam with Eve and Lilith, or Isis supported by Osiris and Set, and Isis supported by Horus and Anubis.

A glance at the vignettes of the "Pert-em-hru" or a study of the wall paintings in the tombs and temples of Ancient Egypt will show how the ancient priest or priestess invoked divine energy into a Temple Ritual. Later, more detailed explanations will be given of the inner meaning of the "Eternal Triangle."

For the Romans, Janus, who, like the Qabalistic angel Azrael, sat at the Gates of the Inner World, is the personified guardian of this knowledge. And here it must be pointed out that knowledge (in such matters) is not the same thing as belief, theory or speculation. Anyone can speculate and theorize about the ancient teaching that is shadowed forth above, but something more than this is necessary in order consciously to pass the blood-red sword of the Angel of Death that guards the ever-open gate that is between the Pillars of the Here and the Yonder. But unlike the gates of the Roman temple of Janus Bifrons (two-headed) this gate is never closed (except to the living by the blood-red sword) for there is never peace between those twin brothers that are Life and Death, Osiris and Set, Vishnu and Siva.

"On the day the silver cord is snapped and the golden bowl drops broken," you will, as it were in sleep, pass the sword of Azrael and the gates of Janus Bifrons, and you will then find that they are each of them the kindly helper who gives to his beloved sleep. But it is quite another matter to face the flaming sword that keeps the way through the Gate of Life and of Death (for they are not two things but one thing viewed from two aspects) and to bring back to this earth consciously tidings of that which in human language is said to be behind or beyond or within this ever-open, yet closely guarded gate.

This conscious entry and return through the Gates of the West is the result of knowledge that can be gained by using this so-called

Yoga of the West; however the method itself can only be learned through the trial and error of practical experience.

In a certain sense Osiris on his bier is the candidate. But in another sense he is the officiating priest. Both have to take the way between the Western portals of night and day. Look closely at this scene, for Lilith, who is the Egyptian Nephthys, must come to the aid of Eve, who is Isis, the mysterious Sister, Mother, Wife of Osiris who may be either the candidate or the officiant at the double altar.

In certain of the mystery rituals Osiris is referred to as the child of Two Mothers and the clue to this aphorism is to be found when and where the functioning priestly unit is triune. In the Old Religion the priest who stands at the altar as mediator between the Great World Mother and her devotees is also in his inner aspect a child of the Two Moon Mothers. For he is the focusing point for the consciously directed powers of Nephthys and Isis as energizing negative and positive cosmic factors. Hints with regard to this point are given in the following quotations from the Litany of Nes-Amsu.

> *Behold the Lord Osiris ...*
> *Are not the two impersonators of the goddess, and Hunnu,* ⊘ *the beautiful, approaching to thy shrine at this moment?*
> *Lo! the Bull* ⊘*, begotten of the two cows, Isis and Nephthys!*
> *He, the progeny of the two cows, Isis and Nephthys, the child surpassingly beautiful!*
> *He* ⊘ *appeareth unto us in thy imnage, like the one beloved.*
> *Behold! He* ⊘ *cometh!*
> (⊘ *refers to Osiris.*)

Quoted from a Wisdom of the East—"The Burden of Isis," *The Litany of Nes-Amsu*, pp. 29 ff.

The proof of a pudding is said to be in the eating of it. It is equally true that the proof of the magical efficiency of a *unit* in any ritual technique is in the working thereof.

"Ho echon ota akouein, akoueto."

* * *

Many popular novels are written around the theme of "The Eternal Triangle," and they are an exoteric presentation of an inner law that holds good in Yoga and in religious psychology.

Here the word Yoga means a graduated series of exercises, chiefly, though not entirely, mental, that offer a practical method by which the microcosm (as the human self) can realize its identity with the macrocosm (as this Great World Self). For the basis of all Yoga (Eastern as well as Western) is the Identity of the Cosmic Principle in the Universe and the psychic principle in man.

"That are thou," and "I am Brahman," said the Indian Yogi of two thousand years ago. And today the same two phrases are repeated all over India, and are true for those who have acquired knowledge.

In the "Gospel of Eve," which is strongly imbued with the teachings of the Old Religion, it is written: "I stood on a lofty mountain (a synonym for deep meditation) and saw a gigantic man, and another, a dwarf; and I heard as it were a voice of thunder, and drew nigh for to hear; and he spake unto me and said: I am thou, and thou are I; and wheresoever thou mayest be I am there. In all am I scattered, and whencesoever thou willest, thou gatherest me; and in gathering ME, thou gatherest thyself." (*Thrice Greatest Hermes*, G. R. S. Mead, Vol. I, p. 85.)

"The Eternal Triangle" is an important part of a yogic process for uniting the self with the Infinite SELF. In the Mysteries the officiating priests and priestesses became the God or Goddess they were impersonating; they identified themselves in the action of the ritual with the conventional personalization of the cosmic forces that were being evoked.

The priest with the mask of Osiris had at his left shoulder a priestess wearing as her headdress the throne of Isis. At his right was another wearing the cup of Nephthys. In other ceremonies Isis functions with Horus and Set as her supporters. In modern psychological terms reason (Osiris) is the focal point for the powers of superconsciousness and consciousness. In ancient times space was conceived of as having Osiris for the horizon line which forever hides Isis, as the seen from Nephthys as the unseen; Time had Osiris, the ever-moving present that divides Isis, as the past, from Nephthys, the dark and ever-hidden future.

Religious psychology has taught that a man has within his soul his Isis and his Nephthys; Adam carries in his bosom both Eve and Lilith. A woman, as the microcosm of the macrocosm WOMAN, the Moon, has within her soul Osiris and Set, those great and vastly ancient gods that are the twin sovereigns of the moon phases. "Hell," it is said, "knows no fury like a woman scorned," a saying easy to understand when Set as the Red Lord of the dark moon phases becomes the ruler of a woman's inner emotional life—for is not Set the slayer of Osiris?

Analytical psychology tells much about these secret moon aspects of the soul, but the habitual working of magical rituals not only tells but also brings into manifestation much more than can the former method. Here is the list of triune divine manifestations that will repay study, provided the processes that have been described in the previous chapters have been brooded upon and used practically and with understanding in meditation.

(A) MALE

Shiva	– Vishnu	– Brahman
Set	– Horus	– Osiris (as moon gods)
Ptah	– Sokar	– Ausar (as the primeval creative power and darkness, the Dweller in the secret place)
Ptah	– Seker	– Temu (the Lord of the hidden place)
Balor	– Bress	– Tethra (the three aspects of Buar-Ainech who is Cernunnos as the wearer of the horned moon)

(B) FEMALE

Hathor – Nephthys – The Green Isis (aspects of Isis)
The Three Bridgets as aspects of Dana
The Three Bridgets (Bride) as aspects of Anu
Aphrodite– Persephone– Hecate

(C) COMBINED

Ptah	– Nefer-Tem	– Sekhet (Sekhmet)
Horus	– Set	– Isis
Sinn	– Merodach	– Ningala
Nannar	– Bel-enlil	– Ishtar
Tammuz	– Belit-Sheri	– Ishtar
Tammuz	– Eresh-ki-Gal, Allatu	– Ishtar
Osiris	– Isis	– Nephthys
Shiva	– Kali	– Durga
Adam	– Eve	– Lilith

The Master Jesus had a friendship with Martha and Mary, and you will not waste your time if you meditate upon the story of Jesus and the two Marys at the foot of his cross. One Mary is the Virgin, one is the harlot, and the cross of Jesus is symbolic of the unfolded black altar of the Universe upon which the divine Manifestor and Architect of the Universe is always being sacrificed in an unceasing ever-becoming. *"Je change sans cesse"* is as true of the mind of the Cosmos as it is of the mind of man.

Again ponder on the fact that the first human being the Christian conqueror of death meets at his resurrection is Mary the Harlot. A very significant point for those who understand that Yesod is the powerhouse of both the universes—the Macrocosmic and the Microcosmic. Why also did Jesus call Mary and Martha to him when he went to the tomb of Lazarus to perform a magical feat upon the dead?

These trinities have nothing to do with the father-mother-child combinations so delightfully explained by some students of comparative religion and folklore. There *are* divine forms for use in magical rituals. They are still potent and can be unpleasant and dangerous if used unskillfully by those who fail to balance Wisdom and Power in Harmony.

Below is given a pictorial method of training the human subconscious mind to link itself premeditatedly with those cosmic factors which Proclus in his *Elements of Theology* called the Divine Henads, or Gods. The practical processes for divine working in the sacred rites that have just been set forth have also been described in principle by Propositions 148, 150, 151, 152, 153 and 155. For Proclus in this book set forth logically the principles which govern the mental conditions that are necessary for actual experience of the merging of the smaller human self into some larger divine self, a self which also in its turn is within that of some still larger cosmic lifestream which flows and ebbs and flows again as described in the (Neoplatonic) triadic scheme of MONE, PROODOS and EPISTROPHE; i.e., abiding, proceeding and returning.

Here it may be added that if the divine Plotinus, as he is sometimes called, told the Neoplatonists of his time WHAT to do in order to realize the yogic axiom—*tat tvam asi* (that are thou), then Iamblichus and Proclus between them must be credited with telling the world HOW to do it: sometimes a much more difficult matter. There is an ancient Greek saying to the effect that anyone can tell you what to do, but it takes an experienced (wise) man to tell you how to do it.

As a method of training the mind to realize through visualized symbols these ideas, draw a large red triangle on a sheet of paper. Put harmony at the apex, wisdom at the left basal angle and power at the right basal angle.

Draw a blue triangle with its apex downwards and label it in the same way. Let the red triangle be considered as Tiphareth, Netzach and Hod and the blue triangle as Netzach, Hod and Yesod. Remember however that these two triangles are in different states of consciousness, or if you don't mind using the terms, on different planes of being. Or again consider the red triangle to be Fire (not physical but metaphysical Fire) and the blue triangle to be Water (also not physical).

Now the qualities named at the angles refer not only to cosmic manifestations of the divine Henads or gods, but also the analogous, psychological factors in the soul of man. Use the red triangle for the positive male gods and the blue triangle for the negative feminine goddesses.

Then draw with its apex upwards a third triangle in green, the fairy color, the sacred color of those who work the moon magic in what the Celtic world calls Tir-na-noge. It too is in yet another dimension as you will soon discover when successful practical work begins.

Use this green triangle as follows. If you have a trinity of two gods and a goddess, place the goddess at the apex. If two goddesses and a male god, then place him at the apex. In a ceremony at the altar this rule is observed by those that wear the priestly masks. Visualize the apex of each triangle as touching the altar, and watch your reactions to the picture when it is firmly built in the astral temple.

Again, in magic the woman is the equal of the man. In the Mysteries of Eleusis the Hierophantissa played a part equal to that of the Hierophant; one of the former was able to boast that she had initiated no less than three Roman Emperors. In the highest of the three grades that the Mystae ordinarily achieved, the roles of the Hierophant and the Hierophantissa were equal even as late as in the Christian era. So picture yourself in the role of your sex, and behind you the two who serve at the altar with you. Every woman has the right to face across the black altar the divine being that she and her assistants personate.

Sometimes the old memories return at such a moment very clearly; so visualize carefully and feel deeply.

Sit down in meditation, and as soon as the mind is quiet, visualize any temple sanctuary that appeals to you. In the center is a black stone altar, a double cube about four and a half feet high. On it is the sacred light. You as priest or priestess stand at the altar facing east. Before you, dimly seen in the darkness of the Sanctuary in the East, are the conventional forms of the three gods, or goddesses, or the mixed trinity you decide to use. Behind you are the two priests or priestesses of the gods or goddesses that form the basal angles of the triangle.

Build that scene until it appears automatically the moment you are seated for your meditation. Now—as the *Watcher*—see what happens when the priestly figure that is you (as the hierophant) invokes.

When the meditation is finished record the results (if any) and your emotional results (if any).

You may get a surprise the first time you try this method. But in all probability (as happened to the author) you will get nothing without many weeks of steady concentrated visualizing with strong desire. So do not be discouraged—you value most that for which you have had to work hard.

Exercise IV

A. As part of Exercise IV and before continuing the vision of Tir-na-Noge, visualize clearly with strong feeling this glorious piece of English rhyming verse. Afterwards, if you are wise, you will buy the book from which it is quoted.

Chorus
Some Maidens

Will they ever come to me, ever again,
   The long, long dances,
On through the dark till the dim stars wane?
Shall I feel the dew on my throat, and the stream
Of wind in my hair? Shall our white feet gleam
   In the dim expanses?
Oh, feet of a fawn to the green wood fled,
   Alone in the grass and the loveliness;
Leap of the hunted, no more in dread,

> *Beyond the snares and the deadly press:*
> *Yet a voice still in the distance sounds,*
> *A voice and a fear and a haste of hounds;*
> *O wildly labouring, fiercely fleet,*
> *Onward yet by river and glen ...*
> *Is it joy or terror, ye storm-swift feet?*
> *To the dear lone lands untroubled of men,*
> *Where no voice sounds, and amid the shadowy green*
> *The little things of the woodland live unseen.*
> (Euripides, *The Bacchae*, translation by Gilbert Murray, LL.D., D. Litt., p. 53.)

B. The Bean Sidhe (banshee) led him back from the pillars to a spur of the heath lands, and they looked not back until she came to a low mound, a fairy rath surrounded by silver-barked birch trees whose thick gnarled and twisted trunks showed their age.

Handing him the branch with the silver blossom, she ordered him to touch the root and trunk of the largest birch which was in the center of the rath. As he did so the tree vanished and in its place was a temple-like portal across which was hung a heavy, dark green curtain through which she plunged and he followed.

They were inside the rath in the transparent brown earth, a great mountain stretched below them and they started to climb its rough, rock-strewn slopes by going down, deep into the rath. Swiftly they climbed ever going downwards in order to reach the top of the mountain upon which a brilliant city of gold and green appeared.

They seemed to be in a land where everything is inverted. In some way impossible to express in objective, three-dimensional language that which is without is looked at as if it were within and that which is below appears as if one had to go up it to reach the bottom.

This world was indeed solid just as is that which is upon the surface of the earth, but one seemed to see the inside as well as the outside. One felt rather like Alice when through the looking-glass.

This city had walls of a semi-transparent green and gold, and it was made of stones that looked like a piece of glass that has been a long time on the seashore and has been marked by the grinding action of the stones and shingle.

At the gate of the city were guards. Each was armed with a golden-headed spear and a round shield. They saluted the silver-like branch and allowed the Bean Sidhe and her companion to pass into a wide street which led to a tree-bordered square on the far side of which was a portal leading into a great palace, where a prince of the fairy people met them.

"Your companion," he said, "had the right of entry, but you have to be vouched for by a guide. By what authority do you come?"

The Bean Sidhe showed the silver-white branch of blossom, the symbol that in the ancient Celtic Mysteries admits the would-be initiate into the land that lies between the *Here* and the *Yonder*, and between the past and the present. It is the dimension that is between the Outside and the Inside, where consciousness is able to transcend the ever-passing present. Here the initiand, like Mohammed's coffin, seems to hang between heaven and earth. This is the Land of the Ever Young, because having no present there is no past and no future. Time as generally understood by man is not, for with the sidhe time is but a graduated scale for the measuring of joy. There is no sorrow, no suffering, only degrees of joy and degrees of beauty, and degrees of wisdom; here, however, wisdom is not just being well-informed.

Yet they lack one thing which mankind has—suffering and the joy that suffering ultimately brings. They live in an unending perfection; and because they are perfect, though in a way that man cannot even faintly comprehend, they can only remain in that state of perfection in which the great World Mother has placed them, who are but the children of one of her many forms of evolution.

Men are mortal because Adam took Eve with him when he left the Garden of Eden, which is fairyland, to seek Mortality as an escape from the timeless, spaceless perfection of Tir-na-noge.

"Now that you will be shown Tir-nam-beo (the land of the ever youthful), will you have me as your guide, or do you prefer to have this woman?" the fairy prince asked his visitor.

There was something in the way that both looked at him that made the man realize that much hung upon that apparently simple and courteously put question. He read in both their eyes something that was almost like human anxiety, an anxiety to escape from perfection it seemed, and he felt an unspoken appeal from the dark fairy woman beside him.

He asked that she might remain with him, and with a sigh the fairy prince left him, and the fairy woman took him into a garden immense as a park.

She sat beside him holding his right hand in her left; she passed her right hand over his eyes and told him to watch the trees and flowers and to try to see how they manifested on the physical plane their real life which is in the fairy world of the moon-plane which some call the Astro-etheric.

The scenery had become just that of an ordinary earthly landscape in a rich cultured man's private park. The fairy woman had grown dim in his sight, he no longer saw her form though he felt the energy pouring from her to him and he heard her anxious whisper, "Concentrate or I am lost for you."

It was difficult to concentrate. Sight had grown abnormal; nothing was clear, and the wide landscape was dissolving in a seeming chaos of color that lost itself in a mother-of-pearl tinted haze. Only one form held—a beech tree, and in despair he compelled himself to see it as he knew it ought to be. A brief struggle, and then the tree and the park came once more into focus as a clear and beautiful astral garden.

"Now try to see the tree as a purposive intelligent entity," he was told, and he felt a hand placed on the nape of his neck.

As he watched, the green of the beech-leaves and the faint silver color of the bole seemed to merge in a form that was not the tree, and yet it was like the tree. He was no longer seeing the tree with his eyes, he was feeling it. He was once again in his inner, subtler, moon-body, and with it he saw and felt the moon-body of the tree. Then appeared the tree spirit, the deva, the shining one who lives through the trunk and branches and leaves of the beech tree as a man lives through his torso, limbs and hair. That beech was very friendly and moon-body to moon-body they met, and as his moon-body merged into that of the lady of the beech tree the sensation of the nature of the seasons, of the caress of the sunlight, of the stimulation of the bright increase of the waxing moon, and of the sleep-time that comes with the decrease of the waning moon were his.

"You can merge thus into all life," he was told; and then he saw, as the fairy sees, the flowers, the waterfalls, the rivers, and the brightly colored holy mountain of Derrybawn, which means the home of the Shining Ones. He merged himself into the roaring life that was at the summit of that great and sacred mountain—and in so doing he took the initiation of the Lady of NATURE—the Green Isis—in her private temple on the heather-clad hilltop that is above the deep ravine.

* * *

The fairy woman stood beside him on a small platform that overhung an immense gorge, the bottom of which was almost lost in the mists that rose from a dark, still lake.

She stretched her arms as if to dive and whispered, "I dare you!" and was gone.

Next moment both were speeding on the wings of thought downwards, and out from the blue mists below came the galloping Host riding from Knock-na-Rea. A pair of riderless horses sped beneath them like a flash. She took a gray horse and he a black mare. And hand in hand, with the flanks of the screaming gray stallion and the whinnying black mare touching, they raced across starlit astral space in the wake of the "Hosting of the Sidhe."

Chapter 5
Diana and Aradia

The Song of Diana
(The Goddess of the Old Religion in Italy)

Endamone, Endamone, Endamone!
By the love I feel, which I
Shall ever feel until I die,
Three crosses on thy bed I make,
And then three wild horse-chestnuts take;*
In that bed the nuts I hide,
And then the windows open wide,
That the full moon may cast her light
Upon a love so fair and bright,
And so I pray to her above
To give wild rapture to our love,
And cast her fire in either heart,
Which wildly loves to never part;
And one more thing I beg of Thee!
If any one enamoured be,
And in my aid his love hath placed,
Unto his call I'll come in haste.

---

* The three should come from one shell. Quoted from *Aradia*, pg. 55, by Leland.

Retrospect and Summary

Sometimes one is asked what is the difference between spiritualism and the teaching given in the modern mystery schools that claim direct descent from those of ancient Egypt, Greece and Chaldea.

Speaking very broadly, it may be said that in spiritualism the main effort both in theory and practice is to establish communion between the humans who are living in this physical world and the humans who are living in what is called the next world. The chief thesis of modern spiritualism is the survival by man of bodily death, and it emphasizes the fact that death makes but little more change in the essential man himself than does the taking off of a wet overcoat on a stormy night when you reach the hall of your own house and are at home among your own people.

It is the human interest, HERE and YONDER, that is the subject of Spiritualism. Of course from time to time one meets cases of the survival of horses, cats, dogs, etc. that have managed to link themselves with humans, and one meets also other and more rare cases of the survival of very primitive forms of prehistoric life; but it can with reasonable accuracy be said that in spiritualism interest is taken chiefly in the human type of evolution.

In Occultism, which is a much-misused term for the teaching given in a mystery school, but little interest is taken in any of the above-mentioned subjects that form the most important side of the public spiritualistic teaching and practical work.

The neophyte (as in the pagan schools of pre-Christian days) is given a particular kind of psychic training; he is taught the nature of his own soul and its relationship to the Divine Souls living and working on planes more subtle than this material plane. He is trained in meditation and in the use of his school's technique for analyzing the nature of his own soul. He is also taught to use a certain technique for concentrating the mind before going to sleep. And he is expected to study modern psychology and its relation to dream states.

His teacher, if the pupil is what is called a natural psychic, makes every endeavor to close down natural psychism, before the student enters on a long period of self-development according to the (ancient) discipline of the Mysteries.

The discipline of the Mysteries is an experience not lightly to be undertaken, for it has as its objective the linking of human and Cosmic consciousness, thus making conscious things that Nature has in most cases buried deep in the modern human subconsciousness.

At the "Twin" doors of the objective Divine Unconscious (as is said to have been the case at the dual-doored Crypt of Ancient Eleusis), stand three vast figures. On the left is that of the Great Queen, the Soul of the World, who is personified as the All-Mother, Saraswati, Aima, Ama, Ge, Demeter, the Heavenly Isis, the Celestial Light and Source of Life—Great Diana and Ishtar.

On the right is a youthful Queen with the "Narcissus" on her brow, the young and ever-virgin bride on the throne of the Underworld, ruler of the kingdoms of sleep and of dreams, She who is Death, and as such also the "Holder of the Secret of Life." Kore, Nephthys, Belit-Sheri, Aradia, the daughter of Diana, are but some of her personifications.

Between these two doors and in the center is the "Lord of the Ivy Crown" holding a winged thyrsus interlaced with two serpents. He is personified as Dionysos who is Life, Death and Resurrection, and as Osiris, the Risen Lord of Death.

It is wise today, as it was in the past, having passed and repassed this dual-doored Gateway, to place finger upon lip, for talking about psychic experiences, except to the Teacher, breaks their magical validity.

* * *

The initiated occultist, that is, he who has stood on the floor of the Cave that symbolizes the Beyond, who is a member of one of the Schools of the OLD RELIGION working under duly constituted authority, is usually chiefly interested in three things:

First, in the training of his earthly personality, both body and mind, so that it shall become as sound an instrument for the work he has to do as he is capable of producing within the limits of his Karma.

Then he spends much time and thought in meditation and in a potent and peculiar type of ritual by means of which he, voyaging into other states of consciousness, endeavors to get into contact with the beings of other evolutions that are progressing along cosmic paths which are, so to speak, parallel to that taken by humanity.

And thirdly he aims at gaining conscious contact with entities that, being more evolved than himself, have for their sphere of operation realms of existence that are supra-physical. The occultist's early studies lie in the sphere of Yesod, which is that of the machinery of this Universe as cosmic energy in action. In the past the initiated called these great beings the Gods, and the Buddhist and Hindus today call them the Devas.

These three objectives were, and are, often pursued more or less simultaneously, though it is, as a rule, wiser to make some considerable progress with the first objective before the second and third are undertaken. All three methods are common to both the Yoga of the East and the Yoga of the West, and are older than either (as we know them today through historical researches) for all true Yoga seeks to teach one HOW to "live in the Universal Soul" consciously.

Thus in all orthodox Occult Schools three levels of the mind are dealt with in the course of the training: the conscious level, the unconscious level that is personal to each individual, and that still deeper and more primitive unconscious level that is common to all humanity and to all "entities" that are part of the evolving life of the Great Mother Isis, Ishtar, Dark Diana of the many breasts.

The more materially minded moderns think, or say they think, that man is the highest of God's creative acts. But in this matter they flatter themselves. In this physical world the human line of evolution may be higher than that of the pig, goat, bird or fish. This however might even be but a matter of viewpoint. The line of the insect evolution may also be lower than that of man. Yet the ant is considered to be wise and industrious by philosophers, and a study of her methods of working and living by modern scientists has proved that in her own way the ant is as pugnacious and destructive as is mankind. But usually occultism is not concerned with the lines of evolution that have externalized completely into physical manifestation. These are subjects for Science.

The activities of the occultist, like those of the spiritualist, are largely directed to certain "ENDS" that exist in more subtle shapes of being than the physical. Both are concerned with the YONDER rather than the HERE. And in this they contrast strongly with the exoteric Churches, which being chiefly ethical in their teaching, stress the living of a good life HERE and say but little of the YONDER, which, for them, is the "Great Unknown."

But here the similarity of their respective tasks ends. For the occultist who KNOWS the truth of the doctrine of reincarnation as taught in the Mystery Schools (which doctrine is not the same as the popular one) does not concern himself with the survival of bodily death. For him, initiation is "a death in life." Also, in many cases, after a certain grade is reached he begins to remember his own past lives, or rather the emotional peaks or crises of these lives.

Now remembering a past life may not be nearly such a pleasant thing as some people suppose. Many of us have died in very unpleasant ways at the hands of others of our own race (which really ought to be called the inhuman race!), and, so far as personal experience goes, it is these moments of pain and terror, emotional suffering and excitement, that first come back into consciousness; and, as with the recovery of the memory of the event are also recovered the pain and fear content latent in the subconscious memory, this re-living of such a remembrance from a past life may leave one shaken and really ill for some time.

It is this unpleasant emotional content and the tremendous physical reaction with which it comes up into consciousness, that determines (for the person experiencing it) the validity or otherwise of this particular recovered memory.

So having died many times, and having often completely lost the memory-tracks of the pleasant events and recovered more easily the not very remote but often very unpleasant ones, and knowing that he is likely to die both pleasantly and unpleasantly yet many more times in the future, the initiate of a Mystery system leaves death alone and gets on with his daily task of contributing his quota of work to the school to which he belongs.

Not much has been or can be said about training. But quite a lot has been said openly about WHAT is done in order to contact "our brethren of the other evolutions," though here again there must necessarily be a reservation of confidence, for nothing can be said as to HOW this is done, except that practically every school has its own method of teaching HOW these contracts should be developed.

In most schools the beings of other evolutions are divided into four classes, those of Earth, of Air, of Fire and of Water. But the terms earth, air, fire and water do not have the same meaning as the man of science or the man in the street give to them. So one starts with the handicap of an incongruous terminology. For example the Tree Spirits are classed under the heading of AIR. Not because they have anything to do with the airy spirits of the storm and evening breeze, but because they belong to the Airy realms of Yesod which is the sphere of the Moon Gods and Moon Goddesses that rule under the guidance of Shaddai El Chai who is the Almighty Living God of the Astro-Etheric plane or state of consciousness. The ancient initiate knew exactly what these terms meant, and they also knew that by using them the unknowing seeker was doubly misled when trying to make use of scraps of knowledge filched from the Mysteries.

Thus far in these articles only the beings that belong to the Sphere of Yesod have been touched upon, and no attempt has been made to develop in the reader the contacts that give access to certain of the Great Devas that rule in Spheres of evolution that are other than human. Nevertheless some readers who are far advanced may have successfully touched certain of these great Beings that in the New Testament are called powers, principalities, rulers, elements or first principles. This leads up to the great truth that in the mystery schools the teacher is not so important as the personality of his pupil—for all development but be self-development.

Masefield has written in one of his poems:

Fate, that is given to all men partly shaped,
Is ours to alter daily till we die.

And he has here put into modern English one of the famous and secret maxims common to the Mystery training processes of all times. AHIEH ASHUR AHIEH, the god of all gods alike in the Microcosm as in the Macrocosm, the "I will be what I will be" of Mystery Schools that long predate the Egyptian initiate Moses. This word secret, however, is used here in a very particularized sense. One great Master has talked of it as seed growing in secret, the grain growing secretly in the dark black earth. Here reference is made to what a certain type of teacher calls a "seed thought," which is what this maxim is.

A seed thought means that if you put with strong intention a magical idea into your visualizing imagination and build it clearly and then with intention consign it to the fructifying darkness of your subconscious mind, it will begin to grow in energy. If you go on repeating this process with strong intention every day even for but a few short moments when rising from and also when going to bed, this magical idea will in time come to energize your life and your expression of life in matter.

Suppose you feel drawn to the Old Religion, to the Mysteries of Diana in the sphere of Yesod. If your circumstances bar you from participating in them, and if you are unable to change those circumstances in the ordinary way, there is no need for you to sit down and do nothing. By working upon your subconscious mind you can change the NATURE of your relationship to your environment—a thing that Omar Khay-yam has hinted at, and Aradia taught in the "Song of Diana" just quoted.

Build the Green Ray pictures that have been given you. Strive to feel within yourself the joy that they are intended to produce in your emotional nature. If you can work yourself up into ecstasy—that is, to a state of consciousness that enables you to stand without yourself—a few moments are all that are necessary—in time you will so change that circumstances will case to hinder for you will have changed their relationship to yourself.

When the students are ready the Masters will come: for usually they are more anxious to find us than we are to seek them. The first step is always preparation, and on its thoroughness depends the speed at which you will advance. So begin upon your own inner self—your first and last task in the Mysteries.

The Ancients used the "Fire of the Wise" to burn away the dross in their own personalities. "The Fire of the Wise" is the visualizing imagination. As a man thinks in his heart, so is he. The modern rendering of that term "heart" is subconscious mind. And the psychological rendering of this saying should be "As a man's subconscious mind *sees* him to be, so is he." The subconscious mind is not the reasoning mind. It is something far more primitive and powerful which works in picture-images and not in words. Its guide is feeling, not reason. In it are hidden the memories of past eons. In it lie also the potentialities that will determine the future, for the cosmic subconscious mind is Aradia, the ever-virgin daughter of the Dark Diana, the Cosmic Mother of the OLD RELIGION.

In the imagery that has been given in the previous articles is hidden a method for doing two very different things: first for developing and maintaining an emotional drive that will enable you to get started on your task of "Finding the hidden Wisdom that contains all the Ancient Wisdoms of the World," as one ancient worthy has declared; and secondly the construction of a FORM which will enable you to link your varying states of consciousness to their appropriate type of subtle matter in the Soul of the Great Mother.

When this form is adequately functioning and when it is filled with the appropriate type of energy you have within yourself an

ENS REALISSIMUM which is as the Philosopher's Stone. It is a magical personality and it is the key to symbolism used in "Woman's Mysteries" when worshipping Great Diana, the Compassionate Mother of the downtrodden man and the "unfortunate" woman.

So long as you remember and act upon the ancient proverb, "The Gods give their reward only to those who sweat for them," you have, by virtue of this key the power to function as a member of the priesthood of THE OLD RELIGION.

Index

Achad, Frater, 45
AE, 75
Alexandria, 24
Amen-Ra, 79
Ambrosius, 25
AnnaRea, 169, 201, 205, 207, 214
Annwn, David, ix, 66
Anubis, 86, 116, 143, 176, 216
Aphorisms of Creation, 16, 17, 25
Argylle, Duke of, 49
Armoise, 132, 178
Asar, 117
Ashcroft-Nowicki, Dolores, ix, 72
Ast, 117
Atlantis, 16, 27, 30, 50, 71, 80, 83, 122, 127, 133, 148
Aurd-na-Rea, 89, 169, 213, 214
Avalon of the Heart, 27, 35
Avebury, 78, 174, 175
Avignon, 74, 123

Babylon, 108, 144
Bacon, Roger, 53
Baldur, 141, 143
Belfry, 64, 65
Besant, Annie, 21, 23
Bifrost, 141
Blavatsky, H. P., 17, 20, 21
Boccaccio, 53
Bond, Bligh, 29
Brean Down, 172

British Colonial Training Institute, 7
Brodie-Innes, J. W., 19, 49, 50, 51, 63, 80
Bromage, Bernard, 37
Budge, E. A. W., 64
Butler, W. E., 11, 37

Carver, Philip and Jan, ix
Casaubon, Meric, 53
Case for Reincarnation, 86, 176, 179
Cheiron, 103, 104, 105, 146, 166
Christian Mystic Lodge, 19, 21, 33
Columba, 77
Co-Masonry, 84
Connolly, Cyril, 14
Cook, Oscar, 54, 56, 60, 176
Cosmic Doctrine, 24, 64
Coward, Noel, 47
Creasy, W. K., 37, 42
Crowley, Aleister, 9, 10, 18, 38, 45

Dante, 53
Dartmoor, 148
Dee, John, 51, 52, 53, 71
Demon Lover, The, 5, 6, 32, 34, 43
Deo, non Fortuna, 2, 18
Dickson, W. E. C., 79
Dionysus, 105
Dukas, Paul, 47
Dzyan, Stanzas of, 17

Eldon, Lord, 25, 26, 27, 50, 53, 69, 71, 128, 129, 130, 131, 162, 163, 168, 178, 180
Ellis, Havelock, 47
Erskine, Lord, 27
Evans, Hazel, 30, 32
Evans, Thomas Penry, xiii, 28, 30, 31, 32, 34, 44, 178, 180
Eversley, 12, 15
Exton, 86

Firth, Arthur, 3, 30
Firth, Violet Mary, 3, 4, 7, 54
Flame, Lords of, 18, 21
Fluff, The, 1, 2
Form, Lords of, 18, 21
Fortune, Dion, 2, 9, 24, 33, 41, 43, 45, 178
Frere, Robert Temple, 47
Frere, Ayme Frere, 57
Freya, 141
Fuller, J. F. C., 32

Gabriel, 177
Gilbert, R. A., x, 50
Gilmore, Mary, 37
Girl's Realm, 4
Glastonbury, 33, 35, 37, 41, 65, 122, 155
Goat-Foot God, 8, 61
Golden Dawn, Order of the, 19, 31, 337, 38, 70
Grant, Kenneth, 36
Gray, William G., ix
Green Ray, 58, 169
Greene, Liz, 54
Guirdham, Arthur, 24, 74

Hammarskjold, Dag, 179
Harper, Clive, x, 8
Hartley, Christine, xi, 88, 89, 176, 177
Hartley, H. A., 74, 86

Hermes, 133, 215, 218
Hermopolis, 141
Hindhead, 7
Hiordis, 143, 179
Hitler, Adolf, 14, 84
Homan, E., 33
Horus, 116
Hughes, Hope, 19
Hugin, 140

Inner Light, Society of the, xiii, 43, 44
Iona, 76
Ishtar, 145, 172
Isis, 54, 64, 100, 130, 145

Joan of Arc, 131, 132
Johnson, Brenda Teresa, 34, 55

Karnak, 27, 116, 141
Kelly, Edward, 53, 71
Kha'm-uast, 23, 33, 39, 68, 80, 149, 153
Khonsu, 113, 176
Killagally, 62, 63, 85, 126, 129, 149, 151
King, Francis, 19, 42
Kingsley, Charles, 12
Kleomenes, 24, 28, 39, 164, 173

Lapithae, 105, 176
Lathbury, Miss, 42
Lawrence, T. E., 47
Leadbeater, C. W., 21
Llandudno, 3
Lonsdale, 151
Loveday, C. T., 29, 30, 42
Loyola, Ignatius, 68
Lumley-Brown, Margaret, 42

Mainwaring, Veronica, 6
Maltby, Edward, 32, 57
Maund, Zoe Oakley, 64

Mathers, Moina, 19, 34, 42, 85
Melchisadec, 18, 20, 21, 22, 179
Merlin, 22, 27, 80, 87, 127, 128, 129, 148, 173
Mind, Lords of, 18, 21
Mithras, 157, 160
Monks Farm, 8
Moon Magic, 41, 61, 64, 177
Moore, George, 47
More Violets, 5
Morgan le Fay, 27, 28, 54, 127, 128, 129, 173, 178
Moriarity, T. W. C., ix, 10, 11, 12, 19, 22, 24, 30
Munin, 140
Mystical Qabalah, The, 38

Nabu, 146
Nefer-su, 110, 176
Ne Nefer Ka Ptah, 68, 176
Nephthys, 75
Nibs, 122, 177
Nietzsche, 79
Nifl-heim, 159

Occult Review, The, 9, 33, 34
Odin, 141, 158, 159, 171, 173
Old Religion, The, xv, 75
Opet, 116, 177
Orton, General, 157, 180
Osiris, 74, 116, 119

Pan, 44, 78, 103, 104, 105, 176
Parker, 116
Pentagram, Ritual of the, 104, 122, 156
Philae, 53
Powys, J. C., 35
Proctor, 113, 116
Problem of Purity, 54
Psychic Self-Defence, 5, 6, 12, 30, 32, 59, 180
Ptah, 22, 73, 142

Ptolemy, 113
Purbeck, Isle of, 26

Ragnold, 139
Ramses II, 22
Reeves, Elsie, 12
Regardie, Israel, 9, 37, 38
Russia, 66

Scot, Michael, 25, 51, 71, 86
Sea Priestess, The, 27, 31, 41, 61, 65, 74
Secrets of Dr Taverner, The, 5, 6, 10, 12
Sekhmet, 59, 142
Set, 75, 119
Seymour, C. R. F., xi, xii, 11, 32, 37, 62, 63, 64, 66, 73, 84, 177
Sharp, William, 75
Sigurd, 143
Smith, Sarah Jane, 3
Sparta, 164
Stafford-Allen, Gwen, 11
Stella Matutina, 19, 34, 37, 80
Steele, V. M., 36, 46, 61
Surtees, Elizabeth, 25

Tabori, Paul, 47
Taphtarthareth, 9
Tara, 78
Thomson, Christine Campbell, 37, 38, 46, 67, 71, 80, 107
Tir-na-noge, 77, 156, 180, 222
Training and Work of an Initiate, 20
Tranchell-Hayes, Maiya, 31
Trevanion, Paul, 37, 73, 76, 156, 168

U.M., The, 161
Urim and Thummim, 114

Valkyrie, 138
Venus, 21, 59
Volens, 63, 112

Wells, H. G., 47
Western Mystery Tradition, The
    87, 88
Wilde, Oscar, 14
Wilson, Margaret, 73
Winter, J. R., ix
Wolfmar, 157

Wynne, Esme, 47

Yates, Lilian, 84
Yeats, W. B., 72, 75, 206
Yggdrasil, 141, 143
Ys, 72, 75

STAY IN TOUCH

On the following pages you will find listed, with their current prices, some of the books and tapes now available on related subjects. Your book dealer stocks most of these, and will stock new titles in the Llewellyn series as they become available. We urge your patronage.

However, to obtain our full catalog, to keep informed of new titles as they are released and to benefit from informative articles and helpful news, you are invited to write for our bi-monthly news magazine/catalog. A sample copy is free, and it will continue coming to you at no cost as long as you are an active mail customer. Or you may keep it coming for a full year with a donation of just $2.00 in U.S.A. ($7.00 for Canada & Mexico, $20.00 overseas, first class mail). Many bookstores also have *The Llewellyn New Times* available to their customers. Ask for it.

Stay in touch! In *The Llewellyn New Times'* pages you will find news and reviews of new books, tapes and services, announcements of meetiongs and seminars, articles helpful to our readers, news of authors, advertising of products and services, special money-making opportunities, and much more.

The Llewellyn New Times
P.O. Box 64383-Dept. 673, St. Paul, MN 55164-0383, U.S.A.

• • •

TO ORDER BOOKS AND TAPES

If your book dealer does not have the books and tapes described on the following pages readily available, you may order them direct from the publisher by sending full price in U.S. funds, plus $2.00 for postage and handling for the first book, and $.50 for each additional book. There are no postage and handling charges for orders over $50. UPS Delivery: We ship UPS whenever possible. Delivery guaranteed. Provide your street address as UPS does not deliver to P.O. Boxes. UPS to Canada requires a $50 minimum order. Allow 4–6 weeks for delivery. Orders outside the U.S.A. and Canada: Airmail—add retail price of book; add $5 for each non-book item (tapes, etc.); add $1 per item for surface mail.

FOR GROUP STUDY AND PURCHASE

Because there is a great deal of interest in group discussion and study of the subject matter of this book, we feel that we should encourage the adoption and use of this particular book by such groups by offering a special "quantity" price to group leaders or "agents."

Our Special Quantity Price for a minimum order of five copies of *20th Century Magic* is $38.85 cash-with-order. This price includes postage and handling within the United States. Minnesota residents must add 6% sales tax. For additional quantities, please order in multiples of five. For Canadian and foreign orders, add postage and handling charges as above. Credit card (VISA, Master Card, American Express) orders are accepted. Charge card orders only may be phoned free ($15.00 minimum order) within the U.S.A. or Canada by dialing 1-800-THE-MOON. Customer service calls dial 1-612-291-1970. Mail Orders to:

LLEWELLYN PUBLICATIONS
P.O. Box 64383-Dept. 673 / St. Paul, MN 55164-0383, U.S.A.

ANCIENT MAGICKS FOR A NEW AGE
by Alan Richardson and Geoff Hughes

With two sets of personal magickal diaries, this book details the work of magicians from two different eras. In it, you can learn what a particular magician is experiencing in this day and age, how to follow a similar path of your own, and discover correlations to the workings of traditional adepti from almost half a century ago.

The first set of diaries are from Christine Hartley and show the magick performed within the Merlin Temple of the Stella Matutina, an offshoot of the Hermetic Order of the Golden Dawn, in the years 1940-42. The second set are from Geoff Hughes, and detail his magickal work during 1984-86. Although he was not at that time a member of any formal group, the magick he practiced was under the same aegis as Hartley's. The third section of this book, written by Hughes, shows how you can become your own Priest or Priestess and make contact with Merlin.

The magick of Christine Hartley and Geoff Hughes are like the poles of some hidden battery that lies beneath the Earth and beneath the years. There is a current flowing between them, and the energy is there for you to tap.
0–87542-671-9, 320 pgs., illus., 6 x 9 $12.95

EARTH GOD RISING;
THE RETURN OF THE MALE MYSTERIES
by Alan Richardson

Today, in an age that is witnessing the return of the Goddess in all ways and on all levels, the idea of one more male deity may appear to be a step backward. But along with looking toward the feminine powers as a cure for our personal and social ills, we must remember to invoke those forgotten and positive aspects of our most ancient God. The Horned God is just, never cruel; firm, but not vindictive. The Horned God loves women as equals. He provides the balance needed in this New Age, and he must be invoked as clearly and as ardently as the Goddess to whom he is twin.

The how-to section of this book shows how to make direct contact with your most ancient potentials, as exemplified by the Goddess and the Horned God. Using the simplest of techniques, available to everyone in any circumstance, Earth God Rising shows how we can create our own mystery and bring about real magical transformations without the need for groups, gurus, or elaborate ceremonies.
0–87542-672-7, 256 pgs., illus., 5-1/4 x 8 $10.95